THE CHANGING FACE OF PEACEKEEPING

The Canadian Institute of Strategic Studies meets a need for a body of informed opinion on strategic and national security issues and stimulates greater public awareness of the significance of national and international developments. The CISS provides a public forum for discussions which enhance the knowledge of the Canadian public on strategic matters. Through educational and informational activities it seeks to improve the basis for informed choice and decisions by the public of Canada and its leaders.

Canadian Cataloguing in Publication Data

The National Library of Canada has catalogued this publication as follows:
Main entry under title: The Changing Face of Peacekeeping

Proceedings of Peacekeeping '93: An Exhibition and Seminar held in Ottawa, March 16-17, 1993.

ISBN 0-919769-62-4

1. United Nations - Armed Forces - Canada - Congresses. 2. United Nations - Armed Forces - Congresses. I. Morrison, Alex, 1941- . II. Tychonick, Russ. III. McNish, Susan. IV. Peacekeeping '93: Exhibition and Seminar (1993: Ottawa, Ont.). V. Canadian Institute of Strategic Studies.

JX1981.P7C53 1993   355.3'57   C93-094287-6

The CISS would like to thank the following for their assistance in the staging of the seminar and the publication of these proceedings: NATO Headquarters in Brussels, the Cooperative Security Competition Program of the Department of External Affairs and International Trade Canada, Baxter Publications, LeBlanc & Royal Telcom Inc., and SEI Industries.

This volume printed and bound in Canada by Canadian Printco Limited.

Edited by ALEX MORRISON

The Changing Face of Peacekeeping

Associate Editors:
RUSS TYCHONICK, SUSAN MCNISH

THE CANADIAN INSTITUTE OF STRATEGIC STUDIES

The Canadian Institute of Strategic Studies meets a need for a body of informed opinion on strategic and national security issues and stimulates greater public awareness of the significance of national and international developments. The CISS provides a public forum for discussions which enhance the knowledge of the Canadian public on strategic matters. Through educational and informational activities it seeks to improve the basis for informed choice and decisions by the public of Canada and its leaders.

Canadian Cataloguing in Publication Data

The National Library of Canada has catalogued this publication as follows: Main entry under title: The Changing Face of Peacekeeping

Proceedings of Peacekeeping '93: An Exhibition and Seminar held in Ottawa, March 16-17, 1993.

ISBN 0-919769-62-4

1. United Nations - Armed Forces - Canada - Congresses. 2. United Nations - Armed Forces - Congresses. I. Morrison, Alex, 1941- . II. Tychonick, Russ. III. McNish, Susan. IV. Peacekeeping '93: Exhibition and Seminar (1993: Ottawa, Ont.). V. Canadian Institute of Strategic Studies.

JX1981.P7C53 1993   355.3'57   C93-094287-6

The CISS would like to thank the following for their assistance in the staging of the seminar and the publication of these proceedings: NATO Headquarters in Brussels, the Cooperative Security Competition Program of the Department of External Affairs and International Trade Canada, Baxter Publications, LeBlanc & Royal Telcom Inc., and SEI Industries.

This volume printed and bound in Canada by Canadian Printco Limited.

CONTENTS

"Peacekeeping '93: An Exhibition and Seminar" was sponsored by Baxter Publications in cooperation with the Canadian Institute of Strategic Studies and was held at the Ottawa Congress Centre on 16 and 17 March, 1993. An audience of over 2,500 was able to view the latest developments in peacekeeping goods and services presented by 100 companies. The seminar featured knowledgable speakers on a variety of topics of contemporary relevance to both the theory and practise of peacekeeping.

Al Geddry
Director of Communications, Peacekeeping '93

Don Macnamara
President, CISS

Introductory Remarks

Al Geddry

On behalf of Baxter Publishing, I welcome you to Peacekeeping '93: An Exhibition and Seminar. Baxter Publishing is extremely proud of this world premiere show, and we certainly are very pleased with the turnout and the interest that has been shown for Peacekeeping '93. Baxter Publishing dedicates this exhibition and seminar to all members of the Canadian Forces who are serving and who have served in United Nations peacekeeping operations. They serve and have served for the cause of peace in very dangerous circumstances in some cases, and we should not ever forget that. I think their professionalism and their humanitarianism is what is setting them apart from all other peacekeepers of the world, and for this we can be very proud indeed, and we salute all the men and women in uniform who are doing that job. Baxter Publishing est très content de vous accueillir ce matin. Nous pensons que le programme est pas mal divérsifié. Nous espérons que vous trouverez les sujets à votre goût. Et, évidement, par l'intérêt qui est indiqué, on peut s'attendre à des discussions très intéressantes. I now introduce Brigadier-General (retd) and Professor Don Macnamara - a friend and colleague - who is the President of the Canadian Institute of Strategic Studies.

Don Macnamara

On behalf of the Canadian Institute of Strategic Studies, I wish to welcome you to our spring seminar, devoted to the subject of peacekeeping. The Canadian Institute of Strategic Studies conducts two seminars each year - one in the autumn and one in the spring. Normally in the autumn the topic is an annual strategic forecast, and in the spring we seek to identify some major topic of current Canadian strategic interest to address in a broadly-based forum. Today we may ask ourselves three questions: Why peacekeeping? Why in Ottawa? And why in conjunction with an exhibition? It is not news to anyone here that peacekeeping has been on the lips of not just military people but also the general public in Canada, particularly in the last year-and-a-half, but actually for a much longer time: basically since the late 1940s. Canada's history with UN observer and peacekeeping missions is second to none. But the intensified interest over the last year, and the questions that have to be asked about Canada's future roles in peacekeeping - the kinds of forces that we have to bring together in this country, what they are going to be made up of and how they are going to be equipped - are questions that should be addressed by a broadly-based audience. Hence, the topic of peacekeeping for this seminar.

Why in Ottawa? Peacekeeping is not just a military activity or commitment. Peacekeeping is a joint military and diplomatic activity, or at least it should be. It also involves the citizens of the countries that are contributing peacekeeping forces and, most particularly, the citizens of the countries that are involved in the conflicts. Therefore, we must - or should - involve all constituencies - those who are participating from a military point of view, those who contribute from a diplomatic point of view, and those of the broadly-based international community which will be part of the forces or indeed perhaps are from the locations of current or potential conflict. Ottawa, our national capital, the location of our National Defence Headquarters and centre of the diplomatic corps for both Canada and other countries, therefore provides the appropriate locus and focus for a discussion of peacekeeping.

Third, why in conjunction with an exhibition? Those of you who have seen the exhibition will know that there is a wide range of equipment associated with the kinds of requirements that one has to address in the context of peacekeeping. Since the end of the Cold War, it has been extremely difficult to predict the kind of equipment that armed forces in any country will be required to obtain, or that will be required to be used. Indeed, it is very difficult for armed forces in any country to know where they are going to go and under what circumstances, especially in the context of peacekeeping. Therefore, it is entirely appropriate that representatives of the Canadian Forces and armed forces from around the world, and the representatives of the diplomatic community - those with and without peacekeeping experience - can meet with manufacturers who can support peacekeeping operations and provide the associated equipment, to discuss the general national, industrial, political and military interests associated with the task of peacekeeping. The Canadian Institute of Strategic Studies is therefore particularly proud and pleased to have the opportunity to participate and to associate ourselves with Baxter Publications in this combined effort here in Ottawa.

Alex Morrison
Executive Director, CISS

Introduction

Alex Morrison

I am pleased to join with my colleagues Al Geddry and Don Macnamara in welcoming you to Peacekeeping '93: An Exhibition and Seminar. You are already aware of the professional nature of the exhibition. The participating companies are to be congratulated on their decision to be here and to show us how they contribute in a very effective and substantial way to UN and other international peacekeeping missions.

As you can see from your programme, the Canadian Institute of Strategic Studies has been able to draw together an impressive array of experts in various areas of peacekeeping. We are sure that their presentations when joined with your contributions during the discussion periods will result in two days of very worthwhile educational activity.

The Changing Face of Peacekeeping is the title of the book the CISS will be publishing which will contain a description of the exhibition as well as the complete text of the presentations and the question and answer sessions. We all know that peacekeeping is changing. Indeed, I think we would be very disappointed if the face of peacekeeping did not change to keep pace with contemporary challenges and opportunities.

One of the many changes that must be made is in the area of peacekeeping research, education and training. Accompanying the rapid and unprecedented expansion of peacekeeping missions has been a corresponding rise in interest of many countries in all aspects of peacekeeping: historical, operational, and what the future will bring. As you are well aware from the historical record, from the speeches of Canadian officials and from the statements of various UN Secretaries-General, Canada invented peacekeeping as it is now practiced. Canadians have been members of every UN peacekeeping mission as well as of many non-UN operations. No other country can claim that record. More Canadians than citizens of any other country have worn the Blue Helmet and the Blue Beret in the interests of international peace, security and stability. We need to ensure that the experience and expertise we have accumulated over the past decades is put to good use in the future. If we do not share it, there is the risk that future peacekeeping will be less effective.

For six years in the 1980s I helped to represent Canada at the United Nations, and I can tell you of the very high esteem in which Canada is held by countries and citizens all around the world. Canada is one of the small, select group of countries to which UN officials constantly turn when they wish valued peacekeeping advice and when they want expert military contributions.

Canada invented peacekeeping in 1956 when Lester Pearson, then Secretary of State for External Affairs, went to the United Nations during the Suez Crisis, personally took charge of the Canadian delegation, and came up with the suggestion which saw troops deployed to the Middle East to help supervise the cease fire put into place as a stop-gap measure in response to the crisis.

Peacekeeping has changed dramatically over the years. One of the major reasons why this change has taken place is that the United Nations is now working and functioning and operating as it was designed to do in 1945, as was foreseen by those who drafted and agreed on the Charter of the United Nations. The Charter begins, "We the peoples of the world, determined to save succeeding generations from the scourge of war..." It is then very clearly outlined how succeeding generations were to be saved from the scourge of war. It was to be through the threat of the use of force, or the use of force itself. In the early years of the United Nations the Military Staff Committee, composed of representatives of the five permanent members of the UN, was drawing up plans for a United Nations military force. That UN military force was to have 2,000,000 soldiers, thousands of airplanes, hundreds of ships and the atomic bomb. It was to be used wherever necessary throughout the world to bring peace, security and stability.

When the members of the MSC were discussing, in the period 1945-47, the structure of the force, it was decided that if the atomic bomb was to form a portion of the UN arsenal then Canada should be a member of the Committee. The reason for this was that at the end of the Second World War, only three countries, in Bernard Brodie's words "knew the atomic secret" - Canada, the United Kingdom and the United States. But in the event - through a combination of circumstances - the Military Staff Committee decided that the force would not have atomic weapons, and so Canada did not become a member of the Committee.

With the onset of the Cold War, it was not possible for the Charter to be implemented as was envisaged in 1945. But with the end of the Cold War, with the spreading of democracy throughout the world, with western countries seeing their policies and practices fulfilled, the UN is now beginning to function as was envisioned in 1945. The Security Council is very active. The Security Council is interventionist. The current Secretary-General is perhaps one of the most active and most interventionist in the history of the United Nations. The Security Council is now mounting peacekeeping missions at an increasing rate. Established in the last four or five years have been more peacekeeping missions than were set up in the first four decades of the United Nations.

Canada is continuing to play a leading role in peacekeeping at the UN. Canadian participation in peacekeeping is immensely popular with the Canadian public. Notwithstanding that almost 100 Canadians have lost their lives in the service of peace, there continues to be a popular misconception that peacekeeping is a neutral activity. Peacekeeping is not a neutral activity. It never has been neutral and it will never be neutral. Peacekeeping is an objective activity. The professional men and women of the Canadian Armed Forces are dispatched to dangerous locations around the world to assess situations and then to take action based on their perception of the requirements. That involves sometimes taking sides; that involves sometimes saying to one party or to one faction: "You are wrong and you must change."

One reason why Canadians are so good at peacekeeping is that they are professional. The men and women that we send abroad are well trained and highly motivated. They have a vast reservoir of experience and expertise on which to draw when faced with new or unexpected situations. In good Canadian fashion they do not suffer fools gladly. When things have to be done, they do them.

There is developing today, in Canada at least, a new peacekeeping partnership. This is composed of the military, the humanitarian aid agencies, good governance officials from Elections Canada, and professional members of the Royal Canadian Mounted Police. They are now cooperating all around the world to ensure that the peacekeeping umbrella is as large as it can be, and to ensure that the resources of this great country of ours are mobilized in the service of peace. Indeed, in Canada I think we will soon see people from the Canadian Armed Forces actually being seconded to humanitarian aid agencies for short periods of time and also aid experts being attached to military organizations. This interchange will ensure a greater degree of effective advance planning and interoperability. When future peacekeeping missions are mounted, people will know one another, they can work together at the beginning, and a truly coordinated plan can be drawn up and carried out.

The face of peacekeeping is changing because the world is changing. A few years ago at the United Nations one of the most repeated phrases was "national sovereignty". It was held that the United Nations ought not to do anything that would interfere with the national sovereignty of a country. But now we feel that we have a greater duty in the world. More countries and the United Nations itself are beginning to realize that citizens and individuals ought not be held hostage to what are rapidly becoming outmoded concepts. In the future I think we will see the United Nations being more interventionist in conducting operations in countries without the agreement of the government itself. Indeed, we are seeing examples of this in the former Yugoslavia and in Somalia. Now if we think about the fact that throughout the world there are thousands of children under the age of five who die every day from disease and malnutrition - each of which is preventable - are we indirect accomplices in their deaths because of a failure to intervene? In other words, ought the United Nations and the countries of the world to consider in the future the possibility of sending in military and humanitarian aid agencies to look after the needs of the people who are sick and hungry even if the governments of the countries do not want it done? Perhaps that is a bit far-fetched, perhaps it is not.

But I do feel that when we think of peacekeeping in the larger sense, when we think of everything we can put underneath the peacekeeping umbrella, we ought not to be bound by conventional thinking. We ought to let our imagination expand. We ought further to consider what it is we can do with our vast national resources, acting in cooperation with one another and in cooperation with countries around the world to ensure peace, security and stability.

Canadians enjoy peacekeeping because they know they are doing something good, because they know they are doing something real, because they are helping people to live and to make their conditions better. But I would wager that there is not a man or woman in the Canadian Armed Forces, in the humanitarian agencies, in Elections Canada, in the Royal Canadian Mounted Police who would wish that we could keep doing this forever. I will wager that each of them would say that he or she wishes that it were not necessary to have peacekeeping forces.

I hope that the face of peacekeeping will keep changing, and I hope that the peacekeepers will be as successful in the future as they have been in the past. I hope that the face of peacekeeping will change to the extent that perhaps in the future there will be no need for peacekeeping forces. That would be a wonderful celebration of the success of the UN. It would be a wonderful realization of the dreams of people around the world. But until that happens we must remain professional and we must remain committed.

At the exhibition there are many goods and services displayed which are used by our peacekeepers. However, there are many goods and services that are also used by our peacekeepers which are *not* displayed. If you read newspapers and magazines and listen to the radio and watch television, you will know of many items of equipment that are used by our peacekeepers and peacekeepers of other countries not only for their own protection, but to ensure that they are able to carry out the United Nations mandate. We ought to reflect on the mindset of people who wish to shut out this aspect of reality, who wish to say, "I do not want to see and I do not want you to show the equipment that Canadians are using this very day in well over a dozen peacekeeping missions around the world."

I would think that every Canadian ought to deem it a right that they see everything that is being used. I would like to think that perhaps during this exhibition and seminar we will undergo a process of mutual education which in the future will not see some Canadians ashamed of and offended by the items of equipment, and the services and the goods that our troops use. We owe it to these tens of thousands of men and women to ensure that they have the best of equipment, that they have the best conditions possible in the theatres in which they are operating. If we do any less we are guilty of neglecting them. I ask you to remember that as you listen to the speakers over the next two days and as you view the exhibition. It is necessary, regrettably, that when armed forces are deployed abroad in the service of peace that they use certain weapons and equipment - that they are protected and that they are able to carry out their mandate. We ought not to bury our heads in the sand and say, "I know it is happening, but I just do not want to see it, I do not want to look at it."

As we gather here for the next two days, we gather not only to see, not only to enquire, not only to listen, not only to speak with one another and exchange opinions and ideas and - dare I say - even argue from time to time. But we are here, I think, in many ways, as a tribute to the very professional men and women of Canada and of all countries who serve the cause of peace.

Gordon Gedge

UN Procurement

Alex Morrison

Lieutenant-Colonel Gordon Gedge (retd) served for over 40 years in the Canadian military. He is an experienced peacekeeper, he was in Cyprus very early on after UNFICYP was established. He has, just a few years ago, returned from the disengagement observer force in the Golan Heights, where he was Chief Logistics Officer and responsible for ordering goods and equipment for that United Nations peacekeeping operation. He is going to tell us a bit about the challenges and opportunities and about the problems of ensuring that a peacekeeping force is well-equipped and well-serviced.

Gordon Gedge

My remarks are from the point of view of one who has served in peacekeeping missions in the field, not at UN headquarters in New York. I will cover four basic topics: (1) understanding the UN bureaucracy within which the UN peacekeepers work; (2) the need to strengthen logistics operations staff in UN headquarters in New York; (3) UN procurement - how it works, together with some hints which may be of use to those who are trying to sell products and services to the UN; and (4) a plea for standardization in peacekeeping missions.

(1) Understanding the UN bureaucracy. I think most of us are aware that many unqualified people work at UNHQ. This is because each country has a quota of positions to fill and is desperately eager to do so - even with those

who do not have the experience or expertise. Many times the aim is simply to fill the position.

Another factor is that of the UN headquarters staff versus the UN field service staff. In military organizations, service alternates between tours of duty in the field and serving in the headquarters. That is the ideal, and that is what should be achieved within the UN, but is not. Why not? One, the field service people become fairly specialized in their line of work and they also receive higher allowances for being in the field. Two, those in New York like being at the HQ and do not really wish to go out into the field. They have their families and are well-established and accustomed to the metropolitan life. Prior to leaving my last peacekeeping assignment in the Middle East I was visited by the UNHQ Chief of Procurement. This gentleman was very well thought of within the UN, managed a fairly large organization, and he was about to retire. In his 30 years of UN service, this was the first time he had visited a field mission. It was an eye opener for him. On the other hand, I met many who had never left the Middle East in 30 years. That is the kind of thing that needs to be changed, but is very difficult to do so because entrenchment is part of the UN bureaucracy.

Once personnel are recruited by the UN, there is no formal career training for them: on-the-job training is the norm. Of course, as they move from mission to mission, they get experience in various jobs, and gradually move up the career ladder. Generally speaking, UN staff are reluctant to support any initiative or concept with which they have not had personal experience. UN field staff are not regarded by UN military peacekeepers as progressive, imaginative, professional or dynamic. It was not unusual to meet a Chief Administrative Officer (CAO) of a UN mission who entered UN service as a security guard at UN headquarters 30 years previously. There are exceptions of course, but these individuals are considered mavericks, and not often given the opportunity to prove their competence and to prove that they can advance by ability alone. Notwithstanding these comments, UN field service senior management personnel are experienced and competent in following UN financial and administrative rules. When they are inflexible, the military peacekeeper has great problems trying to come up with other options and ways of approaching problems. I found that the best way was to write a memorandum to the CAO with my recommendation as Chief Logistics Officer (CLO) and ask him to pass that to New York. That got him off the hook.

I was fortunate when I was CLO of a peacekeeping mission, as my predecessor was in New York, and he was the official responsible for dealing with my requests. This meant that I had somebody there who understood what I was attempting to do, and who would deal with me in a professional manner.

These are the kinds of games that have to be played within the UN from time to time. I am not saying that the CAO was not willing to help, but he did not want to put his neck on the line for something that he had never seen happen before or that was a concept that he did not understand. But this was the way we worked - I was a CLO for three years, and luckily did not have to fall on my sword. It is my perception that at the moment, due to the great expansion in peacekeeping missions, the UN is suffering from a lack of good experienced CAOs and Chief Procurement Officers (CPOs). Some friends of mine who had retired from the UN as civilians - some of them as much as 80 years old - have now been called back into missions where the UN especially needs people. One was formerly the Chief Transportation Officer in the UN Disengagement Observer Force (UNDOF) and was called back last autumn to go to Somalia to help with administration. When he arrived, there had already been two CAOs on the ground, and nobody gave him a job to do. He immediately started writing standard operating procedures (SOPs) for transport. He kept submitting them and they were repeatedly ignored. Finally, two months ago, a new CAO arrived, and my friend became the Chief Transport Officer. He is now organizing matters as they should be, but unfortunately he is at the end of his six months tour of duty. By the way, I have great sympathy for the UN Chief of Staff in Somalia. It will not be an easy job for him to try to take over control from the Americans and to establish a working, competent UN headquarters there.

Recently, I have heard some very good discussion on the upgrading of the UN operations centre to a 24-hour, seven-day basis in New York. I have never personally had an operational problem with the old system, but I knew that if anything went back on the weekend that we would not have an answer until the following week. I would hope if an operations centre is established at UNHQ that it will include a substantial logistics component. As anybody who has been in the field knows, if logistics arrangements are not planned for, there is sure to be trouble ahead. The need for an adequate logistics operations staff in UN headquarters in New York to develop new or update UN logistics contingency plans and policy and coordinate these plans within all peacekeeping missions and nations, whose experience and advice would reduce or eliminate many of the new missions' startup problems, is one that I cannot emphasize enough. If there could be people working at UNHQ on a permanent basis, instead of asking nations to come in quickly on an *ad hoc* basis, there would be fewer problems in trying to implement new missions. Member states have the necessary personnel who are willing to go to New York and carry out this function.

This logistics staff could perform additional roles. When there is a requirement for the quick supply of equipment for an operational mission, such as we are seeing in the former Yugoslavia at the moment, the UN has difficulties meeting the requirement. If we had a logistics staff at UNHQ, its members could be working on cooperative logistics agreements with the appropriate nations and companies to make this type of equipment and the ongoing spare parts support available in very short notice. I am not saying that such arrangements do not exist now, but I do not think that we are putting as much effort as we could into that area.

With the increased number of new missions, there is a greater need than ever before to coordinate properly any logistic policy changes - either originating in UN headquarters, or as suggested from the field - with all concerned to avoid downstream problems for the new and inexperienced peacekeepers.

We all know that they have other startup problems, including morale and the credibility of the UN, with both the participating nations and the host nations. The average peacekeeping soldier is at a mission for six months. To motivate troops and to keep the morale up are very difficult problems for the commander. If troops are under fire it is even worse. Thus we owe it to the operational commander to do everything we can to lighten the load in the logistics area.

Another task of a UN logistics staff would be to review budget submissions and validate (for entitlement and standardization) statements of requirements for equipment from field missions. This would better control expenditures, especially for the so-called "prestigious" missions where the perception among other missions is that budgetary control is not maintained to an appropriate level, due to high-intensity operations and size.

Those who wish to supply goods and services to the UN must be aware that in UN missions, zero-based budgets are drawn up on an annual basis. Whatever the equipment requirements: night scopes, long-range binoculars, new vehicles or mine-clearing equipment, they all have to go into the budget a year in advance. Furthermore, suppliers can go and talk to UN headquarters staff and say "I have got a new widget here and it is fantastic." But, remember that the people you are talking to in New York are there looking after all UN agencies. Military peacekeeping is not their bread and butter. If you want to sell an item, the troops in the field have to see it, have to want it and have to put it in their budget, and if they do not write a tight, comprehensive specification to make sure they get what they want, the UN will buy the cheapest item that is available that meets that specification. My point here is that if a supplier wants to introduce an item to the UN, then he should get it out to the people in the field so that they understand what the capabilities of that equipment are. Some nations have been very successful in introducing items into mission areas so that they can be tested there and those who will be using them can see whether or not they meet the requirement. In order to do that, UN headquarters approval is required. Bear that in mind and work through your national representatives to get clearance. I am not saying that you will be successful, because there are political ramifications of procurement within the UN, as there are anywhere in the world, and UNHQ buyers are very circumspect to make sure that all nations get a chance to bid. So if the UN peacekeepers have a specific piece of equipment they want, and it is ideal for the job, they must write a very good statement of requirement (SOR). Unfortunately, there is no standard UN SOR format.

As I have mentioned, in the UN procurement system all procurement is undertaken within approved annual budgets prepared one year in advance of the requirement. Think of that for a moment. What does that mean? The budget is made up a year in advance. By the time the money is authorized for a particular mission, the commanding officer (CO) has changed twice. The new CO probably wants to change things right away. The first thing the CAO says to him is: "Just a minute. What you want is not in your budget. You cannot spend any money in that area - there is no UN approved money for that particular item. Put it in your next budget." So in theory, he writes it in his budget, and, if approved, the money will not be there for another year. This was one of my biggest problems as a CLO in trying to keep Canadian

COs happy, because they wanted to do things now, they did not agree with what the previous CO had planned - they wanted to do other things. Sometimes I was able to make arrangements whereby the CAO would accept that Canada funded the item, put it in the budget, and they would get their money back a year later. When I was CLO, Canada spent over $1,000,000 in advance of UN budget approval. Happily, the UN eventually reimbursed Canada. These are the kinds of practices in which we have to engage to make operations run smoothly.

Procurement in the UN basically takes place on two levels: local procurement within the field mission, and the centralized international competitive procurement from UN headquarters in New York for capital equipment and high value service contracts such as food. Let us look at local procurement and what it means. It covers consumables, construction materials, laundry contracts, accommodation rental agreements, fresh fruit and vegetable contracts, and locally available spare parts and other miscellaneous services. By and large, local procurement works reasonably well, and to some degree is dependent upon the personality of the UN CPO and the relationship established by the mission military logistics staff. Routine requirements usually take three months to procure locally, although that could be expedited to a matter of days or hours if a strong operational requirement was present.

Centralized procurement by UN headquarters in New York is another story. This is a large organization with about 100 buyers who provide procurement services to all the UN organizations, not just peacekeeping missions. It was not organized to support high priority military operational requirements. Routine capital procurement for peacekeeping missions ranges from six months at best to two years in the worst cases. UN headquarters basically processes contracts and, to the extent possible, competitively shops worldwide for political reasons. This procurement organization has serviced the Middle East peacekeeping missions reasonably well in the past, but was not well suited for immediate operational requirements when timeliness was essential.

Secretary-General Boutros Boutros-Ghali is urging pre-stocking of common emergency stocks for the UN. This would be achieved, if and when it is authorized, at the UN depot in Pisa, Italy. It was originally planned that as vehicles and other common items were purchased for the UN they would be held there and then issued to the various missions as required. The UN personnel at Pisa also have a minimal local purchase capability. The Pisa facilities come in handy when arrangements need to be made to get items out of the US pipeline and onto UN aircraft.

My last point has to do with standardization. Within the UN the possibility of having to create additional new military peacekeeping missions has always been recognized, but due to a very small UNHQ logistics planning staff, that aspect was never well addressed. In the mid-1980s, when the UN Transition Authority (UNTAC) Namibia mission was in the early discussion stages, UN headquarters staff advised each existing peacekeeping mission that it would be required to release ten percent of its non-military pattern commercial vehicles and equipment for the Namibia mission should it be authorized. At first glance, this solution for startup equipment for a new mission sounded very logical. However, at the next Middle East inter-mission logistics conference the impact of the lack of standardization of common requirements was discussed at length. Not every mission had the same types of vehicles. So if four or five different types of vehicles are sent, what is the implication for spare parts? That would be a major problem, as parts for all of them would have to be carried. The lack of standardization became very clear at that time, and there was unanimous support for maximum standardization of common equipment to the degree possible.

One of the initiatives that came out of those discussions was that there should be one ration scale to accommodate all nationalities. Now when we say one ration scale what do we mean? If you have Irish troops, they want potatoes, if you have Fijian troops, they want rice. So we had to come up with a ration scale so that one item could be traded off one for another, but that still would cover the whole spectrum of National Forces. The logical mission to do the field-testing work on that project was the UN Interim Force in Lebanon (UNIFIL). The people there came up with a very good working scale that I suspect is now being used around the world. That we now have one common scale is great for planning, and it makes it much easier for new staff going in on the ground. There is also a requirement for other common scales of issue. When I talk of scales of issue I am referring to an Army logistics term. To explain: a fighter squadron is entitled to have a video cassette recorder in its operations readiness room. So, if new fighter squadrons are formed, the logistician's task is easy. A logistics officer consults the scales of issue and then selects the required equipment. When I was a CLO, we wanted to come up with common scales of issue for such things as stationery, office machines and furniture - pretty mundane items. But, to put it in perspective, one should be aware that the UN does not have any standard catalogues from which to order.

However, there are now common UN scales of issue for accommodation and furnishings, kitchen equipment, communication equipment (including generators) and even UN Military Police (MP) equipment. The point I wish to make is that with greater standardization in the area of logistics, the operational aspects are made more efficient.

Prior to the plea for the standardization of vehicles, using Namibia as an example, we in the field asked that UNHQ establish one vehicle fleet for all missions. But we did not just say to get one vehicle fleet - we told them to 'tie some strings' to it, so that we did not have to carry huge supplies of spare parts and order them only once a year. We asked each company to be prepared to have regional depots spread throughout the world where we can order parts on a 30-day availability basis. Toyota won the contract. I suspect that when we went into the former Yugoslavia the resources just were not available that fast from Toyota. Volkswagen came through and filled the gap.

I will conclude with a comment on the future of peacekeeping. It is a growth industry, of that there is no doubt. However, suppliers will have to be very competitive to compete on the world market. It must be remembered that the UN is constrained by lack of funds in most missions, and when this is the case, economy is the guiding principle. When money is short, only that which is really needed is ordered. So keep that in mind in trying to sell something to the UN. The product will not be purchased unless it meets a specific UN requirement.

Peacekeeping and Defence Procurement

Alex Morrison

Our next speaker is Mr. David Cooper, who has worked at NATO since 1970. In 1980 he moved to the Defence Support Division and was responsible for the establishment and implementation of NATO's Armaments Programming Procedures. He was also the key staff officer involved in the development and proposals for a NATO conventional armaments planning system, and in January of 1988 he was promoted into his present position, that of Executive Policy Coordinator to the Assistant Secretary-General for Defence Support. He will be very heavily involved if there is a NATO force deployed to the former Yugoslavia.

David Cooper

As you have just heard, I am the Executive Policy Coordinator to the Assistant Secretary-General for Defence Support. What that means is that NATO Secretary-General Manfred Woerner has five deputies, one of which is responsible for armaments cooperation, and I am sort of his *Chef de Cabinet*. I am the one that is meant to be coming up with the ideas. I am a supreme non-technician. I was trained as a historian and then as a strategic studies analyst.

Si je peux dire quelques mots à tous nos amis de Canada: c'est avec un plaisir tout à fait particulier que je me trouve à Ottawa, j'ai fait une partie de mes études à l'Université de Carleton, donc c'est toujours un grand plaisir d'être ici, et de voir tellement d'amis dans la salle.

I want to say a few words to set the scene about NATO strategy and then speak about peacekeeping, and the operational concepts which are becoming more relevant to peacekeeping as a theme and as an objective. I will then speak about equipment and NATO's defence procurement policies and programmes.

NATO's new strategic concept was adopted late in 1991. Basically it is a shift from the concept of forward linear defence to one of counter-concentration forces supported by a considerable reserve ability. In accordance with this new strategy, NATO has indicated its willingness to support peacekeeping on a case-by-case basis, and we have already seen certain examples of this, one of them being the provision of our AWACS fleet in support of the United Nations in the former Yugoslavia. One of my main themes concerning defence procurement and the impact of peacekeeping on it is to stress that we are not going to see a radical departure in policies or equipment. Rather, we will see various shifts of emphasis. For example, take NATO's new strategy itself. We must not forget that there is still a paramount requirement for main defence forces. The primary responsibility of any government of NATO and of the Alliance itself is still defence against aggression against territory or aggression against legitimate interests. So we are talking about shifts of emphasis when we talk about peacekeeping. We are not necessarily, in terms of our strategy, in terms of our operational concepts, or even in terms of our equipment - with certain exceptions - talking about radical departures. We are still, therefore, going to require a broad spectrum of military capability. Let us not forget that there are still 23 countries in the world with tank fleets of at least 1,000 tanks apiece. So we are going to continue to need main defence forces, even if, of course, peacekeeping and the capabilities required for it are becoming more important.

In the area of operational concepts, once again we see not so much fundamental change, but shifts of emphasis. Obviously, there will be less emphasis on indiscriminate weapons, area weapons systems and indirect fire support systems, because the objective, less and less, is no longer maximum attrition. Far more emphasis is being placed on what we might call situational awareness, and particularly on urban security equipment. In his presentation, Colonel Gedge queried the qualifications of some of his colleagues in the United Nations. Let me stress that NATO personnel are supremely well-qualified. You will be interested to learn that the entire executive strength of the division in NATO responsible for conventional armaments cooperation is 42 people, supported by an equal number of secretaries and clerks. That is also one illustration of the extent to which defence procurement remains very much a national responsibility. NATO headquarters is not a great big procurement organization.

In the future there will be certainly more emphasis on implementation flexibility: in other words, on the availability of all-weather combat assets, appropriate transportation - one of our major headaches - and command, control, communications and intelligence (C^3I). The C^3I area is one which is going to receive particular emphasis at NATO, because it is in that field, in many respects, that the challenges of peacekeeping present themselves in the starkest fashion. It is an area also where NATO's track record must improve. One area I have in mind is that of tactical battlefield communications. Over a decade ago, individual NATO countries started to put together seven or eight different tactical battlefield communications systems, not one of which was designed to be interoperable with any of the others, and none of which were designed to be interoperable with NATO's own communications systems. A lot of work has had to be done by a lot of very clever people to design all of the clever little black boxes to try to minimize the aggravation. I am talking about systems like Ptarmigan, Zodiac, Hermes, Rita and Autonet. What a scandal that was. And I have not even talked yet about the still-missing NATO identification system. So command, control and communications are very much an area of daunting challenges. In peacekeeping we have a dispersion of small national units over large areas and in remote locations, and thus the need somehow to maintain tight political control. So, communications and information systems assets are going to be critical, particularly between the tactical forces and the higher level strategic authorities and headquarters.

NATO forces engaged in peacekeeping operations will certainly not have the robust infrastructure, in relative terms, that they have been used to in NATO territory. What is this going to mean in terms of equipment? It is going to mean a greater emphasis on things like optronics (to improve all-weather capability) and a greater emphasis on communications and data processing systems - everything from satellites to data fusion - allowing for real-time integration of arms and data control systems. It is going to involve far more emphasis on imagery exploitation technologies, providing new possibilities for target acquisition, identification and tracking. And it is certainly going to require an effective ground surveillance system. I am pleased to be able to say that if all goes well - and I choose my words carefully - I hope the NATO Secretary-General is going to be making an announcement about ground surveillance because there is a strong feeling within the international civil and military staffs that we ought to be trying to construct a common NATO approach to ground surveillance, as was done in the case of the AWACS fleet. I will not possibly predict the outcome of this - NATO members may turn it down. But we are obviously thinking of something like the J-Stars and one or two of the European systems being brought together in some common NATO approach, in a similar fashion as what was done with AWACS, using perhaps even the same cost-sharing formula, trying to get everybody involved and ensuring that everybody gets the data from the programme, and perhaps using the AWACS bases as bases for the aircraft. We think we would need a rather small fleet. We would be able to do on the ground what AWACS does so well in the skies.

In terms of the individual armed services, when thinking of peacekeeping, what does this mean in terms of the relative procurement balance between them against the overall context of this change in NATO strategy? In terms of the navy, a tremendous emphasis is going to be placed and is being placed on the question of sealift and custom-built ships. The US has plans already for this, which some people see as a result of the lessening of the strategic significance of its blue water navy. I think aircraft carriers are increasingly coming under question, and I am sure that there are navy men here who will be happy to argue about this for hours, though it is certainly true that there will be future peacekeeping operations probably beyond the range of land-based aircraft. These scenarios may be fewer and fewer, and it was noticeable in the Gulf that the six US aircraft carriers carried approximately 200 ground attack aircraft, compared with over 700 operating from land-bases. So a slight question mark over the future of carriers.

Air forces for peacekeeping are going to remain popular and useful assets. They continue to provide and will continue to provide a flexible source of immediate firepower. They are also the quickest way of assembling a multinational force. We must also not forget that air power is increasingly popular with the public, particularly as a way of trying to limit the consequences of subsequent ground action. As a generalization, aircraft have perhaps in some ways benefitted most visibly from some of the new technology - particularly stealth technology. I think in the background of what I am saying you will hear that the view at NATO is still very much one, I think, that technologically sophisticated armies are still the armies for peacekeeping. There is not going to be a great transition to simple bits of kit - we will still need a full spectrum of capabilities and of technologies. But it is obviously true, certainly for ground forces, that there will be shifts of emphasis to urban security equipment - things like body protection gear, rubber bullets, personal weapons and all of the other things that we know about.

So as I say, shifts of emphasis, but not really any radical departures in terms of strategies, doctrines, operational concepts, military requirements and, eventually, equipment. One slight area which may depart from this generalization is the one that is being referred to as non-lethal weapons (or disabling weapons, or disabling systems technologies), which is something which is of considerable interest to NATO headquarters, and some work in some of these areas is being conducted by NATO's Defence Research Group. I am aware that I open up here a particular Pandora's Box, because some of these technologies certainly do not look very non-lethal to me. But the objective is to move, clearly, from direct-fire attrition to what somebody has called 'information-age wars', where the objective particularly or increasingly is not to kill the enemy, not to destroy him, but to paralyze him - to put him out of business - for some period of time. There are many technologies which are being looked at with this in mind. Some of them sound absolutely fantastic (and I mean fantastic in the 'weird' sense, but they are being taken very seriously). For example, there are types of crystallizing powder which might be dusted on roads to destroy the tires of vehicles. One idea is to use aircraft to spray polymer adhesives which would literally glue up equipment and prevent its operation. It would be extremely time consuming and costly to remove. It is being worked on very seriously. Another area is that of infrasound, which would consist of very low frequency sound generators which would cause disorientation, nausea, vomiting and, if you are really unlucky, bowel spasms. The good news, apparently, with this particular area of technology is that the extremely unpleasant effects cease as soon as the generator is turned off.

Another area of interest is the one which is called supercaustics. This is a very interesting area and a very interesting development. It is a type of hydrochloric acid, but it is about a million times more powerful. The idea is that this could be sprayed, particularly onto armoured vehicles, and, for example, could destroy optics very quickly.

So these are some of the examples of some of the disabling technologies which are being developed in order to try to promote capabilities which do not result immediately in attrition. When you are not faced with the massed ranks of the Warsaw Pact, but you are faced with kids and teenagers with AK-47s, you do want, if you can, to have capabilities to try to deal with the situation without having to shoot to kill. Of course, ultimately, to protect the soldier, that is what has to be done.

So much for some of the equipment and some of the technologies. Let me just say a few words about the way that we go about our defence procurement. One of the positive factors of the greater emphasis on peacekeeping is that it is going to reinforce the process whereby defence procurement is conducted on a far more rigorous, planned and scientific basis. And this of course is being encouraged by the fact that there is less and less money, and so there is less scope for mistakes.

Since the Second World War, we have continued to operate, in the west, what might be called an equipment replacement process. We have tended to replace tanks with tanks and planes with planes and bridges with bridges. The requirement has often been expressed in terms of "I need a new bridge." "Why do you need a new bridge?" "Well, the bridges that I have got are rather old, and the threat on the other side of the river has changed. I need new bridges. I do not need to be able to take 200 men and 50 pieces of material over in 20 minutes, I need to be able to take 2,000 men and 1,500 pieces of equipment over in 2.3 minutes. Please give me a new bridge."

So you go and give him a new bridge, and then you find that one or two things have happened. First of all, it has taken so long to find the money to buy the bridge that by the time you have found the bridge the threat on the other side of the river has changed again. Second, you find that basically the requirement has been expressed in the wrong terms. There are many ways of getting men and equipment across water. Some of them are less serious than others. If it is summer and the river is not very wide, and you just want to get your rifles across, you can have swimming lessons. You can go across in pontoons, you can go across in boats, you can dig under the river, or you can helicopter people across. If you are really smart, you might be able to reposition your forces in such a way that you do not have to cross the river in the first place. In other words, there has been in recent years, nationally and at last at NATO, more and more of the realization that this process ought to be driven by military requirements which are expressed in terms of operational deficiencies. "Please do not tell me that you need a new bridge - tell me what your problem is." When it is analyzed properly, you will often find that the solution is not a new bridge at all - it is something that you had not thought of. Hopefully the solution may be cheaper than a new bridge!

We are already at NATO running a system called the Phased Armaments Programming System, where this type of approach is taken. Cooperation between the allies starts with mission-need documents, and there is a move to understand the mission and the operational requirements before technology and equipment is identified. In more recent times, we have developed what is known as the Conventional Armaments Planning System (CAPS), and this is really the first ever *ab initio* armaments planning system fielded by the Alliance. For the businessmen in the audience, this is of particular interest, because it means that every two years NATO is going to put together a rather large book which represents an agreed, long-range procurement plan agreed to by all Ministers, so this is going to be an enormous source of information, and it should help some of your marketing work by enabling you, perhaps, to direct the money with a little bit more focus. I obviously cannot give you the two-yearly plan because it is classified, but if you have good contacts with your Ministries of Defence, I am sure that you will be able to get some of the information that you need.

NATO is, of course, an inter-governmental organization, it is not an industrial consortium. But you are going to see, in this conventional armaments plan, the long-term requirements of the major NATO commanders being brought alongside the national plans within those requirements areas, and an agreed NATO plan resulting from the process. If any of you know anything about NATO's force-planning system, this, in a sense, is the armaments equivalent of it. It has only taken 40 years to get there, but we have at last done it. There were amazing national sensitivities in getting CAPS launched, but we have managed to get around them, and I think the nations have realized also that there is great benefit and advantage to them in contributing to this exercise and doing so openly. So, industrialists, you will see in this conventional armaments plan an agreed, long-range procurement plan, certainly agreed on at the level of your Defence Ministers. It will go out 10 or 15 years into the future.

Let me just say one or two things about institutions. It is mind-boggling in Europe at the moment - what my good American friends call the 'alphabet soup'. I would imagine from the viewpoint of North America that it must be even more confusing. There are many institutions that are knocking around, with the general public wondering what they are meant to be doing. NATO is well-known, and I hope that its mission is clear. We have a whole range of other institutions - the CSCE, the WEU, the Independent European Programme Group (IEPG). I think that one of the problems at the moment is that so much of the security debate is being focused on institutional competence rather than on the actual subject and the actual issues involved. And here, without springing to the defence of my own organization, let me just say that of all of these institutions, at the end of the day it is NATO that has got the horses. We have got the troops, we have got the equipment, and I believe that we have the capabilities to contribute - in a decisive way - in any way that is required. But very much the view at the moment at NATO headquarters is that the Alliance is at the disposition of the United Nations, that if the international community wishes NATO to participate effectively in any form of peacekeeping operation, then the Alliance certainly stands ready to do so.

The Future of Peacekeeping

Alex Morrison

Our next speaker is Mr. Ernie Regehr, who is the National Director of Project Ploughshares, an organization which seeks to promote Canadian policies of peace through research, publication and education on problems of disarmament and development both in Canada and internationally. Mr. Regehr has served as the Canadian expert on the United Nations Secretary-General's Committee of Governmental Experts on Transparency and Openness in the Arms Trade. He enjoys an international reputation for the quality of his research, his writing and his speaking.

Ernie Regehr

Introduction: The Context of Decision-Making

When we in Canada explore the future of peacekeeping and our contribution to it, we of course do it in a particular political and economic context - and currently that includes an environment of intense competition for dwindling public resources. Relative to other departments, the Department of National Defence has so far managed to hold its own, but that record will not necessarily be sustained. The maintenance of international peace and security in the post-Cold War world has significant military elements to it, but much more significant, of course, and increasingly urgent, is the need to bolster the non-military foundations of global stability. The Right Honourable

Joe Clark, when he was Secretary of State for External Affairs, put it this way: "A world which is inhumane and characterized by great variations in economic and social well-being will never be truly secure."[1] The demands for resources to create the conditions of enduring peace, for what United Nations Secretary-General Boutros Boutros-Ghali calls "peace-building," will increase and will ultimately, if we are wise, command a large share of the Canadian and global security budget.

A second feature of the present context is that some Canadian military requirements have been sharply reduced (notably a land presence in Europe and a strategic maritime presence in the North Atlantic), while peacekeeping requirements have sharply increased. So the proverbial, and obvious, bottom line is that we must in Canada, as must all wealthy, industrialized, aid donor countries, make some tough choices. How are we going to spend our security dollar? How much of it should be used for social and economic programs to alleviate the inequities which, as Mr. Clark says, are a fundamental threat to peace and security? How much of it should go to maintaining a military capability to respond to military threats to security? What portion of the military dollar can be focused on peacekeeping operations, and how much needs to be retained for territorial requirements and combat capabilities beyond our borders?

It is clear that while each option may have an active constituency of support, what Canada manages in each case is bound to fall short of expectations. I want to raise briefly three concerns relevant to the future of peacekeeping, and then return to the theme of implications for Canadian spending priorities.

Section I: Focus on Peace Making

The first concern relates to "peace making." In that section of *An Agenda for Peace,* his June 1992 report to the UN Security Council, Mr. Boutros-Ghali refers to the accumulation of declarations and mechanisms for the resolution of conflict in the international community, and concludes: "If conflicts have gone unresolved, it is not because techniques for peaceful settlement were unknown or inadequate. The fault lies first," he says, "in the lack of political will of parties to seek a solution to their differences..."[2] Nor, one might add, is the failure to resolve conflicts, as Cyprus, or, more dramatically, Angola and the former Yugoslavia tragically testify, a failure of peacekeeping. Peacekeeping is itself not a conflict resolution mechanism, but it certainly assumes, and ultimately requires, parallel and committed political attention to resolving the conflict. Peacekeeping operations at their best buy time - but the advantage of time is quickly squandered if the international community is unable to fill it with constructive peace making initiatives.

The future of peacekeeping depends on improved peace making, and the recent report of the Standing Senate Committee on Foreign Affairs seconds many of the peace making suggestions in *An Agenda for Peace*. It goes on to counsel increased attention to such "extra-military measures" as sanctions, human rights monitors, and war crimes investigations and proceedings to generate political will and address the roots of conflict. One important resource that has received scant attention is the growing field of non-official or "Track Two" diplomacy. Not only has "globalization" of the non-governmental organization (NGO) community in recent years dramatically increased the capacity for this kind of "citizen diplomacy" (buttressed, as it is, by an extensive and growing academic literature), but the current surge in ethnic or identity conflicts reveals an urgent need for it. Identity conflicts, that is, conflicts in which the rights and political and/or social viability of ethnic groups or national communities are central issues, by definition develop deeply rooted mistrust and antagonism between communities. When one community, usually in response to unmet basic needs for social and economic security, sets out to strengthen its own collective influence, and to struggle for recognition, and power, over against the state or other communities, it produces a level of mistrust, even hatred, which is not readily dealt with at a level of official diplomacy. Political elites cannot cut workable deals on behalf of communities that do not trust each other, or that see each other as having fundamentally conflicting interests (Canadians learned the truth of that not so long ago.) What is required is extensive, long-term, community level contact, consultation and confidence-building to generate a minimal trust between communities.

In some instances, where conflicts have endured for centuries, even millennia, it is obviously a bigger job than in others. Project Ploughshares has for several years now been hosting a series of cross-clan consultations involving the Somali community in Canada. Linked to similar exercises in other countries, and in Somalia itself, these discussions follow two basic assumptions: first, that reconciliation and the resolution of national or regional conflicts, especially in the case of "identity conflicts," require broad-based, citizen participation in consensus building; and second, that Somalis now in exile have an important role to play in planning for, and rebuilding, a reformed Somalia. One of the attractive elements of the earlier UN plan for Somalia (under the leadership of Ambassador Sahnoun), was that it envisioned a vigorous, decentralized, grassroots consultative process to complement the peacekeeping or enforcement actions. The Somali case is a good example of the symbiotic relationship between peace making and peacekeeping. Without peace making, the danger increases that the present military intervention will prove to be a tragic failure. If there is not some measure of real confidence and trust built among the conflicting communities, if there is not significant progress in redeveloping a pan-Somali consensus on the future form of the Somali states, then the route back to chaos will be short and direct. At the same time, without peacekeeping or the present multilateral intervention, without at least a tourniquet to arrest the haemorrhaging, even temporarily, there would have been little will, and even less opportunity, for sustained peace making efforts.

If peacekeeping is to have a future, then the peace making agenda of the UN needs to be extended, and the contribution of the NGO community worldwide needs to be increasingly recognized and encouraged.

Section II: Future Peacekeeping Models

The second concern I want to raise relates to what seems to be the developing conventional wisdom that peacekeeping is evolving toward a much greater reliance on the use of force - that operations that do not have the consent of the parties will become almost routine. Let us not forget that any peacekeeping operation depends on the ability of a disparate, often distracted, international community to forge the political consensus and the will to act together in a contentious, controversial context.

As Norman Cousins has written, the international community is still more an arena than it is a community. It will not be easy, in this arena, to muster broad political support for major military interventions against the wishes of one or more of the significant parties to a conflict. And this kind of broad support will be a prerequisite to action because the major powers (happily) are increasingly constrained. The capacity of the United States, for example, to act unilaterally in the use of force beyond its borders has been substantially inhibited. Of course, that does not deny the fact that, in major operations, the international community also cannot act without the US (for some time to come the US will give leadership to collective operations). And even the five permanent members of the UN Security Council (China, France, the United Kingdom, the United States, and Russia) must retain credibility. One American conference group recently concluded that, "for the United Nations to operate as global 'peace-maker' (a term it wrongly used to connote forceful intervention),...it must co-opt support from medium and regional powers and work closely with regional organizations. Sooner or later the leadership in any UN cause may need at least the acquiescence of two-thirds or more of the member governments voting in the UN General Assembly."[3]

Canada's Ambassador to the UN, Louise Frechette, really made the same point to the Senate Committee when she said that developing countries in particular are wary of UN mandates to intervene without the consent of a host government. Even though most wanted intervention in Somalia, she said, they would have opposed it if directly polled, for fear that consent would be taken as approval of a principle of support of intervention.[4] Gulf-style enforcement actions, whatever one may think of their merits, will remain the exception. Only in the most unusual circumstances will there be the combination of mass indignation and national self-interest that is necessary for the major powers to mobilize the international community to the kind of response that was raised in the Gulf crisis. In most instances, particularly in well-armed regions of conflicts, the international community will be confined to what it is confined to in the former Yugoslavia - operating in a very dangerous environment, but not willing (wisely) to attempt large-scale enforcement because of the uncertainty of either cost or outcome.

Another factor that will continue to dampen the international community's enthusiasm for enforcement actions is the cost. For a long time to come, the UN will be operating with very limited resources. In a brief review of the costs of peacekeeping, Mr. Boutros-Ghali concludes that "the contrast between the costs of United Nations peacekeeping and the costs of the alternative, war..., would be farcical were the consequences not so damaging..."[5] The $60 + billion cost of the Gulf War does not measure up very favourably, in cost-benefit terms, when compared with the $3 billion annual cost of all current peacekeeping world-wide (even when you add to that all the incremental costs of participating forces), but there is to date little indication that governments are prepared to reverse those priorities.

So, when we contemplate the kinds of demands that are most likely to be made on Canada for UN peacekeeping in the future, I think we need to conclude that, all the new conflicts and threats of disorder notwithstanding, the most prominent or frequent model for future peacekeeping will be the traditional form which involves the consent of the parties. To this will be added increasing occasions for assistance to humanitarian relief operations with slightly increased levels of force, but the bread and butter of military peacekeeping will continue to be minimally armed forces in patrol and monitoring situations.

Section III: Conventional Arms Control

The third concern I wanted to raise is the threat to effective peacekeeping that is posed by the continuing proliferation of conventional weapons.

In the introduction to his *Agenda for Peace,* Mr. Boutros-Ghali said that to address the "pervasive and deep" sources of conflict "will require our utmost effort," among other things, "to curtail the existence and use of massively destructive weapons."[6] In this he was really harkening back to one of the original assumptions of those who conceived the UN's original collective security responsibilities; namely, that the international community was moving toward substantial disarmament. Indeed, not only was there such an expectation (the Charter was signed before the first nuclear explosion[7]), but there was an assumption that sustainable peace and security required it. Regulating arms was one of the jobs given to the Military Staff Committee, "in order to promote the establishment and maintenance of international peace and security with the least diversion for armaments of the world's human and economic resources."[8]

The fact that the international community is now better able to respond to regional conflicts with peacekeeping and even enforcement measures does not ease the pressure for conventional arms control. The opposite is the case - the pressure to reduce conventional arms should be much greater because, ultimately, the success of peacekeeping depends on it. The level of resources that the international community is prepared to put into peacekeeping (which is to say minuscule in comparison with what it has recently devoted to collective combat operations - never mind national defence forces) guarantees that peacekeeping forces will be small in number, lightly equipped, and routinely asked to operate in the midst of much more heavily armed belligerents. This means, by definition, that they will be there only with the consent of the parties. Options related to enforcement actions will be severely limited as long as there is no genuine collective effort to control the flow of weapons to regions of conflict.

At the close of the Gulf War of 1990-91 there was a moment of hope that such collective action would be forthcoming. Our own Canadian political leaders weighed in heavily, to their great credit, against the irresponsible sale of still more weapons to regions already dangerously overarmed. It turned out to be a momentary lapse. Exporters scrambled for orders from the cash-rich, conflict-rich Middle East, in a weapons trade that is tragic, not only for its squandering of resources (petro-dollars that should be used in other ways), but also for its further contribution to the insecurity of the region, and for the limitations it ultimately places on the international community's capacity to intervene in the region at minimal force levels.

By most accounts, Middle East countries have placed weapons orders valued at more than $60 billion since politicians collectively wrung their hands in the aftermath of the Gulf War about excessive arms sales to this region of tension. Sooner or later, we will have to learn that you cannot have it both ways. Canadian companies are at it as well - anxious to build commercial viability into a Canadian military industry through export sales. In our case it will not work. I do not have to remind this audience about the rapid decline in the market for military goods worldwide, or about the fact that Canada's share of that market has dropped even more rapidly - in the US, Europe and the Third World (despite some large sales to the conflict-ridden Middle East). In a brand new study, the Stockholm International Peace Research Institute says that the arms industry boom is over, that there will be a steady continuing decline in the industry, and that the strategy of building or maintaining a national military industry based on export orders is a bust. The only truly buoyant markets are in regions of tension that also have a lot of cash (toward which politicians said we should show restraint) - indeed, Canada's best hopes for sales of frigates and ADATS systems are to the Middle East (for which permits would be denied if existing policy were assiduously applied).

Another reason why the strategy of building a commercially viable military industry on export sales is misguided is that the Canadian public does not support it. Already a Parliamentary Committee has put a constructive, forward looking set of proposals before Parliament to make Canada's military export policies much more restrictive than they now are.

And that is good news, because an export strategy is no more desirable, from a security standpoint, than it is feasible from an economic standpoint. Effective peacekeeping, particularly if we want to confine it to minimal levels and to minimize cost, depends on some serious gun control.

Conclusion: Implications for Canadian Policy

Peacekeeping, what Canadians are fond of claiming as their own invention, will remain a prominent responsibility of the international community. And Canada, a country of immense resources (extraordinary wealth and skills by global standards, and possessing a political will that supports constructive involvement in the international community), has a responsibility to carry, to continue to carry, a disproportionate share of that responsibility. It is in our interests to nurture a global security climate conducive to effective peacekeeping, and two ways to do that more effectively are through the nurturing of more broadly based diplomacy, especially in identity conflicts; and through a reinvigorated campaign to control the proliferation of conventional weapons.

Our responsibilities are substantial, but our resources, despite our relative wealth in global terms, are declining - which means we need to take a pretty fundamental look at spending priorities. Among the options that are available for peace and security action beyond our borders, which will best reflect Canadian traditions, values, interests and capabilities?

One question that needs to be revisited is this: what proportion of the security dollar that is available for spending on peace and security measures beyond our borders should go toward military peacekeeping capabilities, and what share should go to peace-building (to what the Department of External Affairs "cooperative security" approach identifies as the need to address effectively those conditions of poverty and abuse which are the conflict producers)? The recent cuts to the Canadian International Development Agency (CIDA) budget, and the current mutterings within External Affairs, for example, to shift the focus of aid away from the poorest countries of Africa, undermine the peace-building agenda, just when it should be a greater priority. There is some hope that Canadians will not stand for it - they may increasingly ask the same question posed by one prominent Toronto columnist. In a discussion of External's interest in cutting and reshaping overseas development assistance, the *Globe and Mail's* Michael Valpy once asked: "Why does External want to rob Uganda to give more to Ukraine? Why doesn't it rob the Defence Department to give more to both?"[9] One could, of course, quote plenty of columnists who would turn the question around - but the point is that it needs to be, and will be, extensively debated.

Besides the question of how Canada's peace and security dollar should be divided between peacekeeping and peace-building, there is also the question of reordered priorities within the Department of National Defence itself. We have been hearing a lot about the fact that DND's resources are stretched to the limit, that the cuts have to stop. Well, there are not a lot of certainties these days, it seems, but there is one you should count on. There will be more cuts to the defence budget. The question is not if, but where. How long, for example, will Canadians continue to tolerate the maintenance of costly surplus military bases in Canada, especially if this is perceived to be at the expense of peacekeeping and peace-building capabilities? I understand that this reluctance to close bases is more properly identified as a failure of political courage than as a DND planning failure - the problem being that shutting down bases is a process with high political cost and very little short term financial saving (while, by contrast, the cuts to foreign aid have so far incurred minimal political cost while yielding more immediate financial returns). But it would be hard to argue that this kind of trade off advances Canada's peace and security objectives.

If peacekeeping is a relatively personnel-intensive enterprise, it is worth asking which ranks have been proportionately trimmed the most in recent personnel reductions. Has there been an effort to preserve lower ranks while cutting back at more senior levels? My impression is that the opposite is the case - the number of people at the level of private has been cut much more than at senior rank levels (and that overall, military personnel have been cut more quickly than civilian personnel).

And then there are the choices about which military roles are in fact the most urgent. Which roles stand to make a genuine contribution to international peace and security? It may be bad form to speak of the EH-101 helicopter procurement programme, but one does need to ask whether current procurement programs are the most efficient response to the most critical security challenges, short and longer term, that we face. For some programs, as in Low Level Air Defence systems, it is obviously too late and we simply have to swallow the fact that we will, at a great public expense, be left with hardware that makes no contribution to our security efforts. In some other prominent cases it is not too late. At the very least, some of these commitments need to be put on hold, removed from the vagaries of party leadership politics, and made the subject of thorough public debate in the context of overall security directions and responsibilities. Such a public debate needs to put the future of our peacekeeping requirements into the context of an overall cooperative security policy. And in this debate we will need to remind ourselves, as the current Secretary of State for External Affairs reminded a recent seminar, that our objective is to contribute effectively to international peace and security, and that we cannot think of these contributions as essentially military operations. Mrs. McDougall put it this way: "When you consider expanded activities such as preventive diplomacy, peacemaking and peace-building, a much wider range of people, expertise and resources is required."[10] Canada's deployment of resources will have to reflect these new realities.

Notes

1. Joe Clark, "Canada's International Relations: Response of the Government of Canada to the Report of the Special Joint Committee on the Senate and the House of Commons," (Secretary of State for External Affairs, December 1986), pp.11-12.

2. Boutros Boutros-Ghali, An Agenda for Peace, United Nations, New York, 1992, p.20.

3. John M. Lee, Robert von Pagenhardt and Timothy W. Stanley, "Strengthening United Nations Peacekeeping and Peacemaking," International Economic Studies Institute, 1992, p.6.

4. "Meeting New Challenges: Canada's Response to a New Generation of Peacekeeping, Report of the Standing Senate Committee on Foreign Affairs," February 1993, p.37.

5. Boutros-Ghali, op. cit., p.29.

6. Ibid., p.2.

7. Erskine B. Childers, "The Future of the United Nations: The Challenges of the 1990s," Bulletin of Peace Proposals, Vol. 21, No. 2, 1990, p.143.

8. Ibid., p.152.

9. The Globe and Mail, March 5, 1993.

10. Seminar Report, "Canada's Agenda for International Peace and Security," February 8-9, 1993, External Affairs and International Trade Canada, Ottawa, p.5.

Forum

Mr. Don Macnamara, President, CISS

Mr. Regehr, I quite agree with you with regard to the whole spectrum of what I would call peace creation as opposed to peace making, because peace making has turned into what we used to call war. The whole matter of how this is going to be done, and by whom it is going to be done, is not outside the military realm. Indeed, if you look at Canada's contribution to peacekeeping over the years, with the exceptions of Cyprus, the hastily withdrawn Queen's Own Rifles at the time of the Suez Crisis, and the Congo, it is only to Yugoslavia and Somalia that we have sent combat troops. The vast majority of our contributions have been engineers, logistics and communications troops. These are the very resources which are part of that peace building or peace creating process. These are the very resources which would be extremely difficult to find in NGOs, and if findable would be extremely expensive to marshall. Yet, within the military, these resources are available, they are at the beck and call of the government, and they have the capability in terms of transportation and sustainability. So I think that we should avoid this confrontation or competition as to what is military and what is peace creation in this process. I think we have to look at where the resources are, how they are going to be expended, and how they are going to be maintained in the best interests of the nation, and for that matter the best interests of the target country. Would you care to comment?

Mr. Regehr

I agree with that. I think that there is a bit of a problem in terminology. I use the term peace building not as being that segment of the operation that is done in the peacekeeping process, but within the concept of overall responsibility and effort to create the kind of conditions of economic equity and the meeting of basic human needs which will alleviate conflict. The problem is that we cannot avoid competition for resources. That is the problem that we have to face now. How much of the international community's resources need to be focused on the more immediate problem? And of course there need to be major resources focused on the immediate problem in Somalia of establishing a basic stability and redeveloping a minimal infrastructure. That I take as part of the peacekeeping operation and using military forces. But then comes the problem of long-term peace building, and that is a very lengthy and extremely expensive proposition, but extraordinarily underfunded. I have some quarrel with the Canadian priorities at the moment. It is easy to cut ten percent from the Canadian International Development Agency (CIDA) budget. You have immediately that expendable cash right on hand. But it is folly in the long run, because in the long run you cannot abandon those countries in Africa, for example, with which we have had a long-term relationship and in which very basic community programmes of clean water and so forth depend upon continued funding. You cannot avoid a competition between those courses of action because there are limited resources. There are not going to be more resources in Canada available for responding to the problems of international peace and security. If anything they are going to go down. So how do we divide them? If we take the CIDA budget and the DND budget as all being part of the package for response to international peace and security, I think that we have to look towards new divisions within that overall peace and security budget.

Mr. Leslie Baylis, CISS Strategic Liaison Officer, Concordia University

Mr. Cooper, will European integration make NATO's job more difficult, or is it going to facilitate it to some degree, from a political context?

Mr. Cooper

Let me show you the dilemma. I have been a European federalist for years. I believe in a United States of Europe, and this is one reason that I have never worked for the British government. I am a strong European federalist - I am in the economic area, I am in the political area, I am in the environmental area. One area that I am not is in defence. There is this great debate at the moment in Europe about the European defence pillar. I have never seen it described clearly in operational terms. I do not know what a European defence strategy would look like. In operational terms, I do not see where western Europe is going to be projecting significant amounts of power out of area without logistics support, cooperation and public combat support from North America. I understand the rhetoric, but I do not see in European terms where all-European forces are going to be fighting in a significant fashion without North American assets. Is it to help the Belgians in Zaire? I cannot imagine that. I think there is a lot of political rhetoric about this. I think it is right that the Europeans want to concert and to discuss defence matters, but in operational terms, European defence to me is intrinsically linked to that of North America, and so you end up with something which is called the North Atlantic Treaty Organization.

Is it harmful? There are many areas which are of concern and which are becoming of greater concern as days go by. The European Community, for example, does not specifically include defence goods within its policy of economic integration. But we all know that more and more of defence technology is becoming dual use technology, that is, both civilian and military. In other words, when it is dual use, the civilian part of that technology does come under the Treaty of Rome and under the Single Act, and this is one area where the European community, with its 15,000 person staff just two kilometres from NATO Headquarters, is beginning to move into my own particular area of responsibility, which is defence procurement.

There are one or two other areas which are of concern. European public procurement regulations are now being devised. They are being devised without reference to North America, and that public procurement process could start to be used eventually in the defence procurement world. Europe is developing European company law. This will be a superb way of excluding North American companies from bidding for contracts, as will Eurostandards. There is a lot of work going on at the moment in standards - there is no easier way to keep a contractor out than to say that his standards do not conform.

There is a lot of work going on at the moment within the European Community, which I personally believe is going to make transatlantic cooperation harder and harder, and that is something which concerns me.

Mr. Allan Dixon, Peace Brigades International

Mr. Morrison, you mentioned how many children are dying from curable diseases, and that it might be necessary to intervene militarily, or that it is almost our duty to do that. I would just like to say that I was in El Salvador last year, where there is a UN operation. My experience there was that, of the different parts of the operation there, the really valuable part was the diplomatic part that happened two years prior to the peace agreement, that is, the negotiations themselves and the human rights contingent that was also there before the document was actually signed. The military presence there, although it was very useful in the logistics department - and I think that the military has something to offer there - was problematic because the soldiers that came were generally from countries which also had fairly poor human rights records. So there was not a lot of trust built up between the soldiers and the population. I think that if we use soldiers in something called peacekeeping, they are going to need very different training from the training we give them, which is for a very different purpose, really. So I think that the logistics part is useful, but the other part really needs some serious looking into.

The other example that I just wanted to mention was this idea of intervening militarily to save people. I think the example of Iraq is a good one, where the idea was to intervene to stop more people from being killed, but one of the side effects was that all of the infrastructure of the country was destroyed. There have been estimates that maybe 100,000 or 150,000 people died as the result of that, and there does not seem to have been much of an effort on behalf of the people involved to try and remedy those effects. So if you are going to intervene militarily to save people, I think that you have to take full responsibility for what you do.

Mr. Alex Morrison

I think that you are absolutely right. What you are pointing out, of course, is the inconsistency and the imperfection of man. We ought not to expect the United Nations to be any more perfect than individual countries. I do think that the United Nations is the best hope we have to present a balanced approach. As long as we have Canadians working on all parts of the spectrum trying to influence the United Nations, and as long as we have the United Nations and its 36 separate and somewhat autonomous agencies and organizations working together, then perhaps in the future we can overcome some of the difficulties that you have described.

Mr. Kevin Hunt

I was interested in what Mr. Regehr said about peace building, and about the cuts to CIDA. CIDA funding is made up of two parts - that which is passed on to the UN and those projects which are funded directly. From my experience in Ethiopia at the same time as everything was going on in Somalia, what I seemed to see was that a lot of UN money had been directed to certain people. For whatever reason there were a lot of people that got very rich, and I was wondering if Mr. Regehr believes if more money should be redirected to the Canadian operations and less to the United Nations?

Mr. Regehr

The main concern that I have is the overall problem of aid fatigue. That is something that is facing Canada, and it is not going to be solved without the international NGO community doing some very serious self-critical reevaluation of the aid effort, because it has not been an overwhelming success in the last four decades. But what we are doing now is moving towards - in times of very serious constraint - limits on the overall budget. You can close down a military base, which will cost you an immense amount of political capital and not yield a dollar of savings very soon. In the long run it will, but not in the immediate future. But you can cut CIDA by ten percent and you get the money in hand immediately and there is no political fallout of which to speak. That is the thing that frightens me, and I think that the danger is that the balance is shifting, ironically, at a time of a post-Cold War world, one of a largely reduced threat in those traditional terms, when the problem is understood increasingly to be one of inadequate development in a sense. But right at this time it is politically easier to cut the peace building budget than it is to cut the peace making budget. I am not promoting the reduction of the peacekeeping budget, but there needs to be some maintenance of balance. The great problem is that CIDA has had to decide essentially to withdraw itself from a significant number of African countries at modest cost saving to Canadian taxpayers and at extraordinary cost to the recipients of those community-based organizations. The NGO-led development agencies are being very badly hurt in this process.

Peacekeeping's Strategic Imperatives

Alex Morrison

As we all know, today is the 16th of March, which means that tomorrow is a day of great celebration, for it is the birthday of Princess Patricia, after whom Princess Patricia's Canadian Light Infantry was named - the last privately raised regiment in the Empire. It was raised here in Ottawa, and it has distinguished itself for Canada ever since. It gives me great pleasure as an officer of Princess Patricia's Canadian Light Infantry and as a Cape Bretonner to introduce to you today another officer of the PPCLI and another Cape Bretonner who has distinguished himself well in the service of peace, security and stability.

I met Lew MacKenzie at Xavier Junior College in Sydney. I consequently studied with him, served with him, and indeed, as with all of you, followed him as he commanded our very professional men and women of the Canadian Armed Forces and those from many other countries around the world. I think he is typical of the Canadian officer that is educated and trained in our country, displaying typical Canadian characteristics - as I said earlier this morning, not suffering fools gladly - irreverent and always ready to tell other people exactly what he thinks of them and what ought to be done. Of course those are the characteristics that have stood Canada and its armed forces personnel in such good stead over the years. Lew is a veteran of nine UN peacekeeping tours, the most recent being as commander of the Sarajevo sector in the United Nations Protection Force (UNPROFOR) in the former Yugoslavia. We have become accustomed to his expert opinions and views on national, foreign policy and military matters. We at the Canadian Institute of Strategic Studies are very pleased that he has agreed to become associated with us as a Senior Research Fellow. Please join me in welcoming Lew MacKenzie.

Lewis MacKenzie

This is my first presentation since retiring from the Canadian Armed Forces, and I have been asked to talk a little bit about the strategic imperatives of peacekeeping. I looked up a few of the key words in the dictionary and wrote a layman's title for my presentation, which is: "The Essential Aspects to be Considered When Developing a Worldwide Plan for Peacekeeping." Up until about 375 days ago - the beginning of March 1992 - that was pretty simple. The UN would be presented with a nice convenient conflict where the belligerents had decided to end the conflict and had pledged to keep the peace. The Security Council sent troops wearing blue berets or helmets riding in white vehicles with "UN" in large black letters on the top and all sides, and a convenient excuse was provided to the belligerents to blame the United Nations, rather than themselves, for not restarting the conflict and winning. The peacekeepers ensured that they established the mechanisms to keep the peace, and that involved everything from liaison officers to hot-lines to conferences and, dare I say, even social occasions where contact would be more informal. Just as long as the UN troops were talking to the belligerents, and they were talking to each other, everyone was satisfied. The UN also avoided civil wars, because they are much too nasty to get involved in, unless they are being fought by NATO proxies in a place called Cyprus.

Matters changed for the UN in the spring of 1992 when it decided to establish its headquarters for UNPROFOR in a bizarre location 400 kilometres forward of the front lines in Sarajevo. There was never any intention that the United Nations would have a mandate in Bosnia. Unfortunately, about three-and-a-half weeks after the commander of UNPROFOR, Lieutenant-General Nambiar of India, I (his Chief of Staff) and the other HQ personnel arrived in Sarajevo, the civil war broke out and we were too slow to leave. The European Community officers, the European Community Military Monitors, the International Red Cross, the United Nations High Commissioner for Refugees and the diplomatic community were all much quicker off the mark than we were and left town within two weeks of the war starting. We tried to maintain contact with the remainder of UNPROFOR which was in Croatia, but we found that to be impossible, as we were spending all of our time under fire in the bunker with a single military telephone connected by a single piece of field cable to a switchboard. So we then moved two-thirds of our headquarters to Belgrade, where we felt terribly guilty and embarrassed - having left Sarajevo - and kept trying to find some way to get back into that city to do some good for the citizens who were suffering. The result was that I was sent back to command the Sarajevo sector and to implement the airport agreement, which very quickly proved to be a counterproductive move. What we did by bringing food into Sarajevo was take the story off the front page of the papers. This upset the Muslim government with a small Croatian participation - the government of President Itzabegovic. What they really wanted was strong military intervention, and we were standing in the way of that. And they started their vilification campaign against the United Nations, and I must say against me. If you have been reading the paper over the last couple of days, you have probably seen reports of the Serbian militia soldier giving evidence in a court in Sarajevo that I was raping and murdering Muslim girls. These actions supposedly took place in August 1992, which gives new meaning to the term 'long-distance relationship', because on 1 August, when the sun came up I flew from Sarajevo and joined Alex Morrison in Zagreb. A few days later I left Zagreb for UN headquarters in New York, and after reporting to the Secretary-General flew straight to Ottawa. I bring up this point to highlight the nastiness of the type of business with which we are involved.

Now the world is sanctioning Serbia for its alleged actions, but no one has confirmed any direct involvement of Serbia in the war. It is the Bosnian Serbs, under Dr. Karadzic, that are fighting Mr. Itzabegovic and his government. Croatia has very large forces and a large number of units fighting in Bosnia, yet so far there has been very little condemnation of the Croatians. Presumably the reason why there is so much talk and so little action is that the situation is so complicated. No one knows what to do - other than try to feed some of the innocent victims - and unfortunately, as in all wars, the priority for food goes to the soldiers. Do not think that those packages being dropped by the American military are ending up in the hands of the old folks and the children. They are ending up in the hands of the people doing the fighting.

Just as the UN and the world community were dealing with the horrors of Bosnia, we began to see pictures of the starving in Somalia, and TV started to dictate foreign policy. This is perhaps not a bad thing, providing we make sure we get pictures from everywhere there is a problem in the world, and then we assign priorities. For if Somalia is to be the precedent for the invasion of a nation's security, then there is no reason to come home from Somalia. We can merely motor up to the southern Sudan and then drive down to Mozambique and over to Angola and then drop in on Liberia. There are many situations in Africa and in the rest of the world that meet the same criteria. So national governments, including Canada's, and the United Nations are scrambling to develop criteria against which they would judge every crisis to see if it qualifies for a peacekeeping force. They are considering all the factors, such as the massive movement of refugees, intolerable human suffering, outlandish civil rights abuses and the favourite catch-all found in the UN Charter, threats to international peace and security. I am not sure that they really have to bother with that cumbersome process, as every UN deployment will ultimately depend on the self-interests of the nations contributing the troops, and those self-interests are very dynamic. They change from day-to-day, and they quite often are dependent upon public opinion. The United States will figure prominently in future peacekeeping missions, as it has done in the past. It is the only nation left in the world with a capability to move large forces anywhere in the world quickly and will continue to play a key decision-making role in the Security Council. Canada will continue to participate because we are good at it, it makes us feel good, and it contributes to creating the type of world in which we want to live.

Now if I am right that peacekeeping is a growth industry, and that Canada will continue to be a major player, then we must acknowledge the fact that we have serious equipment deficiencies that should be addressed within the context of a new defence policy written for the post-Cold War era. It is my opinion that no matter which party forms the next government, peacekeeping will continue to be a major part of our foreign policy. If that is the case, the Capital Equipment Program of the Armed Forces should be reviewed with that in mind. Peacekeeping is basically an army responsibility, supported by the navy and air force. The latter two services are charged with getting the Army personnel and equipment to and from the theatre of operations in an efficient and timely manner, and providing the type of support the army needs while it is carrying out its assigned tasks.

I was asked by the Canadian media in Sarajevo many times if our equipment was good enough. I gave the standard response for a commander in the field and said that it was adequate. It should have been better. Let me tell you of an incident that happened when Lord Carrington paid us a visit during his tour of duty as European Community mediator. We had to drive to Lukavica - the brain of the aggressor, as Mr. Itzabegovic called it - it was the headquarters of the Bosnian Serb army commanded by General Meadic. A very good Sergeant in the Royal Canadian Regiment (RCR) was commanding the armoured personnel carrier in which Lord Carrington and I were riding. I told the Sergeant: "When we go down to the east end of the Sarajevo runway and turn south towards Lukavica, we are going to be fired at from that house about 150 metres from the corner. It always happens - it will happen today. They have got a heavy machine-gun in there. I want you to fire back."

Then I began to think to myself: "By the way, when you do that, unfortunately I am going to have to duck down inside the vehicle, you are going to have to stay up there in the capola. I will be watching you and I want you to know that I have total faith in you. I am really sorry that the multi-role combat vehicle project sorely needed by the Army was cancelled about two years ago, and as a result we do not have the proper vehicle that the Army needs to do this type of work. We have put you in a battlefield taxi with fairly thin protection, and we are asking you to take fire on the move and fire back, and I am really sorry that your .50 calibre machine-gun is on a pintel mount and is going to be extremely inaccurate. But anyway, please fire back and just know that I will be under cover."

And that is exactly what he did. We came under fire, I ducked down and joined Lord Carrington, and the RCR Sergeant stood up in the capola - exposed to the world - and quite bravely fired back, and we got out of there without incident. He should not have had to take that risk - he should have been protected by a turret.

If the much-needed review of Canada's defence requirements - which should not be written by the Defence Department - determines that we need a trip wire defence around Canada, manned primarily by the Air Force and the Navy, then so be it. However, if it determines that the Army is to play the major role well into the next century, then our Capital Equipment Program needs a major rethink, and the Army should be assigned a higher priority for the type of combat equipment it needs to do the job - the job that our soldiers are being asked to do by the Canadian people. That to me is the peacekeeping imperative for Canada.

Don Macnamara

Ladies and gentlemen, this is the third time in the last year and a month that I have sat next to Lew MacKenzie at a meal. The first time, the meal was interrupted by a telephone call from the Commander of Mobile Command telling him that he was going to go to Yugoslavia. The second time was last September when, at the "Canada Salutes its Peacekeepers" dinner in Toronto, he made the stirring speech which I am sure most of you have seen time and again on television where he suggested that the population of Canada might be dropped into the centre of Sarajevo so that we know how uniquely privileged we are to be citizens of this country. The third time is today, when Lew MacKenzie said that this is the first day of the rest of his life - as a retired officer and one free to speak. We are privileged indeed to have an officer with his background who is now prepared to contribute to the further discussion of defence policy in Canada, and to apply his unique experience, along with that of his many colleagues, to the benefit of our country. Lew, your remarks today have been straightforward and worthwhile, as is normal and expected of you, and I hope that the challenge that you have put forth, that the appropriate kinds of allocations for future capital programs for all of the forces, taking into account the interests of Canada and our future peacekeeping commitments, will be in the forefront of whoever it is that writes Canada's future defence policy, within or without the Department of National Defence. On your behalf, ladies and gentlemen, I wish to thank you, Lew, for this address and for your time with us, and we wish you Godspeed in your future career.

David Peel

The Peacekeeping Role of the Conference on Security and Cooperation in Europe

Dr. Joseph Jockel, Director, Canada Project, Center for Strategic and International Studies, Washington, D.C.; Fellow, CISS Pearson Peacekeeping Project

Ambassador David Peel is the Canadian Ambassador to the Forum for Security Cooperation in Europe of the CSCE. During his distinguished career, Ambassador Peel has been Canadian Ambassador to Czechoslovakia and to the Conventional Armed Forces Reductions Negotiations. Just recently he headed a multi-nation mission to the former Soviet Union in search of methods for halting and preventing violence.

Ambassador Peel

You may well ask what someone associated with the Conference on Security and Co-operation in Europe (CSCE) has to do with peacekeeping. Most people who have some knowledge of the CSCE think of it perhaps as the Helsinki process, a talking shop associated with declarations made at its summits of Heads of State and Government, perhaps an instrument that helped in some way to see us through the Cold War by keeping up pressure to improve human rights and, in terms of arms control, brought about the confidence- and security-building measures agreed in Stockholm and in Vienna in 1990 and 1992.

Since the Charter of Paris was signed at the end of 1990, the CSCE has been evolving from a continuing conference of 35 states into the beginnings of an institution that now has 53 members. With the remarkable political changes that we have seen in Europe in less than three years, the character and the activity of the CSCE have also changed. The CSCE has declared itself to be a regional arrangement under Chapter Eight of the United Nations Charter and the governments that belong to it are thinking about and are beginning to take measures that may lead to some kind of collective security. The participating states have given themselves, at least in theory, the capability of engaging in peacekeeping activities quite broadly defined as some of the tools to be used towards keeping the peace in Europe. It is worth remembering too that Europe in this context has been defined as extending the long way around from Vancouver to Vladivostok.

In an address last month on peacekeeping, peacemaking and peace-building, the Honourable Barbara McDougall, the Secretary of State for External Affairs, spoke of six instruments in this context. Drawing from the "Agenda for Peace" issued last summer by UN Secretary-General Boutros-Ghali, the Minister noted that these six instruments reflected a spectrum of ways to handle potential or actual conflict situations. The six instruments for crisis management are preventive diplomacy, preventive deployment, peace making, peacekeeping in the traditional sense, peace enforcement and peace building.

It is the preventive diplomacy end of this spectrum that I want to talk about today, recognizing that the CSCE provided all the examples that the Minister used in describing what can be done to attempt to head off the outbreak of hostilities by dealing with underlying problems and root causes. Preventive diplomacy includes political consultation and such measures as early-warning mechanisms to ensure that potential conflicts can be anticipated; fact-finding missions and monitoring; confidence-building measures, such as mutual military inspections; warnings to potential combatants; sponsorship of consultations; and offers to mediate. Measures like these are perhaps not what we might call "classical" peacekeeping or even "classical" diplomacy but they can be used in serious efforts to keep the peace. A year ago the CSCE did not have an activity in these fields under way, except for its confidence and security-building measures (CSBMs), but today it has ten missions involving well over 100 people on the ground with another three about to begin their work. Of course the CSCE is doing many other things as well, but its role in peacekeeping is developing fast and is worth developing.

I will not try to describe in detail how the CSCE reached the point of undertaking these activities. The CSCE makes all its decisions by consensus and they are not always easy to reach. The diplomatic history of the negotiations that have led us this far and that still continue will no doubt be written some day. It really begins late in 1990 as the CSCE began to respond to the end of communist domination of much of Europe and the east-west confrontation that dominated political life for nearly two generations. One of the roles that participating governments considered could be developed by the CSCE was conflict prevention and some very modest steps were taken in this direction, including the establishment of a Conflict Prevention Centre (CPC). Just as governments through this Centre were beginning to look at the instruments available to them, Yugoslavia began coming apart and the crisis there developed much faster than any instruments could be devised to help control it. In retrospect it is difficult to claim that the CSCE - even with more tools at its disposal - could have done anything to prevent what has happened in Yugoslavia; the crisis was clearly beyond the CSCE's nascent capabilities. As cease-fires were arranged, the CSCE did ask the European Community to take on a monitoring role and Canada, Sweden, Poland and Czechoslovakia, reflecting the CSCE link, joined the EC countries in their monitoring mission in Yugoslavia. A group of countries, including Canada, continued to push the idea of CSCE peacekeeping in the context of giving the restructured institution its own capability of dealing with conflicts in its own region. This was seen to embrace mediation, good offices, early warning and factfinding with the actual deployment of military forces at the far end of the spectrum. During the Helsinki Follow-Up Meeting through the spring of last year, a series of guidelines on peacekeeping was drafted, under Canadian chairmanship, as part of the chapter of the Summit Declaration on early warning, conflict prevention, crisis management and peaceful settlement of disputes.

But preventive diplomacy was also developing in response to events in Europe, particularly in Yugoslavia and what it was possible to do about them. The United Nations was active and the first UNPROFOR troops arrived while the Helsinki meeting was in progress. Governments clearly wanted to do something to prevent conflict from developing in or spreading to other parts of Yugoslavia and were particularly concerned about the situation in Kosovo, the southern region of Serbia where the population is about 90% ethnic Albanian. They asked the Conflict Prevention Centre to send a fact-finding mission to look into the military situation there. Yugoslavia, which was at that time still participating fully in the CSCE, agreed to accept this mission and indeed cooperated with it as did the representatives of the Albanian and other communities. The CPC selected me to lead its mission. Our reports brought no startling new facts to light, but it did lead to recommendations for a mission to be sent to Kosovo for several months to try to promote dialogue to solve some of the problems. It took a few months to get it going but this kind of good offices mission, expanded to include the Sandjak and Vojvodina areas of Serbia as well as Kosovo, was on the ground by October last year.

A similar mission soon followed to the former Yugoslav Republic of Macedonia, designed to work with the authorities there to monitor developments and help prevent possible spillover of the conflict. In the past several months, CSCE missions have also been offering mediation and assistance in Georgia and have been trying to work out what can be done to help end the fighting in Nagorno-Karabakh. A mission has just been dispatched to Estonia and on the recommendation of a rapporteur for the CSCE, a small mission may be in place in Moldavia within the next month. A personal representative of the Chairman-in-Office of the CSCE has just been named to go to Tajikistan; a mission may follow later. In addition, in six countries that are neighbours of the rump Yugoslavia, the CSCE and the EC have provided what are called Sanctions Assistance Missions to help governments enforce the UN trade embargo. These missions are made up of experienced customs officers and Canada provides the Head of Mission and two other officers in Macedonia. All this may not look much like peacekeeping to soldiers who have served in Cyprus or the Golan Heights, but these missions are designed very much with the same objective in mind - keeping the peace. They are trying to do it in most cases before the fighting breaks out rather than after the cease-fire has been arranged. Preventive diplomacy tries to deal with the causes of conflict rather than focusing only on the symptoms of disagreement.

Who are these people and what do they actually do? It is not easy to give an overall description. The customs officers, for example, who of course have no real authority in the countries in which they are stationed, advise and assist the local custom authorities in conducting inspections at borders, supply information on possible violations to a central data system and provide for a kind of international monitoring of the effect of the sanctions on Yugoslavia. Many of the people on the other missions are diplomats including a Canadian serving in Kosovo, one who has served in Macedonia, one about to go to Estonia and no doubt others who will continue the Canadian tradition. The missions have also included military officers and officials with expertise in other areas such as human rights. A major part of their role is simply the establishment of an international presence as a visible expression of concern of the community of nations. They are tasked usually to provide frequent reports on developments and to try to promote dialogue and contacts to bring about solutions to problems as well as undertake fact-finding activities. They are in a sense detectors to provide early warning and in some places clearly act as a deterrent to human rights abuses or the outbreak of fighting. They travel around the countries where they are stationed, usually in small teams, and have been able on occasion to defuse specific instances of tension. They can sometimes act as a go-between to promote settlements of particular disputes. They also act as sources of information and encouragement to assist in building civic societies in areas where former structures are changing. They do not carry weapons or drive around in APCs. For the most part, they travel in locally purchased vehicles and their most sophisticated equipment is lap-top computers, two-way radios and satellite telephones. Since each crisis or potential crisis with which these missions are dealing is unique, it requires a mission designed for the local situation. Each mission has its own mandate with size and composition tailored to it. As some common themes can be seen in problems the missions are dealing with, so each mission offers lessons on how to tackle future problems. Missions can be introduced anywhere along the preventative diplomacy spectrum and the view is emerging that the earlier the better.

The Conflict Prevention Centre has provided basic support for the mission and is now developing a professional support unit. You may have seen its advertisement for staff in *The Economist* a few weeks ago. But this is new territory where the requirements are not easy to foresee and where over the past six to eight months much of the work has been very *ad hoc*, and has depended on the abilities of mission leaders and the generosity of individual governments often working through their embassies. The CPC can manage to support several small teams but will not be able with its present capacities to handle the logistics for large missions.

Despite several affirmations that security in the CSCE area is indivisible, there is sometimes a reluctance to contribute to the preservation of that security if it might cost something. The United Nations is facing a similar crisis: the willingness of governments endlessly to provide people and money is being sorely tried. The costs of CSCE missions are minuscule compared to UN operations or even the operations of some NGOs. But a large proportion of CSCE member states does not pay even this. It is also difficult to staff these missions by secondments through participating states. We have had a difficult time finding the six mission members for Estonia; where will we find the 600 that might be needed in Nagorno-Karabakh?

This is where questions of cooperation with other organizations arise. The CSCE is not a military organization and cannot on its own deploy military forces. If the CSCE as such cannot provide the necessary elements for an operation, can it find a way to devolve the operational responsibility onto some other body while maintaining political control? Could the CSCE ask NATO or the WEU, for example, to undertake peacekeeping operations on its behalf? The structure to do so is theoretically there, having been agreed in the Helsinki document last year. An issue about to be raised in the CSCE is whether it could or should use troops from Russia and other members of the Commonwealth of Independent States in peacekeeping operations and how it would exercise its control over them. Such cooperation with the CIS would raise many questions and problems, especially in view of the strong reaction to recent suggestions from Russia that it have some kind of *droit de regard* over the territory of the former Soviet Union and the Russian minorities therein.

It is also increasingly important that the CSCE develop coordination and cooperation with the United Nations, at the very least to avoid duplication of effort and to define responsibilities, bearing in mind the strengths of each. Perhaps with the CSCE's long history of the promotion of human rights, which in the European context is tied increasingly with questions of minority rights, it would be natural for CSCE missions to concentrate on those aspects of any disputes.

The CSCE has been a forum for political dialogue for 20 years and one of its greatest successes has been the establishment of certain norms of behaviour and the application of pressure to ensure that those norms are met. Looking ahead, there will be a need for just this kind of pressure in an increasing number of foreseeable crisis areas. The CSCE is developing measures of preventive diplomacy, through what we might call its missions to keep the peace, as means of applying pressure short of applying force. Will such measures succeed? It will be hard to tell and difficult to judge whether something worse has been prevented from happening. But the attempt is worth making. It is a small part of Canadian peacekeeping activity but nonetheless a part of peacekeeping where Canada has continued to be among the leaders.

Japan and Peacekeeping: Starting From Zero

Dr. Joseph Jockel

Mr. Jiro Hagi is Deputy Executive Secretary at the International Peace Cooperation Headquarters in the Prime Minister's Office in Tokyo. As those titles indicate, his position is unique, as peacekeeping in Japan is controlled directly through the Prime Minister's Office. Mr. Hagi is probably Japan's foremost expert on peacekeeping. He has guided the government and Japanese Self-Defence Forces as they prepare to participate in the UN Transitional Authority in Cambodia (UNTAC), which is Japan's first peacekeeping mission.

Jiro Hagi

In my presentation I will examine six specific areas. The first is a summary history of Japan's examination of its participation in peacekeeping operations. Second, some important points of the International Peace Cooperation Law, its background and Japan's first experience in peacekeeping operations will be examined. Third, I will speak on the current and future peacekeeping operations in Cambodia. The fourth point is how Japan's peacekeeping participation is viewed within and outside Japan, and the fifth is a look at the controversy over peacekeeping forces or the difference between peacekeeping operations and peacekeeping forces. And last, I would like to touch upon other peacekeeping operations.

First, some words on Japan's examination of peacekeeping operations. Recently we have had very extensive deliberations on whether Japan should send its soldiers abroad to participate in peacekeeping operations. But the very first time the issue was discussed in Japan was in 1958 when the Security Council established the United Nations Observation Group in Lebanon (UNOGIL). Japan was a member of the Security Council at that time, and the Japanese Ambassador to the United Nations was very active in drafting and negotiating the resolution which established UNOGIL.

Secretary-General Dag Hammarskjold then asked Japan to send some Self-Defence Forces officers to Lebanon as military observers. But the Japanese government felt it had to decline the request. You can imagine the difficult position in which our Ambassador found himself at that time.

After that incident, the Government of Japan studied the issue of participating in peacekeeping for many years, but another realistic opportunity did not present itself until the outbreak of the Gulf War in August 1990. At that time, we tried to pass a bill which, if it had been adopted, would have enabled the government to send Japanese units to give logistical support to the coalition forces. But the opposition was very strong, so we had to withdraw that bill from consideration in the Diet.

But in the process of deliberations in and outside of the Diet, the Japanese people became more aware of the need to participate directly by sending personnel to peacekeeping operations or to humanitarian relief operations, instead of just making financial contributions to these UN activities. In 1991 the government decided to present a new bill concerning peacekeeping operations and humanitarian relief operations which was named the International Peace Cooperation Law.

Second, I would like to say a few words about the most important points of the International Peace Cooperation Law, which is the legal framework within which we operate. This law was drafted and adopted on the basis of five principles or guidelines agreed to by the government and the other three political parties which basically favoured the idea of participating in PKOs and sending our Self-Defence Forces abroad for that purpose.

There are five basic principles on which our law was drafted. They are: (1) there must be agreement on the ceasefire among the parties to the conflict;

(2) the parties to the conflict including the territorial state or host country shall have given their consent to deployment of the PKO peacekeeping force and to Japan's participation in the force; (3) the peacekeeping force shall maintain strict impartiality, not favouring any party to the conflict; (4) should any of the above guideline requirements cease to be satisfied, the government of Japan may withdraw its contingent; and (5) the use of weapons shall be limited to the minimum necessary to protect the lives of Japanese military personnel.

These principles have to be met before Japan can participate in specific peacekeeping operations.

But these principles are not really new as they reflect basically the established practice of UN peacekeeping operations over the years. Perhaps these Japanese principles are a little bit more strict than the principles that are applied internationally, but these are the premises on which Japan bases its participation.

In this connection it might be useful for me to refer briefly to the background against which the five principles, or guidelines, were discussed and agreed. Traditional or conventional UN peacekeeping operations are initiated and carried out when there exist certain premises, in particular the ceasefire agreement between the parties and the consent by the parties or the host country to accept UN peacekeeping operations in their territories. It is also an established UN practice that if certain PKO components are allowed to carry small arms, they are authorized to use such arms only when the lives of PKO personnel are threatened or their mission is obstructed by force by other people. On the other hand, Article Nine of the Japanese Constitution is interpreted to prohibit the dispatching of the Defence Forces abroad to be part of a mission which may entail the use of force. In this context, in particular, the following questions arose in the process of drafting the bill on international cooperation.

First, is the use of weapons allowed under the UN PKO practice not considered as use of force which is forbidden under Article Nine of the Constitution?

Second, if the ceasefire agreement is broken or the consent by the host country or parties is withdrawn, will the Japanese infantry units participating in UN peacekeeping forces not get involved if the armed conflict resumes between the parties concerned?

And third, can Japan withdraw its units from UN peacekeeping forces when any of the premises of peacekeeping operations no longer exist while the United Nations still continues the operations?

I do not want to go into too much detail at this stage, but I wish to say that our five guidelines or principles are our answers to such questions and they were also found acceptable by the UN Secretariat. Members of the Japanese Permanent Mission to the UN kept in close touch with UN Secretariat officials during the whole process of the Diet's consideration and adoption of the Peacekeeping Law.

Now I would like to turn to the third point, that is, current and future peacekeeping operations in the United Nations Transitional Authority in Cambodia (UNTAC). Japan has sent eight unarmed military observers who monitor the ceasefire from fixed observation posts. There are also six hundred troops in the engineer battalion currently engaged in repairing roads and bridges in southern Cambodia.

Many countries sent infantry battalions to Cambodia, but under the Peacekeeping Law, Japan does not have this choice. I will touch upon this issue later. Japan has also sent 75 policemen to Cambodia who supervise and give advice to the local police officers.

In addition, the United Nations has asked us to send 50 electoral monitors to UNTAC very quickly because, according to the Security Council resolution that was adopted last November, elections will be held in May for a constituent assembly which will then adopt a new Cambodian constitution. We are in the process of recruiting people from among different fields, including the national government, the local governments and also the private sector. They will be sent to Cambodia in early May.

Japan has also sent three electoral monitors and some diplomatic observers to Angola. That election process was carried out very smoothly and without any major incidents. But unfortunately after the election and after the election monitors had left Angola, when it became clear that UNITA - one of the biggest parties - was losing, it resumed armed attacks. We realized once again that it is difficult to reconcile the parties to the conflict who have, after all, been at war with one another for about 16 years. The situation in Angola is still very difficult.

The present situation in Cambodia is perhaps better than Angola but it is also still quite difficult. The major obstacle is that the Khmer Rouge, or Pol Pot faction, does not observe or respect the provisions of the Paris ceasefire agreement. They did not agree to demobilize their soldiers, or to give free access to their areas for UNTAC activities. There are still many ceasefire violations, mainly by the Khmer Rouge, although some of them are from the Phnom Penh forces. However, although there are violations, we think that the basic ceasefire agreement is still respected.

There are other areas in which some progress has been made. For instance, the repatriation of more than 370,000 Cambodian refugees was carried out rather smoothly. UNTAC has registered about 4.7 million voters, far more than originally anticipated. Of course, UNTAC could not carry out the registration process in some of the areas that are occupied by the Khmer Rouge, but nevertheless this very high percentage was attained.

Now to the fourth point: how Japan's participation in peacekeeping is viewed in Japan and abroad. In Japan, there is still a vocal minority that is strongly against the idea of sending personnel, especially troops from the Self-Defence Forces, abroad. But there has been very extensive and positive news coverage of peacekeeping, especially when we started the UNTAC operations last year. Over 300 journalists went to Cambodia and filed many articles and TV programs. All of that media coverage helped the Japanese people understand better the nature and extent of peacekeeping operations.

However, when the peacekeeping bill was still being discussed in the Diet, Japanese TV programs would feature stories about peacekeeping operations featuring F-15 airplanes and tanks firing their guns and destroyers launching their missiles - activities not at all relevant to PKOs. That kind of broadcasting contributed to a lot of misunderstanding amongst the Japanese people. But now that our military personnel are working in Cambodia, constructing roads, building bridges and monitoring ceasefires, the Japanese people are getting a much more accurate image of actual peacekeeping operations.

In Asia, I think the reaction of the Association of South-East Asian Nations (ASEAN) countries has been rather favourable. Of course, in some countries, such as the Philippines or perhaps Singapore, there are certain concerns that Japanese participation in peacekeeping operations, especially the sending of our Defence Forces abroad, may lead to the recurrence of militarism.

I fully understand the cause of this concern, but I think that even in these countries the reception or the reaction has been rather favourable. Perhaps the same concerns are expressed in Korea and China for the obvious historical reasons. But again, as we continue our activities or provisions in Cambodia or elsewhere, the other countries - especially our neighbouring countries - will understand the purpose of our participation in United Nations peacekeeping operations. Outside Asia, I think the reaction is quite favourable.

Now let me return to another point, that is, the controversy over the difference between peacekeeping operations and peacekeeping forces, which we have just debated in the Diet, and which has come to be known as the PKO-PKF controversy. There is no clear definition of peacekeeping forces in UN practice. But we understand that peacekeeping force means those activities of the peacekeeping operations that are carried out usually by infantry battalions that are armed with small calibre weapons. Their mission is to observe the ceasefire and sometimes they assist in exchanging war prisoners or destroying the captured weapons of the former parties to the conflict.

The guidelines for Japanese participation in UN peacekeeping operations include various definitions and provisions, and these provisions enumerate the different missions of our peacekeeping operations or our personnel. They include the following: (1) Agreement on a ceasefire shall have been reached among the parties to the conflict; (2) The parties to the conflict, including the territorial state(s), shall have given their consent to deployment of the peacekeeping force and Japan's participation in the force; (3) The peace-keeping force shall strictly maintain impartiality, not favouring any party to the conflict; (4) Should any of the above guideline requirements cease to be satisfied, the Government of Japan may withdraw its contingent; and (5) Use of weapons shall be limited to the minimum necessary to protect the personnel's lives, et cetera.

Main Article III of the Law Concerning Cooperation for United Nations Peace-Keeping Operations and Other Operations states that, for the purposes of this Law, the following terms shall have the following definitions:

(1) "United Nations Peace-Keeping Operations" means operations that are conducted under the control of the United Nations, and upon the basis of resolutions of the General Assembly or the Security Council of the United Nations, to ensure the observance of government to prevent the recurrence of armed conflicts among the parties to such conflicts (hereafter referred to as "the Parties to Armed Conflicts"), to assist in the establishment of a ruling apparatus by democratic means after the termination of armed conflicts or to maintain international peace and security in coping with disputes, provided that such operations be implemented by two or more participating countries at the request of the Secretary-General of the United Nations (hereafter referred to as "the Secretary-General") and by the United Nations without any partiality to any of the Parties to Armed Conflicts, in cases where agreement to cease armed conflicts and maintain the cessation has been reached among the Parties to Armed Conflicts and where consent for the undertaking of such operations has been obtained from host countries as well as the Parties to Armed Conflicts, or from host countries alone unless there have occurred armed conflicts.

(2) "Humanitarian International Relief Operations" means operations other than those implemented as United Nations Peace-Keeping Operations, that are conducted in a humanitarian spirit, and upon the basis of resolutions of the General Assembly, the Security Council of the Economic and Social Council of the United Nations or at the request of international organizations listed in the Appendix of the law, to rescue inhabitants and persons who actually or are likely to suffer from conflicts which are likely to endanger international peace and security (Whereas these conflicts are hereafter referred to simply as "Conflicts," these inhabitants and persons are hereafter jointly referred to as "Affected People.") or to make restoration out of damage caused by conflicts, provided that such operations be implemented by the United Nations or other international organizations, or the member States to the United Nations or other countries, in case where consent for the undertaking of such operations has been obtained from host countries and, should the host countries be the Parties to Armed Conflicts, agreement to cease

armed conflicts and maintain the cessation has been reached among the Parties to Armed Conflicts.

(3) "International Peace Cooperation Assignments" means all the following tasks implemented for United Nations Peace-Keeping Operations and the tasks provided for in (j) to (q) below implemented for Humanitarian International Relief Operations, wherein the incidental tasks are included respectively, provided that those tasks are conducted in overseas areas: (a) monitoring the observance of cessation of armed conflicts or the implementation of relocation, withdrawal or demobilization of armed forces as agreed upon among the Parties to Armed Conflicts; (b) stationing and patrol in buffer zones and other areas demarcated for preventing the occurrence of armed conflicts; (c) inspection or identification of the carrying in or out of weapons and/or their parts by vehicles, other means of transportation or passers-by; (d) collection, storage or disposal of abandoned weapons and/or their parts; (e) assistance for the designation of cease-fire lines and other assimilated boundaries by the Parties to Armed Conflicts; (f) assistance for the exchange of prisoners-of-war among the Parties to Armed Conflicts; (g) supervision or management of the fair execution of congressional elections, plebiscites and other elections or votings assimilated thereto; (h) advice or guidance for and supervision of police administrative matters; (i) advice or guidance for administrative matters not covered by (h) above; (j) medical care including sanitary measures; (k) search or rescue of Affected People or assistance for their repatriation; (l) distribution of food, clothing, medical supplies and other daily necessaries to Affected People; (m) installation of facilities or equipment to accommodate Affected People; (n) measures for the repair or maintenance of facilities or equipment damaged by Conflicts, which are necessary for daily life of Affected People; (o) measures for the restoration of natural environment subjected to pollution and other damage by Conflicts; (p) transportation, storage or reserve, communication, construction, or the installation, inspection or repair of machines and apparatus, not covered by (a) to (o) above; (q) other tasks assimilated to those mentioned in (a) to (p) above, as prescribed by Cabinet Order.

There are also Additional Provisions, which are Special Provisions concerning International Peace Cooperation Assignments Undertaken by SDF Units.

Additional Article II states that: "International Peace Cooperation Assignments undertaken by SDF Units, which are the tasks mentioned in (a) to (f) of Article III (3) and the tasks assimilated thereto mentioned in (q) of Article III (3) as prescribed by Cabinet Order, shall not be implemented until the date to be set forth by a separate law."

Additional Article III states that: "Upon the passage of three years after the entry into force of this Law, the Government shall make a review concerning the arrangement for the execution of this Law in light of the state of the execution of this Law."

The activities that are provided for in subparagraphs (a) to (f) of paragraph three of Main Article III are those activities that are considered to be peacekeeping force activities when these activities are carried out by units, not by unarmed officers. So, for instance, in (a), it says "monitoring the observance of cessation of armed conflicts or the implementation of relocation withdrawal or demobilization of armed forces as agreed upon among the Parties to Armed Conflicts." So we understand - and I think that this is also the practice of the United Nations - that if such activities are done by infantry battalions they are considered to be peacekeeping force activities (PKF).

In our deliberations in the Diet the most controversial point was as to whether or not we should participate in such activities by sending our defence forces. And a rather cautious view was expressed from some of the parties who argued that it was premature for Japan to participate in deploying peacekeeping forces because this type of operation may tend to expose the participating units to situations where they would have to use weapons. As a result of consultations among the government and the three parties sponsoring that bill, it was agreed that the provisions concerning peacekeeping forces will be frozen for the time being until a new consent is given by the Diet. At the same time, it was also understood among them that the law will be reviewed three years after its enactment.

Additional Article II of the Additional Provisions says that international peace cooperation assignments undertaken by the Self-Defence Forces unit - which are the tasks mentioned in (a) to (f) of Main Article III, paragraph three - are the assignments that are considered PKF. To review, these tasks include the following: (b) stationing and patrol in buffer zones and other areas demarcated for preventing the occurrence of armed conflicts; (c) inspection or identification of the carrying in or out of weapons and/or their parts by vehicles, other means of transportation or passers-by; (d) collection, storage or disposal of abandoned weapons and/or their parts; (e) assistance for the designation of cease-fire lines and other assimilated boundaries by the Parties to Armed Conflicts; and (f) assistance for the exchange of prisoners-of-war among the Parties to Armed Conflicts. The tasks mentioned in (q) of Main Article III - "other tasks assimilated to those mentioned in (a) to (p) above, as prescribed by Cabinet Order" - shall not be implemented until the date to be set forth by a separate law. So for the time being, we cannot send our units for this kind of mission.

As to the review clause, Additional Article III says that upon the passage of three years after the entering through force of this law that the government shall make a review concerning the arrangement for the execution of this law in light of the state of the execution of this law. So that is the situation about peacekeeping forces.

My last point is about other peacekeeping operations. As you have seen, we have certain constraints as to the type of activities or operations in which we can participate. We have to check every case of peacekeeping operations to see if the operations meet the conditions set forth in our law. And for the time being, for instance, it is impossible to send our forces into a situation like in the former Yugoslavia where there is no clear ceasefire agreement. That prohibition also applies to the situation in Somalia. Although we could give assistance in other forms, such as financial contribution, we cannot send our troops to participate in the type of coalition forces that are deployed there.

However, I think that the peacekeeping operations in Mozambique fall within the classical or traditional type of PKO. Japan is now considering the possibility of participating in this kind of operation, and we have sent a study group to Mozambique. It will report soon.[1]

In conclusion, I would like to say a few words about the future of UN peacekeeping operations and Japan's cooperation. In January 1992, a Security Council summit meeting was held in New York to examine the problems confronting the international community at the highest level. On the basis of those deliberations, the Secretary-General, Mr. Boutros-Ghali, submitted a report entitled "An Agenda for Peace" in June of 1992. In that report, he analyzed the world situation and made very interesting suggestions on preventive diplomacy, peacemaking, peacekeeping and post-conflict peace building. The suggestions include such ideas as peace enforcement units and the preventive deployment of peacekeepers with the consent of one party only instead of all the parties to the conflict. These suggestions are now being examined by the representatives of the Security Council, the Security Council member states, and at other international forums.

UN peacekeeping operations are not mentioned in the Charter of the United Nations but were invented and developed through practice and still continue to evolve to meet changing requirements. It is true that today there are situations which traditional PKOs cannot cope with effectively, and some of the Secretary-General's suggestions have already been put into practice, as in the cases of Macedonia and Somalia. Nevertheless, I believe that the principles and practices of peacekeeping operations upheld by the United Nations for more than 40 years are still both appropriate and valid today and will continue to be so in the future.

As for Japan's participation and cooperation in UN peacekeeping operations: we still need to gain a lot more experience, and since we started our operations only six months ago, we can say we have just started from zero. Although there are constraints in Japan's arrangement and in traditional UN PKOs themselves, I think we can still make more contributions to international efforts for peacekeeping and humanitarian relief. When the bill on international peace cooperation was being discussed in the Diet, somebody in New York was reported to have commented that Japan was behind the other runners on the track. But we had to start from somewhere, and I believe that we made a step forward since until very recently we were not even on the track, but outside the arena.

In 1995, the government of Japan will review the International Peace Cooperation Law in light of the experience we shall have gained in the meantime. It is always useful at any time to discuss new ideas and possibilities, but for the actual review required by the Diet, we need a breathing space of a few years so that the understanding of Japan's peacekeeping operations and humanitarian relief operations will be deepened both domestically and internationally.

Note

1. On 26 March, the Government of Japan decided to send a Defence Forces unit to Mozambique, and Mr. Hagi was appointed Chief of the Advanced Mission.

Japanese Research, Education and Training in Peacekeeping

Dr. Joseph Jockel

Professor Susumu Takai is Professor of International Law at the National Institute for Defence Studies in Tokyo. He is internationally recognized for his work on the legal aspects of peacekeeping. He visited the CISS in September 1992 and also participated in a conference on conflict resolution in New Brunswick at the same time. The CISS and the National Institute for Defence Studies are cooperating closely on all aspects of peacekeeping research and publication.

Professor Takai

I have just returned from a ten day visit to the headquarters of the United Nations Transition Authority in Cambodia (UNTAC) and to the Japanese engineer battalion stationed in Cambodia. The headquarters of the contingent is stationed in Takeo, in the southern part of Cambodia. The temperature was at least 35 degrees centigrade every day. Now I am speaking to you in Ottawa where it is five degrees below zero centigrade, a difference of more than 40 degrees. It is winter in both Canada and Cambodia now, but what a difference there is between the two winters.

In my short presentation, I would like to explain how the Japanese people think about UN peacekeeping and about the dispatch of Japanese contingents abroad.

Japan became a member of the United Nations in 1956. Shortly thereafter, early in 1958, the UN asked the Japanese government to dispatch officers to Lebanon as military observers in UNOGIL. But the government refused this UN request, because the constitution forbids Japanese Self-Defence Forces from serving outside the country.

Since the end of the Second World War, Japanese security has been built on a policy of strong and close cooperation with the United States. In addition, as I have noted, the Japanese constitution forbids the sending abroad of members of the Self-Defence Forces. For these reasons, the number of Japanese scholars undertaking research on the UN and peacekeeping was very small. Of course, most who study, teach and practice international law know about the UN, because they have to teach their students about the world body, but few know much about peacekeeping. Only a few scholars - I would estimate fewer than ten - research peacekeeping from the legal point of view. That is, the origin of peacekeeping, the legal base of peacekeeping, the legal effect of status of force agreements, and so on. There are many scholars who teach international politics and international relations in Japan, but they do not themselves study peacekeeping. It may seem strange to you, but this is true. Most of these scholars do not know of the role that peacekeeping has played in world politics. They only began to treat peacekeeping as a research area a few years ago when it became well known that the Japanese government contributed $130 billion to the multinational forces in the Gulf War.

When that war ended, the government of Kuwait showed its thanks - in the *New York Times* - to the countries which assisted it. But the Japanese government was deeply disappointed when it found that its name was not included. The government and people then realized that it was the strong view of its allies that it should contribute not only money to UN peacekeeping, but also personnel. Money is important, but in order to be regarded as having participated fully, a country must provide troops. It was only at this point that many research works on peacekeeping began to appear. As Japan continues to take part in United Nations peacekeeping, research interest will grow.

I have noted that the Japanese people did not show much interest in peacekeeping before the Gulf War. When the Japanese government signalled its intention to participate in peacekeeping, the argument began in the Diet and among the public as to whether Japan should send or should not send a contingent abroad. Many Japanese people are eager to learn more about peacekeeping. But to educate them is quite a difficult matter in Japan. This is because most teachers in primary or secondary school - or even high school - do not know about peacekeeping at all. They cannot, therefore, teach it to their students. Most Japanese students and citizens have no opportunity to gain access to information about peacekeeping. In addition, I daresay that the media often publishes misinformation on peacekeeping. There is a tendency for the Japanese media to present information with a particular slant. The Japanese people cannot recognize this in the media reports. They are naive people and tend to believe what the mass media tells them. There is no source of information on peacekeeping other than that from the mass media. Moreover, it is difficult for people in general to read and understand scholars' research works on peacekeeping, even if they can obtain them.

This lack of knowledge of peacekeeping has also created confusion in the area of terminology. I think the education of Japanese people in peacekeeping is a very important matter. Properly conducted, it will ensure that Japan continues to participate in UN peacekeeping in the future.

Japan has the experience of being defeated by the Allied forces in the Second World War, and thus the Japanese people have an allergy to war and to armed forces in general. The dispatch of Japanese Self-Defence Forces abroad reminds the Japanese of the last war, and this creates arguments as to whether we should send contingents outside the country. They have mixed up their image of peacekeeping and war, so I believe that it is more difficult to make the Japanese understand peacekeeping than it is to convince the peoples of other countries.

As a reaction to the strong feelings many Japanese parliamentarians and citizens have, when the Japanese government sent a contingent to Cambodia, its functions were limited by legislation.

Peacekeeping education in the Japanese Self-Defence Forces is becoming more extensive. Officers are generally taught the UN system and peacekeeping, but lower ranks receive very little education in the subject. All who were sent to Cambodia were taught about the situation in Cambodia and peacekeeping for a short time before their dispatch abroad. Those who were sent to UNTAC as military observers were treated differently from other officers. The eight Japanese military observers were educated in a military training centre in Sweden before dispatch.

The government's decision to send a contingent to UNTAC seemed to come rather late. That is because of the long process of legislation, and as a result, the Japanese Self-Defence Forces do not undergo special training for peacekeeping functions. The skilfullness and ability of the engineering battalion was excellent, and its leaders thought it could carry out its UN function sufficiently, as the unit members had trained in high level engineering techniques since the time they joined the Self-Defence Forces. I saw the battalion last week, and it was carrying out its function without any difficulty. The only problem that it had was in receiving materials, as many were supplied by UNTAC headquarters, and are slow in being delivered. The Japanese battalion has almost finished its initial work, and is now awaiting the arrival of additional materials such as bridge panels. Because of the advanced construction techniques employed by the contingent, UNTAC and other contingents are asking Japan to expand its area of work. The Commander of the Japanese battalion is anxious to help but awaits guidance from Tokyo.

The Japanese contingent brought much equipment to Cambodia - not only tents but many different types of vehicles, such as dump trucks, power shovels, and bucket and road rollers, to name a few. The engineers thought they might have problems with these machines in Cambodia. However, half a year has passed, and there has been little trouble. The only problem was that the nail points of the graders wore away quite rapidly, as the fine sand of Cambodia acts as a file and wears them down quickly.

It is not as hot in Japan as it is in Cambodia, and the clothing worn by the battalion was made of thick material, so special thin uniforms were made quickly before the deployment. But this type of uniform acquired a bad reputation because it tore easily and mosquitoes were able to bite through the material. This problem is now being solved.

It is clear that Japan has great strides to make in the field of peacekeeping research, education and training. We appreciate the help and suggestions given by Canada and other countries. Our aim is to improve in each of these areas so as to make our total contribution to peacekeeping as effective as possible.

Forum

Mr. Peter Haydon, CISS Senior Research Fellow

Mr. Hagi, there has been a general discussion on the extension of the permanent membership of the United Nations Security Council to include Japan and other countries. Do you believe that this should be conditional on the level of commitment to cooperative security? Alternatively, do you believe that non-support should be grounds for relinquishment of permanent membership?

Mr. Hagi

This is a very difficult question to answer. In Japan we have had some debate about that. Some people, including members of our government, are very much against Japanese permanent membership in the Security Council because Japan does not want to accept responsibility for maintaining security in the international arena. Japan has a very strong peace-like constitution. We cannot send our forces abroad to use force, and we are only now being permitted to send our contingents abroad for the purpose of peacekeeping operations. However, many Japanese do think that Japan should be a member of the Security Council. Some people support the new military activities of Japan, but many also think that it is dangerous and will lead to a new militarism. So there are many for and against, both amongst the government and the general public.

Mr. David Cooper, NATO Headquarters

Ambassador Peel, some people in Europe are beginning to talk about institutional Darwinism. There are so many international organizations around in this new security architecture that there is inevitably a sense of rivalry. I hope that nothing that I said earlier indicated rivalry between NATO and the CSCE. Far from it. But in this complex structure, do you fear that what are designed to be interlocking institutions may be becoming interblocking institutions? One reason for asking this question is that, a short time before I left Brussels, a new body had been set up under the North Atlantic Cooperation Council (NACC), which is a consultative NATO group which brings into the Alliance our former adversaries. This committee of NACC has set up an *ad hoc* group on peacekeeping, and is now working on operational concepts and all the forms of military preparation. I am not arguing on behalf of any one organization, let alone my own, but there is, I feel, a certain institutional confusion which is coming into the picture and I would like to hear what you think about this and what you think about the long-term future of the CSCE if this NACC structure really does take off and function as intended.

Ambassador Peel

I am a bit worried about it, yes. I think we will probably manage to find ways in which the worst of the overlapping or the duplication of effort can be avoided, but there certainly are potential conflicts. I mentioned in my presentation the need for coordination in examining how cooperation can be worked out with other international organizations and, indeed, perhaps finding what tasks some organizations can do better than others. I mentioned the possibility, given its record in the past, of the CSCE being well suited to sticking with the kind of preventive diplomacy that it is pursuing now, focusing on questions that relate essentially to human rights. In the end, I suppose, most of the questions that are facing Europe relate in one way or another to human rights, but there are certain basic understandings of limitations on just what that means. I think that the CSCE is still very much, in an *ad hoc* way, exploring areas of a collective effort to apply pressure in a very quiet way. Canada is not anxious to see the CSCE develop into a large and bureaucratic institution. It is only in the last two-and-a-half years that the CSCE has changed from being a conference into becoming an institution. It will soon have a Secretary-General and it will continue the expansion of its bureaucracy, I am sure, because that is the way that these things inevitably happen. If that is the wish of the 53 governments, then so be it - there will be one more European institution. I do not think that it will ever be a very large one. I doubt myself that the day will come when it ever tries to deploy forces. There are too many risks and difficulties involved in that. A time may well come when it might ask NATO to deploy forces. It may very soon be in the situation that I mentioned, where Russia offers to provide peacekeeping forces in some of the former Soviet Republics, and Russia would very much like to have these forces under the peacekeeping umbrella of the CSCE. This will indeed cause problems, and these are not at all unconnected to the problems that would be involved if the CSCE asked NATO or any other organization to provide peacekeeping forces. These are worrying questions.

Just to conclude, however, I would refer to the fact that there are 53 states that are members of the CSCE. There are certainly possibilities for NACC to be doing the same kinds of things that the CSCE is also interested in doing. However, after all, all members of NACC are also members of the CSCE, and surely we can, without creating institutional rivalries, use the common sense of these governments to ensure that there is not unnecessary duplication of effort. The other point is that there are 53 states - the NACC does not include important countries in Europe such as Sweden, Finland, Austria, Switzerland and a number of others, particularly the states of Central Asia which do actually belong to the NACC but do not participate very actively either in the NACC or the CSCE. There is a much broader membership in the CSCE as well, and I think this will also be important in ensuring that, if not interlocking, at least they are not entirely interblocking. I like the turn of phrase, and I think that it is something of which we have to be very conscious to try to ensure that it does not happen.

Dr. George Bell, Chairman, CISS Board of Directors

Mr. Hagi, I was wondering if you could extend somewhat your description of the kinds of operations which are now possible in terms of peacekeeping and peace observation within Japanese law? When I was in Indochina in 1969-70, your representatives were very concerned and studying the problem then and were looking for opportunities to contribute not military but civil forces. To what extent under your present law can you participate in observer operations, logistics operations, communications operations or humanitarian assistance operations? Could you expand on what you see as the framework of how you could evolve within the limitations before you get to combat units?

Mr. Hagi

As I mentioned earlier, according to our law front line units cannot be dispatched abroad now. It will be three years before we review that law, but the humanitarian relief and the logistics support units can be sent now. Our law also has a limit on the number of personnel - 2,000 - which can be dispatched for logistics support, medical transport, and similar duties. But infantry or front line battalions cannot be dispatched abroad at all.

Major Roy Thomas, National Defence Headquarters

Human rights might involve the question of sovereignty and whether the international community has the right to intervene in the affairs of a national sovereign state. Ambassador Peel, how does the CSCE view this?

Ambassador Peel

The CSCE views this with great difficulty. Clearly the problems are well understood within the context of the CSCE, which makes all of its decisions by consensus. This means, at least theoretically, that all states that are members of the CSCE must agree for the CSCE to take any action. Ways have been found to get around this, and this is particularly the case in human rights. It is not something that I am familiar with in detail because it was worked out in other parts of the CSCE, but the human rights mechanism does allow for action to be taken by the CSCE without the consent of the country concerned in certain circumstances. This is the beginning of the breakdown of the strict consensus rule. There are other ways of doing this, but on the basis of this particular concern in the human rights area there was at least sufficient agreement that the rump of Yugoslavia would not have to consent to certain CSCE activities taking place regarding the human rights situation within what we still formally call Yugoslavia. There was also a suspension from the CSCE of the active membership of Yugoslavia, so that it has not in fact participated in recent decisions regarding what the CSCE is able to do with regard to the situation in that country, which, as I mentioned, has not really been that much.

This is in turn complicated by the fact that it is very difficult, for example, to send a preventive diplomacy mission to the former Yugoslavia without the consent and active cooperation of the Yugoslav authorities. You simply cannot send a preventive diplomacy or any other kind of mission into Belgrade, for example, without the cooperation of the Yugoslav authorities. It cannot be done. So you have to have in a practical sense, if not their cooperation, at least their consent before you can send people to do the various things that I mentioned even in the human rights area - monitoring the situation, trying to get groups together in order to solve some of the problems. The CSCE missions that now exist in the Serbian part of the former Yugoslavia are in fact in four different places. In all of these places, they are clearly subject to the authority of the Serbian government. So that to talk of activity without the consent of these authorities is only possible in a theoretical way - they have to agree that people can be there and that they can indeed use the highways and stay in the hotels and be given visas that allow them to enter. But there is the beginning, at least, of a possibility that consent is not always needed. Where this leads I am not sure. It can certainly lead to decisions without the consent of that country. It is very difficult for it to lead to activities in a country without that country's consent. It could theoretically lead to military action against a country if the situation were serious enough, without the consent of that country, but I suspect, as I suggested earlier, that if it ever comes to action like that, the CSCE will not be the forum for that kind of decision. It would be much more likely that the United Nations would fulfil that role, with the likelihood that NATO would be called upon to carry out the military action. Theoretically, the CSCE could play that role, and it could indeed happen. I think that it is more likely, however, that the governments would choose to operate through the UN. Of course, in the UN, consensus is not the same problem that it is in the CSCE.

Professor Akira Mayama

Mr. Hagi, at the time of the Gulf War of 1991, the Japanese government dispatched minesweepers to the Persian Gulf. Do you think that it is possible to send minesweepers or other vessels under the new Japanese peacekeeping law?

Mr. Hagi

When we sent minesweepers to the Persian Gulf we made a new government order, not a law. So, even under today's law, we can send our minesweepers to other areas, but I do not think that this kind of mission would be considered a peacekeeping operation. It is a very different operation.

Professor Takai

Sending minesweepers is considered peacekeeping in the widest sense. But in Japan, we do not include minesweepers as part of peacekeeping. It is very difficult to explain exactly what the Japanese contingents and personnel can do under peacekeeping.

Mr. Hagi

I would like to add one thing. When we dispatched our minesweepers to the Persian Gulf, we sent them under the Self-Defence Forces Law, not the Peacekeeping Operations Law.

Peter Haydon

Navy and Air Force Peacekeeping: an Expanded Role

Mr. Peter Jones, CISS Senior Research Fellow

Commander Peter Haydon retired from the Navy four years ago. Prior to this he was Director of Strategic Policy Planning. He has an M.A. in Political Science from Dalhousie. He lectures widely on the naval aspects of peacekeeping, and his forthcoming book entitled *The 1962 Cuban Missile Crisis: Canadian Involvement Reconsidered* will be published by the CISS in September.

Peter Haydon

Introduction

I am here today as a simple sailor, trying to understand a complex situation. In this, I start with a disadvantage because the narrowness of the strict definition of peacekeeping is almost prohibitive. However, we have now come to accept peacekeeping as a form of shorthand for military and para-military operations to restore order in the international system. In some respects, perhaps, this shift in definition appears to be an act of self-delusion intended to appease a distaste for intervention or what has been described as neo-imperialism.[1] To some, the change in definition stems from a belief that the peace groups and much of the Canadian media have not taken the time to understand the changing nature of military operations in the modern world.

The Cold War is over, and we have moved into a new era marked, for now, by uncertainty and unpredictability. The Secretary-General of the United Nations has clearly recognized this transition. The military forces of the NATO countries and several other responsible democracies have also accepted the change, and are restructuring so they can respond more effectively to new requirements. The simple fact is that no matter how distasteful it may be for some people, the new world order will not emerge without using force to counteract aggression, anarchy, and abuses of human rights. We have, in fact, embarked on a period of international crisis management, and we are not handling it very well yet. This is mainly a problem of perception of the purpose of intervention and crisis management.

Let me explain my concern by putting three propositions on the table: (1) peacekeeping is the non-violent use of military forces; (2) peacekeeping is essentially an army function; and (3) the UN is able to exercise effective control of military operations.

These propositions, I contend, have become entrenched myths that prevent us from looking objectively at the military requirements for keeping the peace in the world.

To believe that peacekeeping is the non-violent use of military force is to ignore the facts. The lessons of the Persian Gulf, Somalia and Bosnia show clearly that force is necessary to bring stability to some situations. The real issue is, in fact, intervention. If we are not prepared to let states resolve their own internal problems and decide that we must intervene in the interests of order, justice, and decency, then we must accept the use of force and the loss of life in the process.

This is an underlying principle of the Secretary-General's *Agenda for Peace,* in which the functions of preventive diplomacy, peace making and peacekeeping are clearly defined as companion actions to be taken to restore and maintain stability in the world, but under a concept of not using force unnecessarily or as the first option. However, we should not lose sight of the fact that the basic function of a military is to manage extreme violence.

Although other organizations also manage violence, they are not trained and equipped to handle violence at the same level as the military.

The difference between crisis management and warfare is that war is invariably the result of failing to resolve a crisis and restore order. The initial role of the military in a crisis is to be a contingency against further deterioration; a deterrent to escalation; or to coerce an aggressor state into abandoning its actions. By linking military deployments to diplomatic initiatives, the military represents a clear yet controlled potential for violence that serves to reinforce diplomacy.

Under this concept it is clearly wrong to believe that peacekeeping is primarily an army function. Although the final solution to a crisis may require the presence of armed forces on the streets to maintain a stable environment, it takes many military skills to provide that guarantee of security. As seen in Somalia and in Cambodia, the process of restoring order out of chaos requires a wide range of military and non-military capabilities.

The Canadian experience in Somalia is a good example of how modern military operations now depend on several branches of a military structure working closely together. For instance, the Canadian Airborne Regiment would not have been able to carry out its security role without the initial help of the maritime helicopters embarked in HMCS Preserver. Moreover, in the early days, the warship provided medical, logistic, and communications support to the land forces. Had the situation turned sour, the ship would have been able to evacuate the ground forces. Thus, the ship and its helicopters were instrumental in making Somalia a successful operation.

Under other situations or under a different level of threat, a different naval task force would have been provided. A higher degree of direct air support could have been provided once an airfield had been secured. The point is, by having a flexible national force structure the options open to the government are much greater. Flexible force structures are thus the building blocks of the modern military.

Given the resources of the various nations that can be assembled for a cooperative venture, we must ask: "Can the UN exercise effective control of crisis management operations?" I think not. The relative success of some UN operations is, I believe, a reflection of the willingness and inherent ability of a limited number of nations to work together. In this, the UN has been fortunate that those nations are prepared to accept a degree of risk, and that the United States has been willing to act as the principal coordinator. Without this support, the UN would have been in trouble because there is no integral organization able to plan or oversee complex crisis management operations.

Crisis Management

One only has to look at the basic principles of crisis management to realize just how restricted the UN is at the moment. Those principles, which have evolved over time, represent a skilful blend of graduated military and diplomatic measures intended to convince an aggressor state that its actions are imprudent and would result in violence if it persists.[2] The intent is to end the violence so that the rebuilding process can begin. Those measures include: (1) the need to coordinate diplomatic and military moves; (2) maintaining firm political control of military operations; (3) creating pauses in the tempo of military actions; (4) limiting military moves to those that demonstrate immediate objectives in the current crisis; (5) avoiding military moves that might wrongly signal intensified military action; and (6) choosing options that show a willingness to negotiate and that leave the aggressor a way out.

A cooperative, multinational response to a crisis must therefore be planned with the same precision as any other operation in which military forces are taking part. Moreover, it is essential that non-military activities be carefully integrated into the overall plan.

Effective crisis management thus hinges on sound planning that must include such basic factors as: selecting realistic and achievable aims; keeping the plan and its execution simple; establishing unified command and control with provision for coordination at all levels; making the best and most efficient use of available resources; making adequate provision for the security of personnel by establishing clear and appropriate rules for the use of force in self defence (rules of engagement); providing full logistic support and implementing an appropriate public relations policy.[3]

The last factor is particularly important in this age of high-speed electronic media. For instance, is there a point at which the public's right to know, as interpreted by the media, transcends the safety of military personnel and the integrity of the mission? In some cases, it appears the media has become part of the problem as journalists take risks and intrude in their search for a story. All too often, it seems, the quest for the story ignores the need for other people to get on with their jobs. In complex situations such as Somalia, there has to be an understanding between the military and the press corps to prevent mutual interference. Media management is as important in crisis management situations as it is in war.

Naval and Air Force Roles in Crisis Management

Having set the context for my examination of expanded naval and air force roles in peacekeeping, which I will call crisis management unless I specifically mean truce supervision, I can begin to paint the picture of how those forces fit into the larger scheme of things.

The first point to make is that naval and air forces are not just support elements of the operations on the land. They are equal partners in the overall process of maintaining order and stability. The second point is that modern military operations are dependent on technology. The families of ships, aircraft, helicopters, vehicles, sensors, radios, and support equipment that we will take with us into the 21st century have a flexibility and reliability seldom seen before. Used properly, modern equipment will hasten solutions to crises and reduce risks to life. Contrary to popular belief, these are not merely Cold War weapons that have been recycled. For the most part they represent a new generation of technology intended to make modern military units far more versatile and far more efficient than their predecessors. In this respect, what seems to have been missed by the peace groups and much of the media is that western military forces began a gradual shift away from highly specialized roles towards multi-purpose concepts in the mid-1980s.

The present debate over the EH-101 helicopter is an example of how special interest groups have distorted the facts and deliberately misled the Canadian public over modern military technology. By continually portraying the helicopter as a "Cold War, attack, ASW vehicle", those groups show a lack of knowledge of the transition that has taken place in the military forces of most industrialized countries. Moreover, they do not appear to understand modern technology or the related industrial process. Further, their perspective of the post-Cold War world is perhaps somewhat limited, particularly in view of the proliferation of naval and other weaponry that is taking place in what used to be called the Third World.

As I see it, my task is to explain, as simply as possible, the roles of modern navies and air forces in 21st century crisis management. To do this, I am going to focus mainly on the maritime aspects because this is the best way of showing how naval, land and aviation units have become interdependent.

The Maritime Dimension of Crisis Management

There is a tendency today, particularly among theorists, to champion "peacekeeping" wrongly as the great new mission of maritime forces. This misperception is largely the result of not fully understanding the mechanics of how those forces operate. Tasks now being proposed as the key elements of a maritime peacekeeping mission are, in fact, traditional naval tasks that have been undertaken by warships since the days of sail. The important point here is that the inherent flexibility of warships has always allowed them to change tasks quickly and without loss of efficiency.[4] The ability of a state or group of states to deploy deterrent and coercive force quickly by sea has become an important element of crisis management. It is not just a question of getting there, it is one of being able to do something about the situation once you get there.

Many warships, such as our own new frigates, are highly effective in a broad range of functions. In fact, the capability of the modern frigate is often misunderstood. Actually, there is little it cannot do. As a surveillance platform, for instance, one of our new frigates can maintain almost complete surveillance in and over some 20,000 square kilometres of ocean - an area about the size of Lake Ontario. Although the ship itself may not be able to intercept all contacts in that area, it can investigate almost any contact within the area under surveillance by using its helicopter.[5] The frigate can also use the helicopter to extend the size of area over which it is keeping watch. The ship and its helicopter have thus become a highly potent and flexible team.

Returning to general concepts for a moment, it is useful to contrast basic maritime force capabilities with some of the concepts for cooperative security established by the Secretary-General in his *Agenda for Peace*. The three objectives involving the use of military forces, in one form or another, are: (1) to make early identification of those situations that could lead to conflict, and to try through preventive diplomacy to remove the sources of danger before violence results; (2) where conflict erupts, to engage in peacemaking to resolve the issues that led to conflict; and (3) through peacekeeping, to work to preserve peace, however fragile, where fighting has been halted and to assist in implementing agreements achieved by peacemakers.

The other two aims of the Secretary-General's *Agenda For Peace,* peacebuilding and addressing the root causes of conflict, are functions of maintaining stability through assistance whereas the first three serve to restore stability.

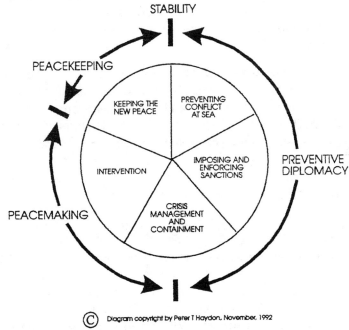

STABILITY

PEACEKEEPING

KEEPING THE NEW PEACE

PREVENTING CONFLICT AT SEA

IMPOSING AND ENFORCING SANCTIONS

INTERVENTION

CRISIS MANAGEMENT AND CONTAINMENT

PREVENTIVE DIPLOMACY

PEACEMAKING

© Diagram copyright by Peter T Haydon, November, 1992

The second dimension of the model is the cycle of maritime crisis management, which has five phases: (1) preventing conflict at sea; (2) imposing and enforcing sanctions; (3) crisis management and containment; (4) intervention; and (5) keeping the new peace.

To explain the inherent flexibility of naval and maritime air forces I want to discuss some of the possible roles of those forces within each of the five maritime categories.

First, in preventing conflict at sea, maritime forces can conduct surveillance and monitor ocean use to provide early warning of a deteriorating situation and to gather general information on the situation. Maritime forces can also be deployed into a region as a deterrent to aggression. Under the heading of naval presence, this is a traditional way of signalling concern over a worsening situation.[6] There may also be an occasional need to use a warship to oversee or take action in humanitarian relief situations or to enforce international law. Examples of these situations are numerous. They range from the deployment of a single ship to the movement of a full naval task force into an area. Submarines and maritime patrol aircraft have also been used in this role, particularly where the operations of other submarines are of concern.[7]

Maritime forces can also be used to impose and enforce economic sanctions, quarantines, or blockades. Under some situations this may require the use of force to make ships stop and submit to search, and so these operations must be conducted under strict rules defining the situations where force may be used and the level of force permissable. Experience has shown that these operations can be done with multinational forces, but only under a unified command structure, particularly where the operations of air, surface and sub-surface units have to be coordinated.[8]

The most difficult maritime tasks are those of containing a crisis and protecting non-belligerents, not only because they require the limited use of force under tightly prescribed conditions but also because of the difficulty of determining what constitutes a direct threat to ships or facilities being protected - the old problem of defining hostile acts and hostile intent. A related problem lies in the fact that under law, a state may only use force to protect ships sailing under its own flag. With some 75 percent of the world's shipping now sailing under flags of convenience, the problem of protecting their cargoes is complex. The 1987-88 Tanker War in the Persian Gulf is probably the best example of just how complex this operation can get. Under some circumstances, military forces may also have to dispose of mines and explosives or undertake other specialist tasks such as controlling the movement of shipping.

The decision to intervene in a crisis ironically simplifies the situation in removing most ambiguities. However, an intervention must have clearly specified objectives with accompanying limits on the use of force. As in other phases, determining appropriate rules of engagement is extremely important and will influence the final outcome. The wrong rules, either too stringent or too loose, can jeopardize an operation.

Finally, keeping the new peace, after a treaty or cease-fire has been signed, may require maritime forces to conduct surveillance, monitor the use of the ocean, and verify that the conditions of the treaty or truce are being respected at sea. Again, this requires a unified command and control struc-

	Patrol Vessel	Frigate	Sub	Aircraft Carrier	Patrol Aircraft
PREVENTING CONFLICT					
– Surveillance	GOOD	GOOD	GOOD	GOOD	GOOD
– Presence	POOR	GOOD	POOR	GOOD	POOR
IMPOSING SANCTIONS					
– Intercept	POOR	GOOD	GOOD	GOOD	GOOD
– Search	GOOD	GOOD	POOR	FAIR	NIL
– Apprehend	POOR	GOOD	POOR	FAIR	NIL
CRISIS MANAGEMENT					
– Protection	FAIR	GOOD	GOOD	GOOD	POOR
– Shipping Control	FAIR	GOOD	NIL	POOR	NIL
INTERVENTION					
– Anti-shipping	POOR	GOOD	GOOD	GOOD	POOR
– Anti-submarine	POOR	GOOD	GOOD	FAIR	GOOD
– Shore strike	NIL	POOR	NIL	GOOD	NIL
PEACEKEEPING					
– Surveillance	GOOD	GOOD	FAIR	GOOD	FAIR

ture if the operations of ships, aircraft and submarines are to be coordinated effectively.

Thus, all types of maritime forces can be used in crisis management, but not with the same degree of effectiveness in each case. This can be seen from the table which matches the suitability of platforms (ships and aircraft) to specific crisis management tasks.

Without going into individual ship and aircraft characteristics, such a comparison is very subjective. To summarize, the smaller patrol vessels obviously have uses, but are less capable than larger warships. Aircraft carriers, on the other hand, are able to carry out most tasks but lack some of the flexibility of frigate-sized vessels. Overall, the value of multi-purpose ships such as frigates, particularly those with integral helicopter support, stands out. It is little wonder that so many of the world's navies are turning their attention to that concept, which, I might add, is a Canadian innovation.

The bottom line is that traditional concepts of naval operations, both multi- and unilateral, are completely consistent with the policies outlined in the *Agenda for Peace.* All it takes to make use of the flexibility of maritime forces is for the political objective to be translated into precise tasks. In other words, the key to effective maritime operations in support of crisis management is good command and control of those forces from the beginning of the operation. Achieving this requires a specialist staff. The UN, therefore, should either acquire its own integral naval staff or be prepared to delegate that function to a single state or to ad hoc or existing coalitions. This is where I believe that the experience gained through the NATO naval organizations, the Standing Naval Forces in particular, has much to offer.[9]

Although the concept of multinational maritime forces is theoretically sound, there are several practical difficulties. The key question is, "Which states can actually form such coalitions?" Again, this is largely a function of experience in multinational operations and general interoperability in such important things as communications, tactical procedures, and logistics. In reality, there are few navies that can effectively cooperate at sea in this way. Today, I believe they are: (1) The western nuclear navies (Britain, France and the United States). The Russians cannot be included because of communications and procedural incompatibility and because the status of their Navy is just too uncertain. (2) The other NATO navies, all of which have considerable multinational experience at sea. Although the larger vessels of Canada, the Netherlands, Germany, Italy, Spain and Turkey are useful for general-purpose tasks, the specialist skills of all NATO navies can be used collectively. (3) After that, there are only a handful of navies with the necessary capability to cooperate effectively, mainly Argentina, Australia, Japan, New Zealand, and perhaps India.

Thus, the potential for effective multinational cooperation at sea is limited at the moment, and it will take time to bring other maritime forces up to required operating standards. But those are not the only limitations.

For instance, for multinational forces to be truly effective throughout the spectrum of crisis management, the capabilities of those ships, submarines, and aircraft should be unambiguous. Simply, ships and aircraft with a nuclear capability cannot be used in crisis management if their capability is seen as a further threat. There is no room for the ambiguity of "neither confirming nor denying" the presence of nuclear weapons or other weapons of mass destruction. Similarly, the presence of aircraft carriers, submarines, and amphibious forces can be misconstrued under some circumstances. Thus the quintessential requirement of effective multinational forces in crisis management is the lack of ambiguity. This is a confidence and security-building measure that the peacemakers and peacekeepers must impose upon themselves.

At the present time, there are probably no more than 15 navies that can be realistically used to support maritime operations within the new UN concept for world peace. For the most part, these are the traditional maritime medium powers, of which Canada is one. This does not mean that the larger navies, which we should now think of as the "major naval powers", have no role to play in maritime security. On the contrary, their resources should be saved for the intervention phase and for specialist tasks such as mine countermeasures, tactical air support, logistics, and amphibious operations. However, the routine work of maritime crisis management should be done by the family of maritime middle powers who have the proven ability to work together and whose forces are unambiguous.

If the "family" of nations able to cooperate in multinational maritime operations is to be expanded, it will need compatible equipment, common procedures, and appropriate training. Until that happens, the burden will fall on the shoulders of the few nations able to coordinate their operations at sea and in the air. If cooperative security is to be a realistic objective at sea, regionally or otherwise, there is a long learning curve and a related modernization program for all but a few navies.

One point that seems to be missed frequently is that through the integration of frigates, helicopters, support vessels, and occasionally submarines, the modern naval task group has become a flexible, multi-purpose structure that can be deployed to crisis areas as the first step in finding a solution. This can include securing port and off-loading facilities and making approach routes safe. Moreover, such a force can be made up of several nationalities. The naval task group has thus become the basic building block of modern maritime forces.[10]

Once port and airport facilities have been secured or arranged elsewhere in the region, the task group can be given additional support by maritime patrol aircraft and air defence fighters. Again, this can only happen when the procedures for command, control and coordination of all forces have been established. Units that cannot communicate or cannot understand orders quickly become a liability.

To summarize, the crisis management roles naval forces must be able to carry out in the future include: maintaining a military presence in an area to prevent or deter aggression and lawlessness, conducting anti-piracy, anti-smuggling and other law enforcement tasks; enforcing a quarantine or a blockade; protecting shipping and maritime facilities, including mine countermeasures; supporting operations on land in many ways, particularly by the use of helicopters and by providing logistic support; restoring order and stability in a crisis; and supervising truces and other such agreements through peacekeeping, verification and monitoring.

Although these operations may not always require the use of force, they do require that warships be prepared to go in harm's way.

Rather than serve as just peacekeepers, naval forces must truly be diplomats, peacemakers, and guardians of security, as they have been for centuries. But we must acknowledge that much of their effectiveness is now a function of modern technology.

Air Force Roles in Crisis Management

So far, I have deliberately restricted my remarks to maritime concepts. However, these have included frequent mention of the vital role played by aircraft in those operations. As I mentioned before, the aircraft has become an integral part of the naval task force. Whether operating from the deck of a frigate, a support ship, or an aircraft carrier, or flying from a base on shore, aircraft are essential to the success of a maritime mission.

Of the various aircraft used in maritime operations, the helicopter is probably the least understood. Rather than being purely for antisubmarine warfare, as many believe, the new generation of helicopters have acquired a level of flexibility not seen before. A modern helicopter, such as the EH-101, can carry out a wide range of tasks without requiring reconfiguration. These tasks include: search and rescue; medical evacuation; reconnaissance and surveillance, including environmental monitoring and reporting; support of land force operations; law enforcement at sea; communications relay; personnel and general cargo transport, and a wide range of specialist military tasks including antisubmarine operations.

The traditional air force role in crisis management has been to provide support for ground operations. This is not limited to transportation, but includes tactical support in combat situations and, more importantly, reconnaissance. Here again, the helicopter has become the most versatile vehicle for providing that support. Like its maritime counterpart, it can carry out a wide range of tasks varying from close support as a gunship, to armed or unarmed reconnaissance, to general transport and medical evacuation.

In the future, the ability to exploit advances made in radar technology will allow ground forces to monitor the surrounding area as often as they wish. On the other hand, resupply will remain a problem that cannot be solved completely by air other than for small groups of people.

Conclusion

In conclusion, we must acknowledge that the post-Cold War era is marked by two features: it has become a period of international crisis management that must take place as a necessary precursor to a new international system, and it is a period in which technology will play an increasingly important part in everything we do. The military forces needed to bring about a more stable world are already part of the technological era. The price of world peace will not be cheap.

Like radical change, military equipment - the purpose is not understood or has not been well explained - is invariably viewed with suspicion and seen as a threat to entrenched beliefs and expectations. Yet in reality, that equipment is part of the means whereby our high standard of living can be offered to even more people in the world. If we do not invest in new technology we will not prosper and will not be able to help others do likewise. In the process, however, the technologists have an obligation to explain the nature of change and the implications of specific changes.

I want to close by bringing the views I have expressed back into a more specifically Canadian context. This can be done by examining three more myths: (1) The end of the Cold War has made the world safe and stable. (2) As the only superpower at the moment, the United States is the natural global policeman. (3) Canada does not need to be involved in putting the new world order in place.

First, it should be quite clear to all that we now live in uncertain and unpredictable times in which several arms races are taking place. Second, there is now every indication the US Clinton administration and the US military are in accord that the United States will not become the global policeman. The emerging US international security policy indicates that the Americans see their new role more as the "Marshal" who will coordinate the posse and provide some unique capabilities to cooperative security operations. In this, they expect the other nations of the world to carry their fair share of the security burden. Last, Canada is still a leading member of the international community. Our economic system is completely integrated into that of the world as a whole, and international trade is essential to our continued well-being. For us to prosper there has to be a stable world order. This requires that we pay our dues to international security. There is no free lunch, as some self-interest groups want to believe.

Canadians have a long tradition of opposing aggression and tyranny, and it would be morally wrong to abandon that role now. It is in our collective interest, therefore, to ensure that we maintain a professional and well equipped military built on the concepts of flexibility and mobility. To keep the costs of maintaining that military structure as low as possible without jeopardizing its effectiveness, two principles must be adopted: the reduction of excess infrastructure so that the greater part of the military is directly linked to operations, and the exploitation of technology to the highest possible extent.

This will not be inexpensive. But if we are to become a respected member of the new international system, we must accept an appropriate level of responsibility for building and maintaining that system. Reducing the military to insignificance in comparison with our trading partners and traditional allies, as the peace groups would have us do, will marginalize Canada and turn us into a Third World country.

Swords can be beaten into ploughshares only when there is no more need for those swords. But turning those swords into social programs means that you have neither swords nor ploughshares. That is shortsighted. A modern, well-equipped military is a necessary extension of foreign policy and an essential element of sovereignty. The technology used by that military is thus an investment in the nation's future.

The Cold War is over, but we do not yet have peace in our time. There is still work to be done in building a better world. The process will be long and occasionally dirty. And Canadians must roll up their sleeves and accept their fair share of the workload if we want to reap the benefits.

Notes

1. Professor Joel Sokolsky has referred to the present trend to widespread interventionism as "humanitarian imperialism." (Joel J. Sokolsky, "How Should the Canadian Forces Be Organized and Equipped for the Modern World?" a paper presented to the Conference of Defence Associations seminar "Canadian Forces for the Modern World", 28 January 1993).

2. There is a wealth of literature on crisis management. Of the more recent works, Alexander L. George, ed., Avoiding War: Problems of Crisis Management, (Boulder: Westview Press, 1991), contains some excellent analysis of the more pertinent case studies.

3. These factors are not new. They are based on traditional "Principles of War" used in strategic planning. Perhaps they are better thought of as "Cardinal Rules" which if broken greatly increase the likelihood of failure.

4. The integration of helicopters and other aircraft into modern maritime force structures has increased this flexibility.

5. This figure may seem incredible. It is, however, based on several logical factors. For instance: the air search radar has a range greater than 150 miles, the surface search capability is less, but can be doubled in a given direction by using the helicopter. The towed array sonar is capable of ranges beyond 90 miles, and the underwater search can also be extended by using the helicopter's sonar systems. On aggregate, the frigate's effective total surveillance horizon (air, surface and underwater) is about 50 miles (80 km) to give a total coverage of 20,096 sq km. Lake Ontario has an area of 19,001 sq km. In circular form this converts to a diameter of 156 km or 96 statute miles.

6. This concept is often referred to as Gunboat Diplomacy and, as such, has been widely studied. The best known examination is that by Sir James Cable, Gunboat Diplomacy 1919-1979: Political Applications of Limited Naval Force, (London: Macmillan, 1981). Ken Booth, Navies and Foreign Policy, (London: Croom Helm, 1977) is an invaluable companion to Cable's work. Also, Eric Grove, The Future of Seapower, (Annapolis: Naval Institute Press, 1990) discusses naval diplomacy in some detail, as do several other authors.

7. For a more detailed discussion of the "presence" role of submarines see Jan S. Breemer, "Where Are the Submarines?", Proceedings, January 1993, pp. 37-42.

8. Again, there are several good examples of the use of maritime forces in this task. Canadian experience largely comes from the Cuban missile crisis and the 1991 Persian Gulf crisis. A good review can be found in Nicholas Tracy, Attack on Maritime Trade, (Toronto: University of Toronto Press, 1992)., and Peter T. Haydon, The 1962 Cuban Missile Crisis: Canadian Involvement Reconsidered, (Toronto: Canadian Institute of Strategic Studies, 1993).

9. This point is well made by Dr. Michael Pugh in his recent paper "Multinational Maritime Forces: A Breakout from Traditional Peacekeeping" (Southampton Papers in International Policy, No. 1, July 1992). The concept of multinational forces has been addressed by several analysts, mainly from a theoretical perspective. For instance: Michael Vlahos, "A Global Naval Force? Why Not?", Proceedings, March 1992, pp. 40-44; Derek Boothby, "Sailing Under New Colors", Proceedings, July 1992, pp. 48-50; and Gwyn Prins, "The United Nations and Peace-Keeping in the Post-Cold War World: The Case of Naval Power", Bulletin of Peace Proposals, Vol. 22(2), pp. 135-155 (1991). Canadian contributions are: Commander Daniel G. McNeil, "Maritime Peacekeeping: A Role for Canadian Naval Forces", (an unpublished paper in the RMC War Studies Program), and Peter T. Haydon, "Naval Peacekeeping?", Canadian Institute of Strategic Studies Strategic Datalink, No. 35, December 1992.

10. The naval task group is comparable, organizationally, to an army Brigade Group in being completely self-sufficient.

John Bremner

Canadian Preparations for Peacekeeping

Mr. Peter Jones

Colonel John Bremner is Director of International Policy at National Defence Headquarters. As such he coordinates the development and implementation of Canada's peacekeeping policy. Colonel Bremner is well-travelled and is often sent by the Canadian government to brief other governments interested in learning our way of peacekeeping. He served with UNEF II in Egypt, and most recently as Canadian Forces Attache in Malaysia.

Colonel Bremner

First I will review quickly some factors which govern Canada's defence policy, and how peacekeeping fits into that policy.

Our present defence priorities are: (1) defence, sovereignty and civil responsibilities in Canada; (2) collective defence arrangements through NATO and NORAD; and (3) international peace and security through stability and peacekeeping operations, arms control verification and humanitarian assistance.

The last of these priorities is, of course, the one that we are focusing on during this seminar and, indeed, the one that is occupying much of our time. The end of the Cold War did not herald a more stable and peaceful world. In fact, it had an opposite, destabilizing effect, with the result that the Canadian

Forces (CF) must now deal with a broad range of operational challenges brought about by the emerging world order.

Today there are more Canadian servicemen and women serving throughout the world on peacekeeping and related duties than at any other time since the Korean War. Approximately 5,000 members of the CF are currently serving on such missions, roughly double the number of a year ago. They are serving in 15 different missions located on nearly every continent. The missions they are undertaking range from traditional peacekeeping, humanitarian relief operations, protection of the delivery of humanitarian relief supplies, an enforcement action in Somalia, and a just-completed preventive deployment in Macedonia. During the past four years alone, the UN has created 15 new missions, which is more than all those missions established in the preceding 40 years. And as the missions have increased in number, they have also increased in size and even more dramatically in scope. The mission in Cambodia, for example, involves more than 20,000 personnel, and is providing a transitional government in that country as well as human rights monitoring, civil policing, electoral duties, infrastructure development, and many other tasks.

As the makeup of missions has changed so too have the type and range of activities. In the case of the former Yugoslavia, the line between peacekeeping and humanitarian assistance has become blurred. In Somalia, Canadian troops are involved in an enforcement action related directly to a humanitarian mission. We have also extended our efforts in some missions beyond peacekeeping to "post conflict peace building" as foreseen by the UN Secretary-General in *An Agenda for Peace*.

Needless to say, planning for such a wide range of roles and activities is a very challenging task. We have always begun our planning by applying a set of criteria to each request for a new mission. These criteria, in various forms, have been used since the 1970s and have been very useful in assessing the likelihood of success of the missions in which we have been involved. To date, they have served us well. Nevertheless, the drafters of these criteria could not have envisaged the scope and complexity of modern missions, and this has caused us to review them. We have recently developed a preliminary set of guidelines to cover the much broader range of missions which are now being conducted. These are: (1) What is the mandate? Is it achievable? (2) In what setting will the mission take place? Do one, or all, of the principal antagonists agree to a UN presence? (3) What is the political context? Have other peaceful means to resolve the situation failed? Is this operation likely to serve the cause of peace and lead to a long-term settlement of the problem? (4) Does Canada have the forces available to fulfil the role that the UN has proposed for us? (5) Will this operation jeopardize other CF commitments and tasks? (6) Is the peacekeeping force that is being proposed adequate and appropriate to the mandate? (7) Are the lines of authority clear? (8) Is the mission adequately funded? (9) Is it logistically supported? (10) What is the risk to peacekeepers? Is the level of risk acceptable? (11) Are the rules of engagement clear and appropriate? (12) Does this operation serve Canadian interests?

These new guidelines have not been formally accepted and may still undergo some change, but we are working with them to see if they meet our needs. So far they seem to, although we will be keeping them under review.

Much has been said and written recently about our ability to sustain the present level of peacekeeping operations. In this vein I can assure you that the Chief of the Defence Staff (CDS) would not have accepted any one of the commitments if it was beyond the Forces' capability to mount and support it effectively. However, it is obvious that the current peacekeeping load is a heavy one, considering the limitations on our present and projected resources. As most of you know, the regular component of the CF is being cut back by 14 percent over a six-year period. In 1989 there were 87,000 regulars. Today the regular force is down to 81,000 and it should be down to 75,000 by 1995-96.

In contrast to the regular force, the reserves are undergoing an expansion. In fact, they have already been enlarged from 22,000 to 27,000 in the last four years, and they will continue to grow, peaking at 40,000 by the end of the 1990s. Most of the expansion will occur in the land forces, which coincidentally bear the largest burden of peacekeeping operations. The implementation of the total force concept has allowed us to increasingly draw peacekeepers from reservists who volunteer. Today a full ten percent of our peacekeeping troops serving abroad are reservists.

Peacekeeping is expanding in another way as well. Many states which have not expressed interest in peacekeeping before are now lining up to provide troops to the UN. Following from this, much has been said about the need for standardized training to ensure interoperability among the diverse forces deployed. Some states have already established training systems for peacekeeping troops and the UN has recently published training guidelines, which are helpful.

There have been some suggestions that our forces should be trained specifically for peacekeeping duty. However, it has been our experience that general purpose combat training produces an efficient, reliable and flexible peacekeeper. Indeed, the best peacekeeper, in our experience, is a well-trained soldier, sailor or aviator. This is not to say that we forego special preparations. Indeed, we follow the UN training guidelines and we conduct appropriate specialized training for those selected for peacekeeping duty. Specifically: (1) Contingency Training. This is conducted annually by the UN standby force using different areas of the world for variety. The timing of this training varies from year to year, as does the location; (2) Replacement/Reinforcement/Rotation Training. This is designed specifically for those personnel posted to the CF logistic unit in the Golan Heights (UNDOF). This training is conducted quarterly and involves approximately 100 personnel each time. It is one week in duration and is conducted at CFB Montreal; and (3) Military Observer Training, which is conducted once per year over an eight day period in accordance with UN standards. This training is for officers warned for postings to existing missions. It is also conducted at CFB Montreal. Military observer training is also conducted on an as-required basis for officers warned for short notice peacekeeping operations. This intensive training is normally conducted over a three-day period at National Defence Headquarters.

Units assigned to peacekeeping missions undergo approximately three months specific-to-mission training prior to deployment to the theatre of operations. Moreover, curricula at most training institutions such as staff schools, staff colleges and advanced training courses also include training on the UN, peacekeeping and related subjects. And in the international arena the CF provides peacekeeping assistance teams to states which request such assistance and conduct or participate in seminars and conferences on peacekeeping from time to time.

We are often asked about standby forces. At the moment a number of nations have forces on standby for UN missions, including Canada. We have informed the UN that we are prepared to formalize these standby arrangements through an exchange of letters as suggested by the Secretary General in *An Agenda for Peace*. Our standby forces consist of an infantry battalion, air transport elements and a communications element.

We are also often asked about the cost of peacekeeping and how it is budgeted and paid for. As a member of the UN, Canada is bound by Article 17 of the UN Charter, which states that "The expenses of the organization shall be borne by the members as apportioned by the General Assembly". Based on this precept, the UN has historically established accounts for each peacekeeping operation. All new missions, in theory at least, are financed by obligatory contributions levied on member-states according to a special peacekeeping scale of assessment. The principal component of the assessment methodology is national income in the form of GNP. Canada's current rate of assessment is 3.11 percent. We (the Government of Canada, not DND) therefore contribute 3.11 percent of the cost of each new operation regardless of the extent of our military contribution. This is expected to be approximately $100 million for fiscal year 1992-93 and more next year. There are exceptions to the assessed contribution rule: UNFICYP is funded on voluntary contributions, UNPROFOR II, which is currently funded nationally by troop contributors (although it will convert to assessed contributions on 1 April 1993), and non-UN missions such as MFO have special funding arrangements.

Of direct impact on DND is the incremental cost of each peacekeeping mission. Incremental costs are the difference between the costs incurred using a unit in a UN operation and using the same unit for normal duties. Needless to say, these incremental costs are high and, in the present expansionary climate, are difficult to forecast accurately. They currently stand at approximately $171 million for this fiscal year - more than three times the amount that was considered normal just two years ago. As a result, we have had to transfer funds from the operating and maintenance budget which, of course, has an adverse affect on other activities. We are trying very hard to avoid taking funds from the capital budget, which pays for the equipment needed by the forces. Next year we expect incremental costs to be more than $200 million.

So what more can we do to contribute to help the cause of peacekeeping, put our experience and expertise to good use, and best assure a sustainable and effective level of participation in peacekeeping operations, considering our shrinking resources? One option is that, in order to emphasize Canadian skill and knowledge to a greater degree, we could place emphasis in providing troops in the early stages of a mission only. Once it was set up and running effectively we could leave its long-term sustainment to other, less-experienced countries. Another idea is to redeploy peacekeepers more frequently to where the need is greatest. For example, we have recently agreed to the shift of some of our peacekeepers from El Salvador and Angola to the new UN mission in Mozambique.

We have also been active in directly assisting the UN. A Canadian Major-General is the military adviser to the Under-Secretary-General for peacekeeping operations in UN Headquarters New York, and we are also providing advice and assistance with UN projects on logistics and organizational requirements for standby forces.

Before closing, I would like to leave you with a few thoughts about peacekeeping and how we must prepare for it.

First, peacekeeping in its traditional form is currently undergoing profound change, and has become only one mechanism within a greatly broadened international system of peaceful conflict resolution. We believe that new organizations, activities, structures and mechanisms will characterize peacekeeping missions in the future: politicians, diplomats, bureaucrats, soldiers, police and civil officials will all have to work together, each with a complementary role. Preventive measures will play an increasing part in the process.

Second, peacekeeping is a high profile and generally popular military task. Although we do not need much specialized training for it, we do need very well trained, disciplined and equipped personnel. It is a demanding military task, not to be taken lightly, and peace comes with a price. It is demonstrably and increasingly evident, in such missions as those in the former Yugoslavia and Somalia, that general purpose combat troops are the best prepared and equipped for the various types of missions in which we are now being asked to participate. Finally, we expect that peacekeeping, as an instrument of conflict resolution, will play a pre-eminent role in the emerging international system. The maintenance of peace is clearly going to be one of the principal challenges as we enter the 21st century, and we must continue to develop the tools to do it well.

I can assure you that our peacekeepers are well trained, well led and well equipped for the task, and are held in the highest regard wherever they go. We are, however, facing limitations on both our human and financial resources, and the growth of peacekeeping comes with a price.

Jeffrey Tracey

The Use of Overhead Surveillance in United Nations Activities

Mr. Peter Jones

Mr. Jeffrey Tracey is a Verification Research Officer with the Verification Research Unit of the Non-Proliferation, Arms Control and Disarmament Division at the Department of External Affairs. He is responsible for all technical matters related to arms control verification, including overhead surveillance, seismic and non-seismic monitoring of underground nuclear tests and verification of outer space activities. Mr. Tracey was a Technical Advisor to the Open Skies Delegation of Canada, and one of his recent studies on overhead remote sensing has just been presented to the UN Secretary-General.

Jeffrey Tracey

Preface

In his speech on 27 September 1989 to the forty-fourth session of the United Nations General Assembly, Canada's Secretary of State for External Affairs, the Right Honourable Joe Clark, announced that Canada would make available to the United Nations the results of future Canadian investigations into the utility of overhead sensing technologies (both airborne and satellite-based) for peacekeeping. The primary objective of the original Canadian research, which was undertaken in 1990 by the Verification Research Unit of

External Affairs and International Trade Canada, was to examine the applicability of such technology for verification of arms control agreements relating to the control of conventional armaments in Europe. In the course of this work, it became increasingly evident that the relevant sensing technologies could also be beneficially employed in United Nations peacekeeping to provide cost effective supplementary information and support to ground-based United Nations forces. My presentation is an updated version of the study that was presented to United Nations Secretary-General Perez de Cuellar in 1990.

I. Introduction

In the past, United Nations peacekeeping efforts have depended on traditional methods of monitoring for the surveillance and supervision of combatant forces. Patrolling and surveillance of borders, demilitarized zones and coastlines has been conducted primarily by use of ground-based personnel in vehicles, on boats or on foot. Aerial patrols, if used at all, have been normally focused on the daytime visual reconnaissance of key areas. United Nations peacekeeping operations, however, often involve extremely large territories which would seem to invite the use of more efficient and effective techniques of large scale monitoring.

My presentation deals with the use of commercially available overhead imagery for the verification of multinational agreements only. While the use of National Technical Means (NTM) satellites does serve an important intelligence assessment function, it does nothing to build confidence and trust between multinational regimes. Only those data and systems that are commercially available to all nations will be discussed here today.

The use of airborne imagery in support of peacekeeping missions is not unprecedented. During the Sinai Disengagement Process (1972-1979), American aerial photo reconnaissance was used extensively for information gathering purposes. In the Yemen in 1963 - 1964, UNYOM was one of the few examples where overhead reconnaissance was used directly in United Nations peacekeeping. In this case, the United Nations had the support of eight reconnaissance aircraft because of the mountainous terrain and difficult accessibility for ground troops. In Central America, ONUCA has utilized eight light helicopters for reconnaissance purposes. Since the writing of the original report in 1990, the use of both satellite and airborne overhead remote sensing has proven itself as a valuable tool in multinational programs. SPOT satellite imagery was extensively used during the Gulf War by the coalition forces as a supplementary overhead data source to National Technical Means imagery. Following the Gulf War, the United Nations Special Commission (UNSCOM) established an overhead image acquisition program using U-2 high altitude photography and low-level imagery acquired by helicopter surveillance to monitor Iraq's compliance with UN Resolution 687. This imagery has proven itself by supplying on-site inspectors with a better understanding of a site before an inspection takes place. Helicopter acquired photography and video imagery assist in real-time portal and perimeter monitoring when an on-site inspection is taking place. The Open Skies treaty, although it is not a United Nations based regime, is an overhead remote sensing confidence building and arms control regime signed in March of 1992. It will undoubtedly be the foundation and framework for many multilateral airborne surveillance proposals to come. While not image acquisition oriented, the United Nations operation UNPROFOR has undertaken the use of NATO AWACS airborne surveillance to monitor the situation in Yugoslavia.

In future operations, the incorporation of airborne imagery sensors into an aerial patrolling program could enable United Nations peacekeeping forces to operate over larger and more remote areas during both daytime and nighttime. Information from these operations could give ground-based United Nations personnel data not normally available to them because of distance or darkness.

Sophisticated forms of overhead imagery are available that could widen the window of observation opportunity. Synthetic aperture radars for an all-weather, day or night capability and thermal infrared sensing to detect heat sources at night are two alternative methods of airborne sensing that could, in addition to photo-optical sensors, provide valuable supplementary information to United Nations peacekeepers in the field.

Although the emphasis of the report is on airborne overhead reconnaissance, the use of commercially available satellite imagery for peacekeeping support is discussed. High resolution commercial satellite imagery, such as that available from SPOT-Image, Soyuzcarta or Russian DD-5, could provide additional preparatory information to ground-based peacekeeping forces for updating existing maps in terms of roads, large structures or camps.

The primary purpose of the report is to identify specific airborne sensor types and aircraft platforms that may have an application in United Nations peacekeeping, and to outline the cost of this equipment. It will also attempt to demonstrate how the use of this equipment could increase the United Nations observers efficiency and, ultimately, their effectiveness during peacekeeping deployments.

II. Peacekeeping and Remote Sensing - Important Considerations

Several key factors must be considered before airborne remote sensing activity could be used successfully as a United Nations peacekeeping support tool. Areas of concern include: the United Nations peacekeeping mandate, the level of political support, the control and command of peacekeeping forces, the type of terrain in which the peacekeeping forces will be operating and the impartiality that the United Nations' role should exemplify.

Peacekeeping Mandate

"Peacekeeping" includes a variety of definitions, all of which incorporate an impartial third party to keep a number of hostile states or communities separated. In the context of United Nations operations the International Peace Academy (IPA) defines peacekeeping as: "the prevention, containment, moderation and termination of hostilities between or within states, through the mediation of a peaceful third party intervention organized and directed internationally using multinational forces of soldiers, police and civilians to restore and maintain peace".[1]

In terms of United Nations peacekeeping missions, the definition would include the following functions within their mandate: observing, reporting, maintaining communication, patrolling and mediating low level disputes and complaints. The sole authority under which a peacekeeping force can operate is the mandate of any operation as devised by the Security Council. A clear and concise objective of the peacekeeping force must be established for it to be effective.

The IPA *Peacekeeper's Handbook* states that mandates set out by the Security Council are commonly broadly phrased in order to meet all requirements and desires of the parties involved. Mandates of a peacekeeping force are also typically short-term. Even so, aerial reconnaissance in support of peacekeeping should be incorporated into any mandates as prescribed by the Security Council. The role of aerial reconnaissance should be defined in the mandate so that this technology is clearly established as a tool to complement information acquired by ground-based observer groups.

Acceptability and Political Support

Clearly, political support from the nations where a peacekeeping force will operate must be obtained. The inclusion of aerial reconnaissance activity as an observational tool available to the peacekeeping forces must be accepted explicitly and have the support of the various parties to a dispute. An airborne remote sensing system, incorporated as support to United Nations peacekeeping initiatives, must be perceived not as a covert means of intelligence gathering, but as a source of informational support to help observers do their job more efficiently. Each party must perceive that the benefits from aerial overflights will apply to every party. By allowing overhead reconnaissance in peacekeeping operations, all parties can contribute to and benefit from increased openness. In this way, aerial overflights can assist in the confidence building process that is indispensable to the re-establishment of a durable peace.

Command and Control

Command and control as it relates to peacekeeping operations involves two separate groups: the United Nations peacekeeping forces itself and the combatant forces involved in the dispute. Command and control of the sort of overhead monitoring program envisaged in this report would be the responsibility of the peacekeeping force.

In peacekeeping operations, information gained from a variety of sources including overhead monitoring must be properly interpreted, analyzed and disseminated to enhance the actions of ground-based peacekeepers. Timely and accurate information can provide the basis for better mediation efforts, conflict resolution and dispute avoidance. The proper command and control of this information is vital in decisionmaking processes. Aerial overflights that gather data from preselected areas within individual sectors or throughout numerous sectors must be capable of providing the information necessary to make effective decisions on the ground. Control of the information gained as a result of the use of these airborne imaging sensors must remain in the hands of the United Nations peacekeeping forces in order for the use of these sensors to be viewed as a fair and impartial tool for decision-making. Dissemination of necessary information and data sharing with other parties should be the peacekeepers' responsibility.

The proper reporting of airborne remote sensing information entails a high degree of organization and structure. Incorporation of such a potentially powerful information source must be carefully controlled and planned so as to maximize its full potential as a useful and effective means of data gathering and to avoid any misuse.

Terrain and Climate

The nature and extent of the terrain in which the peacekeeping force must operate directly affects the efficiency of any operation. Peacekeeping forces in Namibia, for example, contended with huge tracts of land in their border monitoring activities and coastal surveillance duties. Frontier areas in Namibia consisted of vast open desert, semi-desert areas, bushland and woodland. The reduction in the initially planned size of the UNTAG forces combined with this large land mass inevitably required prioritizing zones where United Nations forces could be active. The inherent dry climate and open land characteristics of the area made the jobs of the peacekeepers easier. Given these same conditions, however, overhead remote sensing would probably have contributed to the more efficient use of UNTAG resources.

As another example, in a climate and topography like Central America, a much different operating procedure in terms of peacekeeping is required. Major obstacles will be encountered as a result of the extremely mountainous terrain, dense vegetation and tropical climate. The mobility of peacekeeping missions will be restricted by the dense jungle and mountains within the area. Vegetation will hinder verification and observation procedures. In Central America, as in many other locales, peacekeeping forces must often contend with poorly developed road networks which greatly obstruct needed transportation.

There are thus many natural obstacles facing peacekeepers which could impede their activities. Aerial patrols using carefully selected imaging sensors can be part of the answer to the challenges that the United Nations peacekeepers will face in a variety of geographic terrains and climates. Aircraft and their associated sensors can monitor large areas in a short period of time. While their effectiveness depends in part on characteristics of terrain and climate, such airborne sensors are far more mobile than ground observers and can be put to good use in a wide variety of geographical situations. Lengthy borders can be patrolled and large coastal areas can be mapped in a fraction of the time it would take ground-based or ship-based personnel.

The use of airborne surveillance in support of the United Nations Special Commission in Iraq is an ideal example. Long periods of clear, unobstructed weather conditions and lack of vegetation provide an optimum climate for the use of overhead surveillance techniques.

<u>Impartiality</u>

Peacekeeping forces within an area of conflict must be perceived as impartial. This is indispensable in gaining the confidence of the parties involved. Information gained by United Nations peacekeeping missions has been traditionally handled in such a way as to settle disputes as amicably as possible. In the past, the information used in this mediatory function has been generally gained by observations and reports from various ground-based observers. The introduction of airborne sensors should be considered as merely an additional source of relevant information available to United Nations peacekeepers. It is important to emphasize that the way this information is handled and disseminated should not be significantly different from the way data is handled by ground-based observer networks. It should be characterized by the same impartiality with which other information is treated. The method in which airborne sensor data is collected must be viewed as a non-covert activity and as merely providing support for the United Nations peacekeeping forces in performing their objectives as stated in the mandate for the peacekeeping operation in question. All parties within a region of conflict must be made aware that the incorporation of airborne patrolling into a peacekeeping operation, like the peacekeeping operation itself, is of benefit to all.

III. Sensor Systems

Many airborne platforms can be outfitted with off-the-shelf, commercially available sensors capable of producing high quality images which can play an important role when their data are utilized for peacekeeping purposes. Imagery from several satellite systems offer some utility for peacekeeping and are currently available for purchase. The basic principles of these sensor systems and their data products must be understood for a full appreciation of the strengths and weaknesses of each.

For the purposes of this report, sensor systems that are proposed for incorporation into United Nations peacekeeping efforts are restricted to commercially available imaging sensors only. Signal intelligence gathering sensors and NTM imagery have no direct role in promoting neutral and impartial decisionmaking in peacekeeping since the use of these systems can arouse fears of spying.

Airborne Sensors

Airborne remote sensors can provide useful information for peacekeeping observation missions in a number of applications. The ability to respond quickly in order to gather information on a particular area of concern as well as regular monitoring sorties over widespread areas enable airborne imaging systems to be very effective. Real-time on-board processing of images gives the peacekeeper an ability to react very quickly to developing situations.

There are four airborne mounted sensor systems which can be of use for United Nations peacekeeping operations. They are: (1) Airborne synthetic aperture radars (SARs), (2) Airborne infrared linescanners (IRs), (3) Airborne forward looking infrared systems (FLIRs), and (4) Airborne photographic or electro-optical cameras.

Table One describes how each of these systems could be utilized as tools in support to peacekeeping forces.

Table One
Advantages and Applications of Airborne Remote Sensing Systems

SENSOR	ADVANTAGES	APPLICATIONS
Synthetic Aperture Radar System	Day/night, all weather capability; stand-off imaging sensor; wide swath coverage	Wide area coverage of borders, coastal areas; monitoring of large scale construction projects, transportation.
Infrared Linescanner	Day/night capability; high thermal and spatial resolution; realtime imagery	Monitoring of heat sources from vehicular activity, buildings, human activity.
Forward Looking Infrared System	Day/night capability; very high spatial resolution; low level data acquisition	Detection and monitoring of heat sources from vehicles, humans, buildings; tracking of moving objects.
Photography and Electro-optical System	Day capability; very high spatial resolution	Monitoring of buildings, vehicles, large scale troop movement.

Synthetic Aperture Radar (SAR)

Imaging radar systems are unique in their capability to provide useful information under conditions when other sensors are rendered useless because of adverse weather or absence of light. Microwave radar systems are considered active sensors, in that they illuminate the terrain by a series of carefully timed microwave pulses of pre-set length. The reflection of these microwave pulses from the terrain is recorded on the aircraft. It is the reflection capabilities of specific targets on the ground that determine radar imagery characteristics.

There are two types of Side Looking Radar Systems (SLAR) commonly used for remote sensing purposes: Real Aperture Radars (RAR) and Synthetic Aperture Radars (SAR). Each system has basic differences which directly influence data quality. As the name suggests, SLAR systems operate by illuminating the terrain to the side of the aircraft, at significant stand-off ranges of 25-100 km away from the target. The earliest airborne radar surveillance systems used unfocused Side Looking Airborne Radar techniques known as Real Aperture Radars (RAR). Resolution of RAR systems are determined by the length of the antenna which transmits and receives the microwave pulses.

In RARs the antenna length is limited by the ability of an aircraft to support and carry it. Hence, most RAR antennas are not less than six metres in length, limiting the overall ability of the system to resolve objects not less than 20 m in size.

Synthetic Aperture Radars (SARs) were developed to overcome the serious resolution limitations of RARs as a result of restrictive antenna lengths. By performing computations on the received radar signal which incorporate the aircraft's own forward movement, SARs create the effect of focusing the radar image through creation of a "synthetic" antenna up to a kilometre or more in length. SAR resolution is virtually independent of altitude and stand-off range, unlike the earlier RARs. SAR has an improved resolution over RAR by a factor of one hundred or more. Early SARs were limited because of the cumbersome optical processors required for the synthetic focusing operation. The newer commercially available state-of-the-art SARs are now capable of processing real-time synthetic aperture information onboard relatively small twin engine turbo-prop aircraft. SAR systems can also incorporate a Moving Target Indicator (MTI) that automatically cues the operator to moving targets within the radar scene. The wide swath coverage enables very large areas to be searched quickly and comprehensively.

SAR systems can acquire data in two modes; high resolution mode (23 km swath width) or wide swath mode (46 km swath width) from an operating altitude of 11,000 m above ground level. The base system parameters for commercially available SARs are as follows:

Frequency:	X-band (Three cm wavelength)
Polarization:	HH, parallel
Pixel Size: Azimuth:	Six metres
(Resolution) Range:	Six metres (23 km swath width) or 12 m (46 km swath width)
No. of Looks:	Seven
Weight:	450 kg, including antenna and recording systems

The SAR systems use real-time, on-board digital processing. The data products and replay capabilities include an interface for on-board, real-time display and digital recording, as well as the capability to downlink a digital data stream to a ground-based receiving station. In other words, the operator on the aircraft can see immediately an image of what the SAR sees. The data can also be transmitted to a ground station or recorded on tape for further processing.

Interpretation of SAR Images

Synthetic aperture radar systems illuminate the terrain with a series of microwave pulses. These pulses reflect from the surface objects on the ground and are returned back to the aircraft. The brightness of the objects on the SAR images directly correspond to the amount of microwave energy reflected back to the aircraft sensor. Smooth objects such as water or pavement will appear very dark to black on the radar imagery because most of the microwave radiation is reflected away from the aircraft, much like shining a flashlight beam from an angle onto a mirror. Rough objects, such as cobbled roads, corn fields, or trees, will reflect much of the transmitted radiation back to the SAR sensor receiver on-board the aircraft and, therefore, will appear as brighter targets. It is this surface roughness characteristic of an object that determines how it will appear on SAR imagery.

Many objects appear on SAR data that are below the theoretical resolving capabilities of the system, which is usually three to six metres. This is possible when their edges react as "corner reflectors", thus acting as high reflectors. Often power lines and hydro poles will be observable because of this phenomenon.

Shadows can be large enough to disrupt interpretation of the data in hilly or mountainous terrain. Therefore, to overcome this effect, the orientation of the imaging radar must be carefully planned during mission planning procedures. For on-board interpretation purposes, SAR imagery can be printed onto film negatives or onto a dry silver paper product. This would enable United Nations on-board observers to view the target area and commence preliminary interpretation and analysis.

The SAR data is recorded onto video or magnetic tape for archiving and later digital processing if required. The SAR data can be downlinked via a digital data stream to a ground receiving station for immediate analysis if the situation requires real-time tactical decisions.

SAR for Peacekeeping

Airborne SAR imaging systems have considerable potential for patrols by peacekeeping groups particularly when large areas are to be covered. Since the swath width covered by SAR systems is typically 25 km in the high resolution mode, this airborne sensor can be utilized to monitor those areas where normal ground-based observing may be impractical due to manpower or time constraints.

Environmental conditions, nature of the terrain and vegetative cover will determine the effectiveness of SAR overflights for patrolling large areas. In locales where climatic effects result in persistent cloud cover, SAR overflights may well be the only practical means of surveilling large areas. This would appear to be the case for an area such as Central America where cloud cover is common. The application and interpretation of SAR imagery is somewhat more difficult, however, in mountainous terrain or over areas of dense vegetative cover. SAR imagery cannot penetrate foliage cover, and its use would prove limited if specific target areas were hidden under a canopy of vegetation.

SAR imagery could be particularly useful in support of United Nations peacekeeping groups for border surveillance activities in certain contexts. The ability of this sensor to image a wide swath of 25 km at a time from a considerable stand-off distance would provide the peacekeepers with an alternative means of border monitoring. The surveillance of large land masses, frontier areas and long border zones can typically drain available manpower resources from a peacekeeping force. Regular SAR overflights of these large land masses would not only lessen the strain on available resources, but would facilitate the establishment of a United Nations presence in isolated and remote areas; something which may be very important for the objective of the peacekeeping mission.

The information provided by SAR imagery is readily transferable to established verification centres either by down-linking of the data to a receiving station or by landing with the imagery that was produced on the aircraft. This is particularly important when time sensitive information is acquired within a frontier zone or isolated area. Dissemination of the results of the SAR overflight to ground-based observer teams would be a vital component of the operation.

SAR can be very effective for locating the position of large military equipment such as aircraft, tanks or ships except when they are under cover. Because these objects have highly reflective microwave characteristics, they appear quite readily on SAR imagery. SAR data would be useful United Nations peacekeeping missions for airfield reconnaissance, coastal surveillance and the monitoring of important installations. The lengths of runways can be calculated, port utilization can be mapped and new construction determined. SAR does have limitations with respect to the detection of ships in rough water, however, due to the highly reflective nature of wave activity and the constant motion of the target.

Thermal Infrared Sensors

Everything radiates energy at thermal infrared wavelengths both day and night. The ability to detect and record this thermal radiation in image form at night has obvious reconnaissance applications that are relevant to peacekeeping.

The ability and efficiency of an object to radiate thermal infrared radiation is termed as that object's "emissivity". Emissivity is defined as the ratio of radiant flux from a body to that from a black body at the same kinetic temperature. Materials with a high emissivity absorb and radiate large proportions of incident and kinetic energy. Thermal infrared remote sensing systems, therefore, are considered as passive sensors since they merely record this energy emitted by all objects without generating any energy pulses like radars.

There are two types of infrared sensors that are commercially available and could be useful in terms of support for United Nations peacekeeping operations. They are classified as infrared linescanners and forward looking infrared (FLIR) systems.

Imaging thermal infrared linescanners have been developed and utilized for a variety of military, commercial and scientific applications. Airborne linescanner systems consist of three basic components: an optical-mechanical scanning subsystem, a thermal infrared detector and an image recording and printing subsystem.

Most infrared linescanners collect infrared data by flying directly over the target. A rotating scan mirror reflects the emitted radiation from the ground surface onto a super-cooled infrared sensitive detector. The infrared detector utilized is dependent on the ground target of interest. Generally, for "earth" temperatures between -50 degrees Celsius and +50 degrees Celsius, an 8.5-13.5 micrometer infrared detector is used for imaging purposes. The area covered by the swath of the rotating scan mirror is from 1.6 to 2.5 times greater than the altitude of the aircraft. From an airborne operating altitude of 600 m above ground level, a swath of between 1,000 m and 1,500 m can be obtained.

The spatial resolution of infrared linescanning systems is dependent on the size of the infrared detector utilized within the linescanner. Optimum size infrared detectors for reconnaissance purposes for peacekeeping operations would be 1.0 milliradians or less. Using a 1.0 milliradian detector from an operating altitude of 300 m above ground level would result in a spatial resolution of 0.3 m. The resolution is inversely proportional to the aircraft operating altitude, that is, the lower the sensor platform, the higher the spatial resolution.

Airborne thermal infrared linescanning systems have the advantage of operating at night at low level (300 - 1,000 m above ground level) to provide high resolution images of the infrared emission of objects from the terrain below. Real-time, on-board high resolution imagery can be produced in this way to help peacekeeping observers in tactical reconnaissance situations.

Closely related to the airborne thermal infrared linescanning systems is the forward looking infrared system (FLIR). This imaging infrared video system is typically mounted in a low level reconnaissance aircraft or helicopter. Detector types and spatial resolution for FLIR systems is similar to that of the infrared linescanners. FLIR's have the advantage of identifying small targets such as people or vehicles for confirmation of ground activity. The infrared images from the FLIR are recorded directly onto videotape with latitude and longitude positional information. The FLIR has the capability to rotate 360 degrees around the aircraft as well as 180 degrees in the forward and aft directions. Thus, FLIR systems have an advantage over linescan systems in that they are capable of tracking a target by movement of the sensor. This movement is controlled by the operator within the aircraft through the use of a real-time monitor image and sensor controller.

There are many commercially available FLIR systems. All operate very much alike with respect to data acquisition parameters. The main scan head is mounted on a gimbal and turret configuration and its direction is internally controlled by the system's operator. Most FLIR systems have several field-of-views (FOVs): wide FOV, medium FOV and narrow FOV.

The FOV is selected by the on-board systems operator. An important characteristic is the FLIR's ability to retain a high spatial resolution in the narrowest FOV. This is very useful when the monitoring of the movements of objects on the ground is required. Superior FLIR systems retain their very good resolving capabilities in their narrow FOV. The better FLIR systems are built to military specifications and are considerably more expensive than inferior commercial grade models.

Interpretation of Thermal Images

Thermal infrared imagery records the heat emitted by objects as black and white tones. The intensity of the tones is directly proportional to the amount of thermal radiation being emitted by the object. Warm objects or areas will appear dark on thermal infrared imagery negatives and cooler areas will be represented by lighter tones.

Temperature variations as little as 0.2 degrees Celsius can be differentiated using airborne thermal infrared sensors. This is termed as the thermal resolution of the system. The spatial resolution of thermal sensors refers to the ability of the system to differentiate between two objects of a specified size. This characteristic of thermal sensors is determined by the size of the infrared detector element used. Most infrared linescanning systems and FLIRs have spatial resolutions of 0.5 m to 0.25 m from an operating altitude of 300 m above the ground.

The use of thermal infrared imagery is optimized when collected at night, after sundown and before sunrise. During the day, solar radiation causes a thermal "blanket" to be cast on the terrain. As a result, everything on the ground appears relatively warm and it is difficult to measure the natural infrared radiation emitted by objects during daytime operation. Thermal imagery is also affected by water vapour and aerosols in the atmosphere between the sensor and the target. These result in attenuation of the infrared radiation emitted by the object, which could play a role in hindering the identification of a target in extremely humid or dusty situations.

FLIR imagery is recorded onto videotape as black and white tones similar to linescanner data. FLIR data generally provides an oblique view of the objects below, thereby making identification and interpretation of the ground scene easier than vertically acquired images such as linescanner data.

Infrared linescanner imagery can be printed in real-time onto film, dry silver paper, or videotape for immediate on-board interpretation and analysis. The data is stored onto tape for further analysis if necessary.

Both the infrared linescanner and FLIR data can be downlinked in real-time to a ground-based processing station for further digital image analysis on computer processing equipment. This is an expensive option and probably not necessary since the on-board observer will be trained in interpretation skills. The aircrew will be in radio contact with ground-based patrols at all times, therefore, having the capability of transmitting important tactical information readily, if required.

Thermal Infrared for Peacekeeping

Airborne thermal infrared sensing equipment, because of its ability to operate usefully at nighttime, would be extremely valuable to improve the efficiency and effectiveness of United Nations peacekeeping forces. Thermal infrared imagery can be used to map normally unseen objects such as camps, aircraft engine heat or heat produced from boats. Since all objects emit varying amounts of infrared radiation, nighttime activities of personnel, ground-based vehicles or aircraft can be determined. Thermal infrared sensors could be considered as a second pair of "eyes" for use at night by peacekeeping forces.

Using FLIR sensors from an aircraft, a moving ship, a ground-based vehicle or a group of individuals can be identified, tracked and followed for an extended period of time. Ancillary aircraft data such as time, date and present position are recorded automatically on the infrared video images. This could prove to be an important feature if reports of violations are disputed.

UNSCOM would find the use of thermal infrared linescanner or FLIR data very useful in extending the United Nations monitoring capabilities of Iraqi sites into the night. From an operating altitude of 610 m above ground level, the FLIR's resolution is sufficient to resolve individual people and their activity.

Airborne Optical Sensors

Normal daytime aerial photography using films or electro-optical sensors must be considered as a prime method of reconnaissance information for incorporation into the United Nations peacekeeping operations. Photographic systems including aerial photography and especially today's sophisticated electro-optical systems have extremely high resolution capabilities. Black and white photographic negatives can provide useful images of high resolution. Electro-optical images are digitally produced and can be enhanced and processed on specialized computer equipment.

Traditional photography using a standard aerial camera is a relatively economical and reliable aerial reconnaissance method. Film is inexpensive and has the advantage of being capable of enlargement for interpretation purposes. A darkroom capability is required, however, which could prove to be a difficult provision in remote or isolated areas. Aerial photography is restricted to fairly high light levels and must be acquired during daylight hours, usually between 10:00 a.m. and 2:00 p.m. Cloud cover can also pose a serious problem for aerial photography.

Recently, a relatively new concept in solid state signal processing and imaging has given rise to electro-optical systems known as charged-coupled devices (CCDs). Unlike aerial photography, CCD systems record imagery onto a magnetic tape and is viewed on a television monitor. CCD imaging systems are available as small, lightweight portable units which can be readily installed for aircraft operations. Compared to aerial camera systems, CCDs are relatively expensive, but very effective and reliable sensors.

The acquired imagery from CCD systems is normally in the visible portions of the spectrum, but can be filtered for specific applications. The imagery produced is recorded onto videotape for immediate use as a very high resolution source of surveillance information. Ancillary information such as positional information and time/date can be overlaid on the CCD image for cataloguing purposes.

CCD imaging systems have similar restrictions to those for normal photographic cameras. Their use is restricted to the daylight hours in relatively good weather conditions. There are CCD systems which can operate in low light level conditions but their resolution characteristics are reduced as a result. CCD data is recorded digitally, however, and has the capability of being manipulated for interpretation purposes by computers.

The evolution of CCD camera systems has led to the development of long range optical photography (LOROP) systems. These cameras can produce very high resolution imagery from a considerable stand-off distance from the target. The average cost of three to five million dollars per system, however, may be a prohibitive factor.

Multispectral camera systems, one form of electro-optical sensor, consist of electromechanical linescanning devices or pushbroom scanners. Several channels of multispectral data can be recorded or viewed simultaneously. These scanning systems can image and record very narrow spectral wavelengths, a feature that is particularly useful when imaging camouflaged targets. The data reduction and image processing required to produce imagery from these sensors can be a complex operation requiring radiometric and geometric corrections.

Resolution from airborne optical sensors is determined mainly by the altitude of the aircraft platform during data acquisition. A spatial resolution of 0.15 cm is obtainable from flying heights of 305 to 915 m above ground level.

Optical Sensors for Peacekeeping

Aerial cameras, charged coupled devices and multispectral scanners have great potential for United Nations peacekeeping operations. Airfield activity, selected installations, tank storage areas and ship docking areas can be readily monitored. Base camps along border zones and military activities of ground-based groups can also be monitored. Because of their high resolution these systems are highly recommended, despite the limitations on their use posed by adverse weather conditions and darkness.

Interpretation of Daytime Optical Imagery

The interpretation of daytime optical imagery, whether it is normal aerial photography or charged coupled device (CCD) video data, is based on seven basic principles. These are: shape, size, tone, shadows, pattern, location and texture. Using these concepts as an interpretation guide as well as understanding the situation on the ground, an on-board observer or an interpretation specialist should be able to obtain information readily from the imagery provided.

Interpretation of aerial optical imagery will be conducted from either photographic negatives or prints, or from videotaped CCD data, depending on the system used during data collection. The electro-optical imagery has the capability of being downlinked in real-time from the aircraft to a ground processing station if required. An additional advantage of an electro-optical sensor over photographic systems is that the on-board observer can conduct immediate analysis of the imagery on the aircraft; normal photography requires processing of the negatives and prints on the ground. CCD sensors can also be used in low light level conditions while aerial photographic systems require a high sun angle to produce useable imagery. The cost of electro-optical systems may be a prohibitive factor, however, with typical prices of approximately (US) $250,000.

Satellite Imagery

Current overhead commercially available satellite imagery might be used to provide some kinds of information to support United Nations peacekeeping operations. There are, at present, two sources of commercially available satellite imagery which have sufficient resolution to be of use for United Nations peacekeeping support: the French Systeme Pour l'Observation de la Terre (SPOT) satellite program and the Soviet Soyuzcarta satellite program. Imagery from the American LANDSAT satellite program is also available, but with resolutions of not less than 30 m this imagery would not be useful in mapping smaller features on the ground.

SPOT

The French SPOT-1 and recently launched SPOT-2 satellites supply digital satellite imagery with a high spatial resolution. The two High Resolution Visible (HRV) sensors provide three-channel multispectral images with a resolution of about 20 x 20 m or single-channel panchromatic images with 10 x 10 m approximate resolution on the ground.

Table Two outlines the general spectral, spatial and radiometric characteristics of the SPOT HRV sensors. The panchromatic mode is intended for users requiring fine geometric detail as would be required for peacekeeping support. The bands provided in the multispectral mode were optimized for analysis of vegetation which will typically have a response peak in the green band, strong absorption in the red band and a pronounced response in the near-infrared band.

The HRV instrument operates as a pushbroom scanner. Entire lines of imagery are collected at once using 6,000 charge-coupled device (CCD) detectors arranged in linear arrays. The motion of the satellite provides the second dimension for the image. Use of a pushbroom scanner eliminates geometric distortions caused by acceleration and deceleration of the oscillating mirror used in mechanical scanners.

The HRV sensors have the capability to operate over a range of look angles out to 27 degrees from vertical. A strip selection mirror for each sensor can be instructed from the ground to observe areas of interest which are not directly beneath the satellite, providing a 950 km wide observable corridor centred on the satellite's ground track. The width of the imaged area on the

Table Two Characteristics of SPOT Satellite Data		
	PANCHROMATIC	MULTISPECTRAL
Swath Width	60 to 81 km	60 to 81 km
Spatial Resolution	10 to 13.5 m	20 to 27 m
Spectral Bands	0.51 to 0.73 um	0.50-0.59 um (green)
		0.61-0.68 um (red)
		0.79-0.89 um (near IR)
Radiometric Resolution	64 gray levels	256 gray levels

ground will vary from 60 km if the area was directly beneath the satellite to 81 km if the image was acquired obliquely. Lengths of the imaged scenes remain constant at about 60 km.

If the satellite were only capable of vertical viewing, it would be possible to image a particular location only once during the 26-day orbital cycle of the satellite. Oblique viewing provides the means to collect images more frequently for a particular site.

Soyuzcarta

Recently, the Soviet Soyuzcarta satellite program has made data available for public use. Data is available for all areas of the world. Three types of photographic imagery are available, the KFA-1000 imagery and the MK-4 photographic data, both having approximately five meters resolution capability. Table Three outlines the characteristics of the MK-4 and KFA-1000 camera systems. Recently the release of high resolution degraded Russian National Technical Means data has been approved. The Russian panchromatic DD-5 satellite imagery has approximately two metres spatial resolution. Because of the high resolution, the swath width is restricted to

Table Three Characteristics of Soyuzcarta Satellite Data		
	MK-4	KFA-1000
Number of Channels	4	1
Focal Length	300 mm	1000 mm
Frame Format	180 x 180 mm	300 x 300 mm
Scale (depending on altitude of survey)	1:650,000 1:1,500,000	1:220-280,000
Longitudinal Overlap	60%	60%
Width of the Survey Band	120-270 km	120 km
Possible spectral bands of channels (nm)	635-690 nm 810-900 515-565 460-505 580-800 400-700	560-670 nm 760-810
Resolution	6 m	5 m

approximately 15 km by 15 km. The availability of data and area coverage provided by the DD-5 satellite program includes all countries with the exception of Russia.

The KFA-1000 photography is available in both panchromatic and colour formats at a purported 5 m resolution. The KFA-1000 images are taken by the satellites' two photographic camera systems and are jettisoned back to Earth and retrieved and processed for subsequent distribution. Each image covers an area approximately 80 km by 80 km in size, on a negative of 30 cm x 30 cm. There is 60 percent north-south overlap for stereoscopic coverage. The colour film is spectrozonal in nature, with two individual emulsion layers. The colour of the final photographic product depends on the number of filters used during film processing.

The KFA-1000 is a photographic product, but work is now underway to digitize the negatives to provide a digital format compatible with SPOT data. All digital data is produced from the original film positives or negatives.

The MK-4 system is the most sophisticated of the Soviet Union's large format topographic cameras. This system is a multispectral camera recording four separate black and white images which may be combined to produce a colour image. The resolution of the MK-4 imagery is approximately 6 m.

Photographic products are available in either film negative or positive format or prints. The area covered on the ground by the MK-4 data is 160 km by 160 km. Digital products are available for the MK-4 data and are produced from the digitization of the first generation film positives or negatives.

Satellite Imagery for Peacekeeping

Commercially available satellite imagery can be usefully incorporated into the United Nations peacekeeping operations for some ancillary applications. The Verification Research Unit has conducted a number of studies for various geographic areas directly influenced by United Nations peacekeepers, looking at ways SPOT satellite imagery could be of benefit. The use of combined multi-spectral and panchromatic multi-temporal SPOT scenes has proven to be useful in monitoring the Soviet troop withdrawal and removal of related military equipment in Afghanistan in the late 1980s. Other studies using SPOT data of various locations throughout Namibia, Angola, Western Sahara, and Iraq have demonstrated the usefulness of this imagery to update existing maps and for identifying general features such as non-identified military facilities or airports which are not always delineated on maps provided to peacekeeping troops.

Before the peacekeeping forces first arrive on site, they should become familiar with the area in which they will be operating. For example, it would be desirable to have a complete and accurate record of the existing road network to facilitate their own operations, such as organizing patrols to monitor for potential infiltration of military forces into a buffer zone. Existing maps may be inaccurate and will almost certainly not include some specific types of information which would be of interest to the peacekeeping forces.

Useful information could be interpreted from panchromatic SPOT imagery in the form of 1:200,000 scale transparencies. Using this small scale, features such as roads and encampments could be interpreted but any fears regarding potential use of the imagery for intelligence gathering purposes could be largely avoided. Results of the interpretation could be transferred to the existing basemaps for use in the field. Optionally, photographic prints of the imagery could also be made for use in the field.

Satellite imagery can be acquired for a specific location of interest for which precise latitude and longitude coordinates are known. A photographic print of such an image could be used by patrols as a guide to the locations of buildings and other features which would be large enough to be evident on commercially available imagery but are not usually marked on maps.

Satellite data could be used to detect change over a specified target area over a period of time. If large scale changes were scheduled to occur at a specific site, such as the construction or destruction of buildings, satellite imagery could be used to confirm or refute that such changes were occurring. Limitations on the spatial resolution and timeliness of commercially available imagery precludes its use for change detection applications which might be considered intelligence gathering, such as the detection and tracking of convoys of military vehicles. In this way, the use of commercially available satellite imagery might be acceptable within a peacekeeping context.

There are several factors that must be considered if satellite information is to be used for map updating purposes for United Nations peacekeeping. Time to order and process the satellite images for a specific site can be a limiting factor if speed is required. Satellite images can take as long as one month to arrive once ordered, although special requests are sometimes considered. The frequency of the satellite overpasses of an area of interest is dependent on the repeat cycle of the particular spacecraft. For example, the SPOT satellite overflies the same point on the ground approximately every 26 days. Therefore, a careful catalogue search must be done before any data is chosen and ordered. The spatial resolution of satellite imagery restricts the use of such data to large scale mapping such as major construction projects of large buildings or transportation systems.

In contrast to commercial satellite systems, airborne imagery is much more versatile and flexible. It can be acquired over any particular area at almost any time required assuming an aircraft and sensors are available. Delays in obtaining the information are minimal and the resolution of the images is generally superior to that provided by satellite data.

IV. Airborne Remote Sensing Platforms

The characteristics of an airborne remote sensing platform for peacekeeping forces is of considerable importance. The aircraft must be capable of carrying a sensor payload which could be effectively used in a specific terrain environment and it must be able to safely transport the crew in order to conduct its mission. Long range endurance must be provided with sufficient fuel capacity to ferry the crew and sensors to the target, conduct a particular mission, and return the crew to a predetermined base. It is most probable, for peacekeeping support, that the aircraft would be operating from remote airstrips and would therefore require a short take-off and landing (STOL) capability. It should have sufficient power to quickly climb to a safe altitude away from any mountains below.

The type of sensor systems and data acquisition parameters have a direct influence on the type of aircraft suited for a particular peacekeeping surveillance role. High level synthetic aperture radar missions above 9,000 meters require aircraft pressurization. Lower level FLIR and IR missions require slower operating speeds (100 knots) and low flying altitudes of 300 m in order to obtain high resolution thermal images.

On patrolling missions where the detection of an aircraft may seem threatening to some parties below, it is desirable to have a relatively quiet aircraft. This is not to imply that the operation is a covert activity, but only to ensure a measure of safety for the flight crew if operating in an area of possible hazardous confrontation.

Other airborne platforms that are available for monitoring purposes include helicopters, balloons, dirigibles and remotely piloted vehicles (RPV). Helicopter mounted sensors systems could be considered as an optional platform for obtaining overhead imagery for peacekeeping applications in some contexts. The relative operating costs to fixed wing aircraft, however, should be recognized: helicopters are approximately twice as expensive to operate and maintain than fixed wing aircraft of comparable size. Helicopters are also generally restricted to visual flight rule (VFR) conditions and are restricted in their ability to fly in adverse weather or instrument flight rule (IFR) conditions.

Balloons or Small Aerostatic Surveillance Systems (SASS) are now operating in reconnaissance modes for aircraft surveillance purposes in the United States. These SASS platforms use a high resolution air to air radar system for the tracking of suspicious aircraft. They are tethered by a cable which doubles as a data link route to a ground receiving station. The main disadvantage of these systems is their limited ability to move to a different area. As a result, a series of SASS balloons is required to provide overlapping coverage. The cost for such a program is so high that it would be hard to justify its use for United Nations peacekeeping operations.

Manned dirigibles might be of use to a United Nations peacekeeping force for reconnaissance purposes. These platforms can carry large payloads, have a long flight duration capability, and would be cost effective in terms of maintenance and operation. Dirigibles, however, are very susceptible to weather conditions due to their size, require large ground support resources and are relatively slow in moving a crew and sensors from one location to another. Storage of these platforms requires a large facility, one which may not be available in some of the remote locations where the United Nations peacekeepers operate.

Remotely piloted vehicles (RPVs) have been used for tactical surveillance in situations where the threat to human life is high enough to warrant no direct human interaction. RPVs are restricted to line-of-sight to facilitate their effective launch and continuous control. Therefore, in hilly or mountainous terrains RPVs would be virtually useless. RPVs cannot carry large payloads and have a limited range and endurance due to fuel restrictions. Maintenance and staffing for an RPV is similar to that required for an aircraft.

Airborne platforms discussed below for United Nations peacekeeping operations will be restricted to fixed wing aircraft. This is not to say that some of the unmanned platforms and balloons mentioned previously are without potential in peacekeeping activities. But these systems do not have the flexibility required in terms of mobility and costs that fixed wing aircraft can provide to United Nations peacekeeping.

Reconnaissance operations for United Nations peacekeeping activities would require two classes of aircraft; light to medium twin engine fixed wing aircraft (up to 6,800 kilograms) and specialized high powered single engine aircraft.

Twin Engine Aircraft

Aircraft capable of carrying a SAR sensor as its prime payload must have two engines. SAR systems weigh typically on the order of 400-500 kilograms. This weight, combined with the additional weight of a systems operator, a pilot and perhaps on-board United Nations observers and their associated supplies, justifies the requirement for a twin engine turbine powered platform. The airframe must be spacious enough within the cabin to allow for the installation of SAR system equipment. The aircraft must also be capable of carrying an externally mounted antenna system with sufficient clearance beneath the fuselage for adequate aircraft performance.

Proven examples of aircraft types which could adequately carry a SAR system are the Cessna Conquest 441 and the Beechcraft King Air 300. These platforms are turbine powered aircraft which have sufficient power and space for a complete SAR installation package. There are a variety of other suitable twin engine platforms produced internationally which could be used for a SAR platform. It should be noted, however, that there is a substantial amount of structural engineering work required for installation of a SAR into an aircraft platform.

The average maximum operating altitude of these twin engine aircraft is 9,300 meters with an average cruise speed of approximately 250 nautical miles per hour. Typical endurance is five to six hours at cruise speed, with long range capability of seven to nine hours possible with the addition of extra fuel tanks.

There is a broad array of used twin engine aircraft available within the aviation industry. A used, fully functional twin engine platform with avionics could be acquired for approximately (US) $750,000. A new aircraft would cost between (US) $1-1.3 million dollars.

Single Engine Aircraft

The second category of appropriate aircraft includes a very specialized, high powered single engine platform. There are very few of these type of aircraft available but one example is the Turbo Thrush. This aircraft was originally designed for agricultural crop dusting and seeding purposes. Special models have been produced with reconnaissance and surveillance applications in mind. The Turbo Thrush is an ideal platform for such imaging systems as an infrared linescanner, a FLIR or an electro-optical camera system.

In peacekeeping operations in remote locations, the Turbo Thrush provides a short takeoff and landing capability, under 230 m at normal surveillance mission weights. The Turbo Thrush can fly at very slow airspeeds (70 knots), a requirement for maximizing the usefulness of FLIR imagery. The endurance of this aircraft is seven hours, an essential characteristic when patrolling requirements are addressed.

The Turbo Thrush has a very high powered engine with 1376 horsepower. It has been designed to climb rapidly to ensure the safety of its crew if operating in a mountainous environment or in places of possibly hazardous confrontations. The maximum speed of the aircraft is 200 knots.

The cost of the Turbo Thrush, compared to the price of a twin engine aircraft is relatively expensive at (US) $750,000. This is mainly due to the modifications required to configure it for surveillance applications. Maintenance costs, on the other hand, are minimized for the Turbo Thrush. Approximately ten minutes of maintenance per flight hour is required.

The Turbo Thrush seats two people, a pilot and a systems operator. During a reconnaissance mission, the operator typically provides instructions to the pilot based on the imagery provided by the FLIR, linescanner or optical camera system.

V. Costs

Remote sensing technology has provided many countries with support in environmental and engineering monitoring studies. Canada, for example, has developed a very strong base in the development of sophisticated remote sensing hardware, their operation and in the processing of data. There are many private commercial airborne remote sensing firms with a strong base in data acquisition, image processing and interpretation, and analysis of a variety of remotely sensed data products. While the description of many of the sensor systems and the airborne applications described in this report is based on what is available from Canadian commercial remote sensing companies, similar capabilities exist in other countries. These airborne remote sensing services are a result of decades of sensor and program development for specific applications.

The United Nations has three general options in terms of acquiring airborne remote sensing for peacekeeping operations: (1) purchasing off-the-shelf remote sensors and installing them into aircraft and operating the systems itself; (2) leasing complete sensor outfitted aircraft including the service to operate and maintain these systems; or (3) having the system contributed by member states to particular peacekeeping missions.

The following discussion will focus on the first two options. There is a considerable difference between the cost of purchasing versus the cost of leasing commercially available remote sensing systems.

Purchasing

Buying remote sensing systems and aircraft platforms is the more expensive option open to the United Nations because of the capital costs involved. If the sensors are to be installed into a new aircraft, there is a considerable cost to modify the aircraft before sensor integration can occur. (Of course, this capital cost could be reduced if a suitable aircraft platform or sensors was contributed by a member state.) Another expense that the United Nations would incur with buying sensors and aircraft would be the cost of training pilots, sensor operators, engineers and image interpretation specialists. Proper and adequate training of personnel is a time consuming venture with an expected duration of three to four months required for a staff of fifteen to twenty people. The skills required would also require very specialized training.

Other costs to consider if a remote sensing system were purchased and operated by the United Nations would be annual carrying costs of the capital equipment, miscellaneous sensor and aircraft parts and spares costs, aircraft operating costs and staffing costs. Table Four summarizes the estimated costs for the provision of two aircraft outfitted with a SAR, a FLIR, an infrared linescanner and an optical camera system. The cost includes the aircraft, the sensors (including sensor integration) and parts and spares.

Table Four
Typical Airborne Remote Sensing System Costs

	ANNUAL LEASE ESTIMATES*($US)	PURCHASE ESTIMATES**($US)
Sensors		
Synthetic Aperture Radar (SAR)	4,500,000	7,100,000
Forward Looking Infrared (FLIR)	500,000	800,000
Infrared Linescanner	400,000	600,000
Photographic/E/O System	200,000	300,000
Aircraft		
Two aircraft platforms, one twin engine, one single engine including parts and spares	2,000,000	3,900,000
Training	19,000	200,000
Staffing	2,500,000	2,500,000 /year
Carrying Costs	--	1,700,000
TOTAL	10,119,000	17,100,000

*These costs include all associated costs to provide a complete turn key service for a one year airborne reconnaissance program including 300 missions for a total of 2,000 flying hours.

**These costs do not include costs for maintenance, depreciation and operations.

A principal disadvantage with the purchasing option is the problem of keeping the aircraft and related systems busy when not directly involved in a United Nations peacekeeping program. One possibility could be to utilize the systems and the imagery provided for environmental monitoring or mapping applications.

Leasing

Leasing complete remote sensing reconnaissance services on an annual or pre-selected time basis has several advantages for the United Nations. Leasing of aircraft and sensors together with imagery interpretation services would free the United Nations from carrying a financial burden for an extended period of time. Leasing would also enable the United Nations to use an airborne system only when required. Contracting a commercial firm which specializes in airborne remote sensing services would provide the United Nations with the least overall cost with maximum flexibility in terms of required operating timeframes. Provision and training of staff would not be necessary if a leased system were used. The contractor would be responsible for a complete "turn-key" service, providing the United Nations with a package that could be designed to meet the needs of the peacekeeping forces, including the analysis of overhead imagery. A United Nations on-board observer or sensor operator should be trained, however, to act as the liaison between the contractor and the United Nations force.

Table Four shows the estimated annual lease costs for a remote sensing system and the costs associated with the purchase of a facility. The costs are not directly comparable, but they provide a relative perspective of the expected expenses.

A third alternative for the acquisition of an overhead sensing system would be the borrowing of the necessary equipment and related resources from a contributing United Nations member. Expenses associated with this option for the United Nations would likely include the manpower, operating and maintenance costs of the remote sensing program for the duration of the peacekeeping mission.

VI. Organizational Structure

The framework, structure, and organization of an overhead reconnaissance program for United Nations peacekeeping operations are important considerations. Guidelines and methods by which an effective and efficient operation is to be implemented must be outlined so standard procedures are ensured.

Standard Operating Procedures

Standard operating procedures are generally designed for every peacekeeping operation to suit the particular requirements and circumstances of the situation. In the case of the initiation of a regular airborne patrolling network as well as *ad hoc* aerial reconnaissance missions, standard operating procedures would include several key aspects. Command and control of the operation by the Force Commander must be understood - the airborne observation team must know to whom they report and from whom they take orders. United Nations control of all aspects related to the operation is essential and can be accomplished with regular briefings given to operations headquarters and newly arrived contingents or units within an area.

The standard operating procedures for an airborne reconnaissance program should also include a complete section on information reporting. Aerial surveillance and patrolling techniques can gather a tremendous amount of information covering a wide area of interest in a relatively short period of time. To use effectively the information gathered by this method, standardized reporting procedures must be implemented. Speed, accuracy and proper analysis of this data is essential. Operational information may have to be transmitted laterally, as well as vertically, to all United Nations officers who could be affected and concerned.

Basic instructions for night flights, limitations on flying and any special directions given for specific types of missions must be outlined in the standard operating procedures. Night patrols have traditionally been frowned upon and discouraged in United Nations operations, mainly because of identification problems and the understanding that information gained during night observation missions is minimal. However, airborne patrolling using imaging infrared sensors can provide a safe means of acquiring very useful information at night.

Flight restrictions over areas of possible danger must be outlined and understood to ensure the safety of the United Nations airborne patrolling mission. In the case of UNSCOM, for example, where aircraft and helicopters might be flying through dangerous airspace, arrangements with host countries' authorities might include: (1) establishment of visual corridors to cross borders; (2) identification of flight plan routes; (3) proper use of colour, marks and call signs; (4) adequate communications; and (5) the location of refuelling services.

VII. Airborne Operations

Structurally, an airborne reconnaissance system operating as support for a United Nations peacekeeping mission could be part of the Air Operations component of the force. Air Operations would be under the command of the Force Commander located at the Force headquarters.

For an airborne reconnaissance program to be effectively used, a United Nations Air Liaison Officer (ALO) should be assigned. All requests for overflights would be addressed to the ALO. The ALO would be the direct link between the aircrew and the United Nations peacekeeping force. The ALO would be responsible for briefing the pilot and on-board observer to ensure the aim and purpose of the mission is fully understood and all flight parameters are outlined clearly. It is the pilot who ultimately makes the final decision on conducting the mission, based on his analysis of the situation, to ensure safety for the crew.

Information received as a result of the overflights would be relayed by the ALO or, possibly, by the on-board observer to individual sector commanders. The utility of the information gained will determine who would receive the information. This decision should be made immediately by the ALO or the on-board observer to ensure the timely use of the information collected. "Operations Immediate" information must be effectively transmitted to all who will be affected. If appropriate, this information should be reported vertically to the higher ranking peacekeepers, especially if deemed as "Operations Immediate." The reporting of relevant information should include copies to the Military Information Officer and his staff. The Military Information Officer would be responsible for updating maps with the latest information. Imaging airborne sensor and satellite data could prove to be useful in this regard. Routine information of a general nature gathered during overflights would be archived in an appropriate database under procedures established by the United Nations for a specific area or topic.

Possible Airborne Patrol Procedures

Before any airborne patrol can fulfil its mission as effectively as possible, a particular and well defined set of procedures must be established. According to *The Peacekeepers Handbook* there are three phases to a patrol operation: (1) Mission planning, preparation and briefing; (2) Mission execution; and (3) Debriefing and reporting.

Mission Planning, Preparation and Briefing

The objective of the aerial patrol should be understood by all individuals involved, most likely including the Air Liaison Officer, the pilot and the onboard United Nations observer. These objectives and aims will be determined by the nature of the original request for overflight reconnaissance support. The sensor selection and the time of day for the flight will be a direct function of the target of interest and the type of information required over that site. For example, a nighttime mission using the FLIR or infrared linescanner would be appropriate, if most of the type of activity previously reported had occurred after sundown.

During mission planning, the transit routes to be followed, flight lines and altitudes over particular targets of interest would be determined. Existing information on the patrol area and imposed restrictions over these areas or enroute to the target would be checked. Each member of the aerial patrol would be briefed prior to departure.

Mission Execution

During the execution of the mission it is important for the crew to follow the patrol flight plan as closely as possible. Continuous radio contact with an established ground-based patrol base or verification centre would be maintained. Observations of ground-based activity would be made and recorded as a written record.

Sensor information would be acquired over the previously designated target areas and recorded onto the appropriate medium for further processing and analysis. Observations made from any real-time imagery available on-board the aircraft would be made, recorded, and if necessary, transmitted via radio link to ground personnel.

Debriefing and Reporting

After return of the patrol aircraft, the crew would report immediately for a debriefing session. Detailed written reports would be provided on observations made and the flight parameters followed. Log sheets for aircraft and sensor usage would be completed.

Sensor data such as FLIR or electro-optical video tape or aerial photographic negatives would be processed, reviewed and interpreted as soon as possible at the operations base. A summary report detailing basic information gained from the sensor data would be compiled by the on-board observer and forwarded to the Air Liaison Officer for distribution to appropriate personnel.

Flight Limits

The time that the aircrew could effectively operate could be determined by the rules and regulations as adopted by the air survey industry. In general, aircrew members are restricted to 120 hours of air time per 30 day period, 300 hours of air time per 90 day period or 1,200 hours total air time per year. Crew members normally operate on a 15 hour duty day with a 24 hour rest day provided if a duty day is exceeded. The United Nations on-board observers/sensor operators would fall into this category and be considered as air crew.

VIII. Conclusion

United Nations peacekeeping operations can benefit substantially from the use of overhead imagery, particularly that from airborne reconnaissance aircraft. Commercial satellite imagery can be used to update pre-existing maps of an area in advance of deployment of a peacekeepers force. Aerial reconnaissance could increase the ground coverage by observer groups and could confirm information already received from other ground sources.

The incorporation of special night and all-weather imaging sensors could radically increase the time in which peacekeeping forces can operate effectively within a given territory. Finally, and perhaps most important in the long run, the increased network of observation provided by an airborne reconnaissance program could also help build confidence between the parties by demonstrating the commitment of the parties involved to reducing tensions.

Real cost savings in terms of manpower could also be realized, especially when compared to traditional methods of peacekeeping observation methods. The costs of aircraft operations are relatively modest when weighed against some proposals for traditional style United Nations peacekeeping operations. An airborne program for the United Nations peacekeeping forces could be purchased and operated by the United Nations itself, donated by a host country, or be leased from a commercial firm.

Notes

1. International Peace Academy, Peacekeeper's Handbook (New York: Pergammon Press, 1984), p. 22.

Forum

Colonel Murray Johnston, CISS Member

Colonel Bremner, in your list of guidelines you included acceptable risk and you also included logistics support. But you did not include acceptability or adequacy of equipment. I am referring now to the comments made by General Mackenzie concerning the Armoured Personnel Carriers our soldiers are using in Yugoslavia. Adding to that, in your presentation you talked about training, standby forces and funding, but you did not talk about logistics support and preparations for those activities. In many peacekeeping operations the Canadian mandate has been to provide logistics support not only for Canadians but for the whole mission. That fact is not well known.

Colonel Bremner

My initial reaction to what you say is that the equipping of the force is largely an internal thing - internal to the Canadian Forces. When we send a force abroad, we commit to the United Nations or the requesting organization a complete package of people, equipment and resources to do the job. It would be unacceptable for the Department of National Defence or the Chief of the Defence Staff to make a decision to send a force abroad that did not have the correct equipment for the task, because obviously that would make the risk unacceptable or would render the force unable to achieve its mandate. I would consider that to be an elementary condition of providing the forces to the UN. Now it is true that, depending on the type of mission, some of the equipment is ultimately provided by the United Nations, and I suppose one would have to satisfy oneself that the equipment provided by the United Nations was acceptable. From that point of view I guess one could legitimately include it on the list. I think, however, on the types of missions in which there is a high degree of risk, or a moderate degree of risk - the missions such as the ones we are doing in Somalia and Bosnia - we do send a complete package. Those are not UN APCs over there, they are Canadian APCs. They are not UN weapons, they are Canadian weapons. So I think that is under our control. It is not something that we would have to include on the list in every case. But I do take your point.

With regard to your second point: you are absolutely right that Canada has provided logistics to a number of forces, not only in UNEF I, but also in UNEF II. We provide logistics to UNDOF in the Golan Heights, we have a transportation role in UNTAC in Cambodia. So this is reasonably common, yes. I think it is worth highlighting that Canada does provide this type of role to the United Nations frequently. I think, however, that this reflects the fact that we are good at it, and that the UN has in the past quite frequently asked Canada to provide this type of commitment to their forces because Canada has a relatively sophisticated logistics capability and one which we are capable of providing to the UN. And it is very important. In this respect, however, it should be noted that although for years we were providing communicators and logisticians and in some cases air transport elements to UN forces, in the last year or so, it has been more common for us to provide combat arms, as we are now doing in Croatia, Bosnia-Herzegovina, Cyprus and Somalia. The reason, of course, is that for a number of years, the missions to which member-states were invited to send troops were often relatively low intensity type missions. It was not hard to obtain relatively unsophisticated infantry battalions from countries other than Canada and send them to those areas, whereas it was quite difficult to get obtain air transport units and logistics units and communications units. So countries like Canada, possessed of well-developed armed forces, were often asked for those units, whereas some less-developed countries were asked to provide the battalions. Now it is a changed situation as the missions have become more complex, difficult and dangerous, and require a higher degree of sophistication at the combat level. The UN is now frequently looking to nations such as Canada to provide the combat capability in the force because our battalions are professional, well-equipped, sophisticated, well-trained, well-led and capable. The UN is also "contracting out" many logistics tasks. We have seen a change in the whole method of operation. But I do take your point. The reason why we have on standby the units that we do is because we reckon that on short notice, a combat capability such as an infantry battalion is the essence of getting to a place quickly to provide some stability. We think to support that battalion immediately a communications element in the sense of a long-range communications terminal is the first thing that has to go in, and that we need the air transport to get it there. So that is why those are the standby forces. That is what the UN is happy with and that is what we are providing.

Mr. Peter Jones, CISS Senior Research Fellow

Commander Haydon, you made the point that one must exploit technology to the extent possible in future peacekeeping operations, and Colonel Bremner made the point that even the unsophisticated infantry battalions are now becoming very much more sophisticated given the types of operations we are involved in. I am wondering if, on a political level, we are not running the risk of dramatically reducing the number of countries that can take part in peacekeeping operations, and I wonder if either of you would like to comment on whether you see this as a problem and if so, what you think could be done about it.

Mr. Haydon

Yes, it is a problem, because as I mentioned, there are probably no more than 15 navies that can effectively work together, taking into account equipment limitations and the ability to exchange information. If the operations become more complex, the basic requirements for command, control and coordination go up accordingly. It is not a problem that we can circumvent, it is a problem that has to be faced head on. What I did not say in my prepared remarks was that I think there is a very significant requirement to put in a second generation of naval forces through an equipment modernization process and a related training process. In that manner, the number of military units that can conduct operations in a complex situation without running foul of orders and without misunderstanding the intention of other people can be increased. I am sure that what is valid on the ocean is equally valid on land, and certainly in the air.

Colonel Bremner

I would agree, although I think it is fair to say that more and more countries are prepared to become involved in peacekeeping. There is now an increasing number of UN member-states that can provide sophisticated forces. Within peacekeeping or conflict resolution situations, just as in any other military operation, there are more difficult tasks and less difficult tasks. You might need a sophisticated infantry battalion to do task A, but you might need a much less sophisticated battalion to task B, so I think the UN commander has a degree of flexibility there. I think, although I agree with Mr. Haydon that in terms of navies there are relatively few in the world, that increasingly the newly industrialized countries are quite capable of providing a pretty good package in terms of personnel carriers, communications, et cetera. As peacekeeping expands, the number of countries capable of providing forces expands as well.

Mr. Haydon

There is also a planning consideration: which countries can actually effectively do the job at hand? As Colonel Bremner said, there are some tasks which are sufficiently easy so that almost any unit available can be used. It is when you get to the difficult tasks that the question is going to come up. I think this is where the UN staff system is desperately in need of overhaul to allow those decisions to be analyzed and taken correctly.

Colonel Bremner

And, I might add, the UN is doing some overhauling. As we speak the UN is examining its requirements in New York and other places. It is a slow process and sometimes a frustrating one, but it is making strides in getting this sorted out.

Colonel Johnston

Colonel Bremner, in your reply to my first question you slipped in the term 'contract out'. That concerns me a lot, because that has been used quite a bit in the past, particularly in UNEF I and UNEF II as you explained, and it was even used in Namibia. But we are now in very intense operations in Yugoslavia and in Somalia. I would like to hear your comments on contracting out under the circumstances we find ourselves in in the former Yugoslavia, where much of the infrastructure has been destroyed, or in Somalia, where it has always been at a very low level.

Colonel Bremner

I am not an expert on this, and the benefits of contracting out versus not contracting out would be the subject of a very interesting discussion. Increasingly, if one goes to Cambodia and looks at the very large operation there, the organization providing aviation support in the form of helicopters is not a foreign military unit from Canada, France or Britain, it is Russian helicopters flown by contracted Russian crews. The UN tells us that it can provide this aviation support much more inexpensively by doing it that way than if they were to obtain a unit from us. I guess it makes good business sense for the UN to do that. I do not think that there is any argument. As long as the service can be provided, and it can be provided safely, then that is the best way to go. I am not a member of the UN and I do not work on the logistics side of the house and I do not know what the result of this contracting out process is. The reports that we get is that the support is being provided, and I have not heard anything too alarming about the system. I would think that it is a logical way to go if the service can be provided adequately.

Colonel Johnston

Commander Haydon, in one of your tasks for naval forces you talked about support of land forces. I would like to focus on just one aspect of that because I think you alluded to it slightly. You talked about the evacuation of land forces in the case of trouble. My question is this: how do you see the troops being brought to the shore and then loaded over open beaches and taken out to the ships? Do you have provisions for that?

Mr. Haydon

Yes, by helicopter.

Colonel Johnston

How do you do that with only one helicopter on each ship when you have large numbers of troops?

Mr. Haydon

One support ship can have three or more helicopters, and you could fly a number of sorties from that. It is a slow process, but an orderly extraction operation can be planned with one or two helicopters using one or two or more decks. I think that this is one of the beauties of the flexibility of a naval task force. Within the structure of a naval task force you may have as many as eight helicopters, perhaps even ten. If you have built that possibility into your initial planning, then you can do it as a contingency should it come along. All these missions should be very carefully planned. My concern is that I do not think that in all cases the planning is being done in sufficient detail or in sufficient depth.

Dr. George Bell, Chairman, CISS Board of Directors

Mr. Tracey, I think in the development of your presentation on verification we moved a long way, but I wonder if you could expand in two areas. First, what is the condition within the body of nations now in terms of the acceptability to those involved in conflict of a regime of verification? Second, in terms of your cost factors, how do you see the process of imagery interpretation taking place? Where does it take place? What are the costs involved in that over time? It seems to me that this is a high cost item in itself, requiring a lot of specialization and a centralized capability of dealing with it.

Mr. Tracey

Certainly the acceptability of verification using remote sensing is a very contentious issue within the UN. I think what might be commercially available to the western nations might not be considered commercially available to some of the lesser developed countries. I think it is going to be a long and slow process to educate some of the developing nations on the techniques and to convince them that this data should be used as a confidence-building tool rather than as a spying or espionage tool. That is what we have seen in the Open Skies talks. In the initial round of the talks we had to stress the importance of confidence-building as opposed to intelligence gathering. In terms of the costs of imagery interpretation, you have a very good point, because the imagery that is collected from many of these sensors is only as good as the interpretation that is carried out. Much imagery can be interpreted quite easily. Aerial photography does not require a lot of interpretive skills. Many times, however, there are many people on the ground-based side that do require in-depth information as a result of the interpretation. There have been proposals put forth by France for an international satellite monitoring agency. Canada has put forth a proposal to look at satellite imagery and establishing two satellites for arms control monitoring. The costs involved are fairly high - there is no doubt. From an airborne point of view, a couple of imagery analysts with some half decent image processing equipment can do quite an adequate job of putting out a report that could be used for ground-based observers. I do not think that the imagery is the be-all and end-all in an overhead regime, but the information that comes out of that imagery and is put into report form can give a commander in the field some sort of decision-making capability.

Mr. Jones

Colonel Bremner, I can remember reading things ten or fifteen years ago saying that the Canadian Forces was always very proud of the fact that it always sent regular force personnel to do peacekeeping jobs. There was a feeling that reserve personnel might not be up to the task. As the number of tasks expands, and the size of the force shrinks, you made the point that reserve forces are going to be used more and more. They are already comprising more than ten percent of our peacekeeping effort. I wonder if you could tell us a little more about that? What sorts of jobs are the reserves doing these days? What sorts of jobs are envisaged for them? How is the process coming along? How are they doing in the field?

Colonel Bremner

I do not remember reading that we did not want reservists in regular force units, but certainly the total force concept on which we work now is a relatively new concept and one which is the basis for the armed forces for the foreseeable future. It represents the reality of fiscal restraints and the economical way in which reserves can be fitted into the system. Indeed, within a total force concept one does not differentiate between the regular force and reserves and the type of tasks that each can do. The two forces are complementary to one another. Most of the reservists now are coming into our combat arms units on rotation over to one of the peacekeeping units. The reservists are not drawn from a specific unit, they are drawn on a regional basis from a number of units. They are brought into a central training area with the regular unit that is deployed abroad, and they are used to fill out the unit to its war establishment, keeping in mind that our units at peacetime are normally at something below war establishment and we need the reservists to fill up the units. In most cases, that is what the reservists are doing. They take about 90 days of training with the regular force when they come in, so that when one takes the amount of reserve training that they have had prior to joining the regular force, and then the training with the regular force, they are only slightly shy of the amount of training that a regular member of the unit would have had on joining the unit. They are then fitted into where they are needed in the unit. They do the identical tasks that the regulars do. Our experience to date has been extremely good - we have experienced no difficulties with integrating reservists, and from all reports they perform exceptionally well and we see no reason that we cannot sustain units with a mix of regulars and reservists in the future.

Dr. George Lindsey, CISS Board of Directors

Both yesterday and today we have heard people talk about peacekeeping being much broader in its scope, and of all the good things that we should be able to do to help countries that are in trouble as the result of violence and so on. It struck me that there is one area that we have not talked about, and that is the business of mine clearance. Both when sending troops into a place where there has been trouble, and especially when trying to clean up afterwards, I think mines are one of the most awful things that are left behind. I would like to ask Mr. Tracey if there is any way that they could spot either marine or land mines with these overhead techniques, and I would like to ask Commander Haydon if minesweeping and mine clearance is something that can be done by a small country. Does it really mean that the country has to have long distance ships that could travel a long way, even if they are going to operate in coastal waters? Colonel Bremner, are we prepared to send out engineers and the sort of people that can deal with minesweeping? It seems to me that you can receive a lot more credit in a country by having arrangements made so that children do not get their legs blown off than by having a lot of the other things that have been suggested.

Mr. Tracey

Of course the detectability and the identification of any particular thing on the ground using a remote sensing system depends on its spatial resolution and the capability of that system. I guess the highest resolution sensors that we have available today are aerial photography ones - low-level photographs. Now whether these mines are land-based in an open area, and whether they are large enough to be detectable, will determine whether they can be spotted or not. They must also be in a non-cluttered terrain. If you have mines in terrain beneath a canopy of vegetation they are very difficult to detect. In an area like Iraq, with fairly consistent sand, detectability is quite good. In the water it is another story. I do not know much about mines and the size of them in the water, but if they are floating on top of the water, radar systems can provide some fairly useful information. One additional problem is that some of the mines are so small.

Mr. Haydon

That is a nice question on sea mines. The Americans and I believe the British, Dutch and the Belgians have done quite a lot of work on craft of opportunity, and the conversion of the standard basic trawler or small vessel into a mine hunter. I think the business of sailing a 150 or 170 foot vessel from a North American or European port some 6,000-7,000 miles adds a lot of delay to the process. I think the whole business of 'pack up and go' modules is one that is well worth pursuing. It is a logical process and yes, you are right, I think that is where the smaller navies can come in in specialized roles. Those are just one of the building blocks that I think a professional military staff is able to draw on depending on the mission they have at hand.

Colonel Bremner

Dr. Lindsey, your point is very well taken about the mine clearance task and the magnitude thereof in peacekeeping missions. In almost every mission that results from any form of significant or long-term conflict, the mine problem is one of the most serious ones. We do it, in fact, in UNIKOM, which is the force on the Iran-Iraq border that went in after the Gulf War. Our initial contribution to that was a combat engineer unit of 300 engineers, and it did indeed clear mines from the buffer zone. In Croatia, in UNPROFOR I, we have a combat engineer unit, and it has been carrying out mine clearing tasks as well. In fact, the one unfortunate fatality we have had in the territories of the former Yugoslavia was the result of a mine clearing task. The trouble with mine clearing, quite frankly, is the scale. In most countries the scale of the mine clearing task is simply so overwhelming and would eat up so many resources that it almost has to be given to the whole of the population to carry out. What the UN has focused on normally is the initial cleanup tasks within buffer zones and routes that must be used by the UN force to get the civilian infrastructure operating again and to return refugees, et cetera. They then focus on programs of mine awareness and mine training - teaching the people how to recognize mines and how to deal with them in order to try and prevent death from mines and to try and get a cadre of people who are capable of dealing with them. That is also going on in Cambodia in UNTAC. We have some engineers on the staff there and the New Zealanders and the Australians are carrying out that task with great success. I think, however, to suggest - and you were not suggesting this, but I am just putting it out - that the UN could actually take on the mine clearing task when we are talking about millions and millions of mines in some cases, covering most of the land where the conflict took place would just be beyond the capability of the

UN, and some long-term program resources outside of the UN force would have to be found. But we are engaged in it, and we recognize it as the problem that it is.

Kenneth Eyre

The Need For Standardized Peacekeeping Education and Training

Mr. Peter Haydon, CISS Senior Research Fellow

Dr. Kenneth Eyre is a Research and Development Specialist with Adga Systems International Limited. He has had a long interest in peacekeeping education and training systems almost from the time he participated in his first peacekeeping mission in Cyprus. Dr. Eyre has designed a concept for a fully computerized peacekeeping education and training system called ORION. Located in Canada, ORION would be linked to national and regional centres of excellence, and would ensure that peacekeeping Staff Officers are exposed, before deployment, to the types of problems that they will encounter when they arrive at the mission location.

Kenneth Eyre

Introduction

My presentation has three specific objectives. First, an attempt to identify and to understand the current Canadian Army position with respect to training and education in peacekeeping. Second, a comparison of that position to what Canadian soldiers appear to be increasingly required to do in far flung UN missions. Finally, an examination of the applicability of some of the new information technologies to facilitate peacekeeping training.

The Conventional Wisdom

The Pearson-Hammarskjold model of interpositional peacekeeping deployments dominated the international scene from 1956 until the early 1990s. Peacekeeping operations in these environments involved truce stabilization operations between belligerent parties that had agreed to stop fighting and who at the same time were able to exercise a real and effective control over most elements of their population as well as subordinate military commanders. By and large, the official Canadian Army position is that training soldiers for general war also serves to prepare them fully for peacekeeping operations. Within the context of the Pearson model, there is much to support this contention.

Soldiers: The Ideal "Raw Material" for Peacekeeping

There is much about traditional army organizations in general and soldiers in particular that make them ideally suited for classical peacekeeping operations. (One might also be tempted to make the same case for an organization such as the Royal Canadian Mounted Police, but police forces tend not to have personnel available in sufficient numbers to meet the requirements of a major peacekeeping deployment. In addition, to put it bluntly, police constables are considerably more expensive than private soldiers.)

Armies have mass troops that are typically available in quantities of hundreds or even thousands. Added to this mass is mobility and a modular command structure. Armies can be moved with their equipment over strategic distances and their range of light and medium combat and logistic vehicles typically allows them to range move over virtually any terrain. Soldiers also come in convenient "packages" be they sections, platoons, companies, et cetera, making them incredibly flexible in meeting a range of peacekeeping tasks.

The list goes on. Army units come with organic communications systems, and if need be, they can create additional systems. A combat arms unit, to say nothing of the larger formations, has an extensive skill spectrum in its sub units and individual members permitting the organization both to be self-sufficient and to be able to take on a wide array of specific tasks.

At the end of the list are the unquantifiable characteristics of a military unit that are perhaps the most important of all. Canadian army units are disciplined troops at all levels and can be relied on to do what they have been told to do and to do what should be done. Because of the unwritten "unlimited liability clause" in the soldier's "contract", it is also possible to require soldiers to do what needs to be done in environments that are dangerous or even, in the extreme, lethal.

The Gendarme Spectre

All of the military attributes listed above are not unrecognized within the general population or within the political arena. There is a significant element of the Canadian population which seems to be content to ignore the warfighting capability of the army and which wishes to "get their money's worth" out of soldiers by assigning them a wide range of "quasi-gendarme" roles. Included in this group would be such tasks as environmental monitoring, border patrol, drug interdiction, disaster relief, election supervision (in other people's countries), peacekeeping, peace making, peace enforcing and so on.

An army that exists solely to do these sort of useful and humane tasks might well have an extremely difficult job in converting to its original purpose of fighting should the need arise. While this notion is grasped intuitively by most members of the military establishment, it is not as well perceived by some vocal and articulate members of the general public who object to seeing (and paying for) soldiers training for war and who would prefer to see them train for gendarmerie operations.

Given the threat to its professionalism posed by the gendarme spectre, it is easy to see why the army has traditionally (and successfully) resisted pressures to train for non-military tasks. With respect to peacekeeping at least, as long as the Pearson model held, peacekeeping ability appeared to be a cost-free by-product of training for general war. There is every indication, however, that in the future the Pearson Model of international peacekeeping will be more the exception than the rule.

Peacekeeping in the 1990s

Given that the peacekeeping model is changing, it is fair to ask if the tasks that soldiers are now being required to do are still covered in training for general war or if the changing face of peacekeeping now raises the imperative to train soldiers at all levels in skills that are beyond those needed to successfully prosecute combat operations. Based on experiences from the unstable environment during the Cyprus War in 1974, media reports from events in the former Yugoslavia, Cambodia and Somalia and an informal survey conducted with several hundred troops who served in Sarajevo with the Canadian Contingent in UNPROFOR, the answer is tentatively "yes".

Humanitarian Tasks

Media reports frequently describe UN troops as conducting operations such as prisoner exchange, civilian hostage exchange, evacuation of non-combatants, evacuation of casualties, provision of relief supplies, and provision of escorts. Some of these tasks may well have anchors in conventional military training. It is appropriate to find out which. Furthermore, one can imagine that certain techniques have been devised to execute these various tasks, and that certain other techniques have been attempted and found to be wanting. It is important to have both the will and the mechanism to capture both successful and unsuccessful techniques and the process to incorporate this new knowledge into the formal documented organizational memory.

Tension Diffusion Tasks

Terms such as "negotiate", "mediate", "conciliate", and "arbitrate" frequently appear in media descriptions of the activities of Canadian soldiers on peacekeeping operations. These terms apply to complex technical competencies that are taught in various institutions of higher learning in Canada. As far as is known, they do not constitute part of the curriculum of training Canadian soldiers for general war. Allowing for the occasional soldier who possesses this information "naturally", it would appear that there may be a gap in training. Negotiating skills are best learned at places other than "on the job". At what levels do soldiers do these things?

Is negotiation something that only officers tend to do? What about other items such as arbitration and mediation? It would appear that there may be a need to examine more closely the specific nature of tasks undertaken by soldiers and to determine honestly if they have been adequately trained to do these things within the minimal use of force/media intensive environment of a typical peacekeeping operation.

High Intensity Peacekeeping

It would appear that peacekeeping operations in the 1990s carry with them a higher level of threat than have similar deployments heretofore. The following sorts of phenomena appear to occur with some frequency: accidental engagements, denial of freedom of movement, encounters with freebooters and brigands, outposts being overrun, peacekeeping forces coming under direct attack, peacekeepers being taken hostage and encounters with mines and booby traps. At first glance, high intensity peacekeeping seems to be akin to combat operations, but the peacekeeping environment is radically different from that of the modern battlefield. Military responses to these sort of encounters are severely constrained by the specific or the generalized peacekeeping mandate. Again, it is important to determine what has been proven to work and not to work in these sorts of situations.

The Non-Hierarchical Theatre of Operations

Canadian troops are used to working within the structure of military alliances but contemporary peacekeeping operations are characterized by significantly more players and significantly less precise definitions of relationships than are typically found on the modern battlefield. Dealing with other national contingents, a multinational force headquarters and the national headquarters back in Canada fits within the general NATO alliance model, although the multinational force headquarters may have less refined procedures and doctrine than various NATO command structures. Peacekeeping clutter includes other UN agencies such as the High Commission for Refugees, non-governmental organizations (NGOs) such as the Red Cross/Red Crescent, diplomats, tourists and refugees, non-combatants, and factions and multiple belligerents. Each element has "turf" and an agenda. This would suggest that there is an imperative for some sort of mechanism that provides "cultural assimilation" to the theatre for troops both prior to deployment and on call in theatre when the need arises.

Some Thoughts

There are several ideas or notions about peacekeeping that could almost be considered as being embedded in the Canadian psyche. It is often stated that Canada is the most experienced peacekeeping nation in the world and that Canadian troops are among the best (if not the best) peacekeepers to be found.

While not denying either of these propositions, it is fair to ask, "How do we know?" What is the standard by which "good peacekeeping" is measured? How does Canada's peacekeeping experience manifest itself? It can be argued that experience is only relevant if it resides in the organization's accessible memory. Put another way, we do not simply learn by experience; we learn by thinking about our experiences. (That is why Napoleon's mule, after twelve campaigns, was still just a mule.)

Adapting Modern Information Technologies
to the Changing Face of Peacekeeping

There is a traditional pattern according to which one completes training for an operation and then deploys to an operational theatre. The characteristics of several modern information technologies suggest that this no longer need be the case. Interactive multi-media computer-based training allows soldiers at all levels to acquire knowledge and understanding of previously unknown fields in a rapid and effective fashion.

The management of high intensity peacekeeping operations is not some intellectual abstraction. It is a complex and difficult skill that, like all other skills, can only be mastered through practice. Computer supported command and control simulators allow intermediate and higher level commanders and their staffs to practice the management of some of the complex situations that peacekeeping field forces are increasingly obliged to face.

Performance Support Systems (PSS), a system shell encompassing several linked information technologies, offer the potential for units deploying overseas to take a performance enhancing capability with them. Performance Support Systems are much more than just computer-based on-the-job training.

An effective PSS provides on-job support when it is needed, in the most useful form, and at the same time provides evaluation feedback on both itself and the system user. Typically, a PSS would include such component parts as multi-media computer based training, an on-line reference (hyper text) system, expert systems/artificial intelligence, data bases, as well as a simulation for training and for modelling operational options.

A full fledged PSS would have a "diagnostic" function to help the user decide what needed to be done and to identify the appropriate time to do it. It would also have a "tutorial" function to support the user, if required, in learning how to do something, and a "rehearsal" function that permits users to practice complex or dangerous processes before attempting them in reality.

Performance Support Systems can be built today. The technologies are there. The task is to analyze the various functional relationships and establish the working linkages between these technologies to make a useful composite tool. They could be used both to support a unit working up for peacekeeping and physically go with that unit when it deploys overseas.

Summary

It has been argued here that soldiers trained for general war have, in the past, proven to be perfectly adequate to the needs of peacekeeping operations conducted under the format of the interpositional deployment "Pearson model". However, with the changing face of peacekeeping, it would appear that there is increasingly a range of new and different tasks required of peacekeepers that take them beyond the technical skills of conventional soldiering. Hence, I have maintained that the time has come to rethink the traditional Canadian position and provide various modules of peacekeeping-specific training and education to the soldiers who are obliged to take on these increasingly dangerous and stressful tasks. There are several new technologies available today that permit this training to be conducted within the context of general army training and which are sufficiently flexible and portable that they are suitable for deployment in theatre. Lastly, there are seemingly radical approaches such as Performance Support Systems that have the potential to make learning and performance enhancement an ongoing function that is conducted within the operational environment.

Professionalism has nothing to do with the length of the work week. With respect to soldiers, professionalism is a state of mind. The full-time members of the regular force, and the part-time troops of the militia, are professionals. If they are, in the future, provided with incremental training and support to meet previously unencountered requirements, there is every reason to believe that they will meet the challenge of the changing face of peacekeeping.

United Nations Peacekeeping: Under the Blue Flag or the Stars and Stripes?

Mr. Peter Haydon

Dr. John Mikulaninec is the Director of the Global Studies Institute of Jersey State College. He writes and lectures frequently on all aspects of Canadian defence policy. He is the founder of the Global Studies Institute, and has established its reputation firmly as a source of expert information on matters Canadian. His most recent publication is "The Canadian Effort in the Persian Gulf," which appears in the latest issue of *The McNaughton Papers (The Canadian Journal of Strategic Studies)*.

John Mikulaninec

Global Leadership

Craig Whitney wrote in The *New York Times* that

> *Since it was established after World War Two, the United Nations has been only as effective as its most powerful member states allowed it to be. The Soviet Union, for most of its history, opposed the United States in the Security Council and in almost all cases blocked the United Nations from meaningful action. In those instances where the United Nations was able to act, from Korea to the Persian Gulf, it always did so with the*

> *strong backing and the military influence of the United States.*
> *Where the United States did not provide the wherewithal, the*
> *United Nations has seldom been effective.*[1]

Undoubtedly, this is somewhat of an overstatement.

But with the collapse of "the Evil Empire," the United States has assumed the mantle as the world's only legitimate superpower and with it, some argue, leadership and control over the United Nations. Some might even say that the United States has molded the United Nations into an instrument of American foreign policy. With some degree of accuracy, those suspicious of America's international intentions point out that the United States seems to be calling the shots in the Security Council, for in the recent past did not President George Bush create the coalition that freed Kuwait (in order to keep the oil flowing) and bring humanitarian aid to millions of starving Somalis in order to show that it had an interest in Muslim lesser-developed countries (LDCs)? To these cynics, let me reply that the United States will not abandon its global responsibilities. As President Bush remarked, "We must engage ourselves [globally] if a new world order, one more compatible with our values and congenial to our interests, is to emerge. But even more, we must lead.... We need not respond by ourselves to each and every out-rage of violence. The fact that America can act does not mean that it must."[2] Clearly alluding to the Bosnian crisis, he set forth his criteria for the use of force by the United States:

> *Using military force makes sense as a policy where the stakes*
> *warrant, where and when force can be effective, where no*
> *other policies are likely to prove effective, where its applica-*
> *tion can be limited in scope and time, and where the potential*
> *benefits justify the costs and sacrifice.*

> *Once we are satisfied that force makes sense, we must act*
> *with the maximum possible support. The United States can and*
> *should lead, but we will act in concert, where possible, involv-*
> *ing the United Nations or other multinational groupings.*[3]

Addressing the Bosnian crisis squarely, he explained that even though "important and strategic" considerations were at stake in the region, it was not clear that "the application of limited amounts of force by the United States and its traditional friends and allies would have had the desired effect, given the nature and complexity of that situation."[4]

There is little reason to fear that the United States will exercise its vast political and military power capriciously in order to establish a 20th century version of *Pax Britannica.* As Mr. Bush remarked as early as September 1991, "the United States has no intention for a *Pax Americana,* ... we seek a *Pax Universalis* built upon shared responsibilities and aspirations."[5] The truth is that the United States currently lacks the economic power to impose any kind of *Pax Americana.*

The more cynical will undoubtedly argue that, due to America's increasing use of the United Nations for promoting its national interests, the United States has been able to bend the will of that body in its direction: (a) through the leverage provided it as the largest financial contributor to the organization and (b) through its control of the Security Council. Paying over 25 percent of the UN's regular operating budget assuredly gives the US leverage. Even though seven seats on the Security Council are normally held by developing nations which, in theory, can block any Council decision, they have been reluctant to jeopardize relations with the more powerful, aid-giving countries such as the US. One is reminded that a Yemeni vote against the United States in the Security Council cost that country American aid. Surely, the cynics would say, the LDCs were not blind to what happened to Yemen. In short, once France and the UK are on America's side, a weakened Russia, desperate for aid, joins their ranks, while China, even if it has reservations, abstains rather than irritating the other permanent members.

The cynics are engaging in sophistry. The United States is powerful, but it does not control the Security Council and through it the United Nations. The power accruing to the United States in the UN is the result of other members defaulting on their obligations to the world community rather than the consequences of any American conspiracy. The situation in Bosnia clearly indicates that the Europeans are not meeting their responsibilities to a people in crisis. Germany protests that it cannot contribute peacekeeping troops anywhere, much less to Bosnia, because of its constitution. France, even though it has committed 5,000 troops to peacekeeping in Bosnia, could not prevent the death of a Bosnian Deputy Prime Minister - whom a French peacekeeping unit was escorting - at the hands of the Serbs. Even President

Mitterrand seemed to acknowledge that it would take the Americans to mobilize the Europeans against the horrors in the Balkans. Russia is obviously weakened. Moreover, historic sympathies with the Serbs prevent it from playing the role of an honest broker in the Balkans. Until the political and economic situation stabilizes in Russia, little can be expected of it as a leader of the international community. The UK, while enthusiastic in its support of the Persian Gulf War, has shown little inclination to involve itself in the Balkans. China, one of the Big Five, seems to be preoccupied with economic development. It has shown little interest in taking positions on issues outside it historic sphere of interest. The only other member state that could play a major peacekeeping role is Japan. But Secretary-General Boutros Boutros-Ghali touched off a storm of protest in that country when he dared suggest that Tokyo change its constitution to permit it to participate fully in UN peacekeeping operations. Yohei Kono, the Chief Cabinet Secretary, went so far as to suggest that the Secretary-General was close to interfering in Japan's internal affairs.

With a change of administration in the United States, many are wondering if America will remain as internationally-minded under President Clinton as under his two Republican predecessors. Media commentators such as Leslie Gelb of *The New York Times* have already cautioned the new President not to back-track toward isolationism as he presses forward with his domestic economic agenda. "If Mr. Clinton fails to lead in Somalia, Bosnia, Iraq, etc., no other nation can or will. And if trouble spots grow still more troublesome, as some surely will, he will be blamed."[6] Fortunately, there is little to suggest that the US will abrogate its global responsibilities. "The trick for the new President will be to lead in ways that persuade and compel other nations to assume much greater responsibility for their own security - so that, in time, he can focus on domestic priorities."[7] In actuality, the United States will have little choice but to continue shouldering an inordinate number of international problems. The global recession from which the developing countries and LDCs are slowly emerging will, for a while, inhibit a wider distribution of burden-sharing. But this does not mean that other nations will not be encouraged to bear far heavier responsibilities in addressing their local and regional problems.

Introduction and Defining United Nations Peacekeeping

Under the Charter of the United Nations, the Security Council has "primary responsibility for the maintenance of international peace and security." But the Charter does not mention the word "peacekeeping." Yet since 1948, the United Nations has established 25 peacekeeping operations, including eight in 1991 and 1992.

Since the creation of the United Nations Truce Supervisory Organization (UNTSO) in 1948, the United States has found peacekeeping to be an important tool in peacemaking, conflict resolution, and dispute settlement. But one may legitimately ask, just what has the United States been supporting? There are several definitions of peacekeeping on the table. General Indar Jit Rikhye explained that

> *In United Nations' peacekeeping ... enforcement plays no part. It is a concept of peaceful action, not of persuasion by force. The fundamental principles are those of objectivity and non-alignment with the parties in dispute, ideally to the extent of total impartiality from the controversial issues at stake. The "weapons" used by the peacekeeper ... are those of negotiation, mediation, quiet diplomacy, tact and the patience of Job - not the self-loading rifle. Thus, the United Nations peacekeeping is designed to end hostilities [and to create] a climate within which the peacemaking process may be successfully applied.[8]*

Sir Brian Urquhart defined peacekeeping "as the use by the United Nations of military personnel and formations not in a fighting or enforcement role but interposed as a mechanism to bring an end to hostilities and as a buffer zone between hostile forces. In effect, it serves as an internationally constituted pretext for the parties to a conflict to stop fighting and as a mechanism to maintain a ceasefire."[9] The International Peace Academy has defined the term as "the prevention, containment, moderation and termination of hostilities between or within states, through the medium of a peaceful third party intervention organized and directed internationally, using multinational forces of soldiers, police and civilians to restore and maintain peace."[10] In the UN publication *The Blue Helmets*, a peacekeeping operation is defined as one "involving military personnel, but without enforcement powers, undertaken by the United Nations to help maintain or restore international peace and security in areas of conflict."[11] The United States has its own definition. The Congressional Research Service, in its *Report for Congress*, defined peacekeeping as "the placement of military personnel or forces into a country or countries to perform basically non-military types of functions in an impartial manner."[12]

But as is evident today, the situations in places such as the Western Sahara, Cambodia and Bosnia seem to be calling for a redefinition of the term. Recently, *The Economist* said, "Though still called peacekeeping, the concept of a true peacekeeping unit interposed neatly between two dormant belligerents has evolved into an untidy and intrusive host of soldiers and civilians who are supposed to demobilize guerrilla armies, run or monitor elections, train police forces and rebuild shattered infrastructures."[13]

Even a casual review will clearly reveal that there are differences among the definitions. But more importantly, there seems to be a consensus that peacekeeping is an organic term continually adapting itself to changing conditions, not a mechanism. Secretary-General Boutros-Ghali's *Agenda for Peace* is already pointing a new way for defining the term. Even though the United States has defined the term for itself, it apparently has little argument with the definitions that others may want to use since peacekeeping has evolved and, in most probability, will continue to evolve on an *ad hoc* basis.

The United States has supported UN peacekeeping operations for a number of reasons, including their role in filling a political vacuum and preventing Soviet intervention (the Congo), in cooling down a conflict situation between NATO allies (Cyprus), in monitoring the implementation of agreements negotiated by American officials (the Middle East and Angola), and in serving US foreign policy goals of the moment (southern Lebanon and Somalia).[14] Today the challenge for both the United Nations and the United States is to make UN peacekeeping a stronger, more effective and more efficient instrument of peace. In America's opinion, this means developing a more reliable financial base for the UN, giving the UN some access to advanced technologies, and improving the planning and management skills of personnel at UN headquarters, as well as the training capabilities for the military forces of current and potential troop contributing countries.[15]

Whenever the UN is asked to initiate or renew a peacekeeping operation, US policy makers take into account a number of factors in assessing it. Among them are: (1) whether the establishment or renewal of a peacekeeping operation accords with overall US interests; (2) the estimated effectiveness of the operation; and (3) the cost of the operation to the US.[16] The last factor has become increasingly vital to the US as the number of new UN operations have increased and the pressures on the US budget continue unabated.

Usually, the United States would not support the establishment/renewal of a peacekeeping operation in the Security Council unless the following factors were present: (1) consent of the host government(s); (2) agreement of the Security Council, especially the Big Five, to create the operation, approve its mandate, and continue the operation; (3) availability of troops provided on a voluntary basis in response to a request from the Secretary-General in consultation with the host governments, members of the Security Council, and other parties involved in the action; (4) agreement to a ceasefire or cessation of hostilities by the parties in the conflict; and (5) unrestricted access and freedom of movement by the force or mission within the countries of operation and within the parameters of the mandate.[17] Other principles considered vital to the success of a UN peacekeeping operation include (6) a totally neutral stance on the part of the forces and (7) avoidance of the use of force to carry out the mandate.[18] But as recent UN peacekeeping operations suggest, these principles may not be as important as they had prior to 1988.

Financing UN Peacekeeping

Generally speaking, not much has been written about American peacekeeping. Yet, the United States consistently supported UN peacekeeping operations. The United States played an important role in creating these operations through its participation on the Security Council. In addition, through its contributions to both the regular and peacekeeping budgets of the UN, the United States helped to underwrite these operations since American interests were "best pursued within a stable, peaceful international community."[19]

According to American law, Sections Six and Seven of the UN Participation Act of 1945, as amended (Public Law 79 - 764), authorize the United

States to provide up to 1,000 armed personnel to serve as observers, guards, or in any noncombatant capacity, and to supply facilities, services and equipment for UN peacekeeping operations. Airlift and sealift, communications, local transport, arms and ammunition, food, and such items as maps, phrase books, inoculations, clothing, blankets, and medical services are some of the types of services and necessities that have been supplied by the United States.

Traditionally, American policy has been to provide "initial" airlift services for peacekeeping operations at no cost either to the United Nations or to the country providing the unit. For example, for the initial deployment of UNIFIL to Lebanon in 1978, the USAF flew 117 missions carrying 2,462 troops and 3,281 tons of cargo at no cost to the UN.[20] The value of these airlift services was $8,000,000 and it was listed as a voluntary contribution to the UN. For whatever reasons, the international community had grown accustomed to this largesse, much to the chagrin of American administrations and Congress. This American tradition has not been followed on a consistent basis in the more recent past. For example, the US Department of Defense (DoD) provided $224,000 in air transport services to move UN observers and equipment to the Afghanistan - Pakistan region for UNGOMAP in 1988 at no cost to the UN. On the other hand, when it provided $7,060,020 worth of initial airlift services for UNIIMOG, it requested a reimbursement from the UN in the form of a credit against the US assessed contribution to the special account financing the operation.[21] In the UNTAG operation, services valued at $3,988,255 were provided at no cost to the UN but the eight airlift flights between March and May 1989, valued at $2,431,088, were provided on a reimbursable basis.[22] As they stand, these numbers are not overly large or impressive, but when put into the context of UN peacekeeping, they clearly show an America that has remained very much involved in peacekeeping despite a deteriorating economy. Looked at another way, the United States has contributed approximately $1.3 billion, or 27 percent of the total costs, to the ten UN peacekeeping operations funded from special assessed accounts or from voluntary contributions since 1956. And this does not include the contributions to the six operations funded from the regular UN budget.

Is the United States becoming tired of being the principal underwriter of UN peacekeeping operations? Probably. When UN General Assembly Resolution 46/221 regarding the scale of assessments for apportioning UN expenses was adopted by consensus on December 20, 1991, in addition to accepting the scale proposed by the Committee on Contributions for the period 1992 through 1994, it authorized the Committee to examine new methodologies that looked beyond the traditional formula based on "capacity to pay." In fact, the Committee was responding to a statement by the US Representative made on November 21, 1991, before the Fifth (Financial) Committee, in which he stated:

> Unfortunately, the reliance on capacity to pay, and the methodology that has gone into quantifying it, have resulted in distortions in the scale. Some delegations have suggested that this is simply the best formula available on which we can all agree. The simple fact that this committee now faces such a dispute over the application of that methodology demonstrates that there is a basic flaw in the concept.[23]

He might have added that the United States is increasingly finding it more difficult to ante-up the type of support for UN peacekeeping operations that it had traditionally provided given the increasing number of peacekeeping operations since 1991 and the state of the American economy.

The United States is not trying to avoid paying its UN obligations. As explained by John R. Bolton, a State Department official,

> Strong support of UN peacekeeping activities has long been a basic tenet of U.S. foreign policy.... We have requested an FY 1992 budget amendment totalling $350 million in the foreign assistance bill to meet FY 1991 and 1992 unfunded requirements for the UN Iraq/Kuwait Observer Mission, ... the UN Angolan Verification Mission, ... the UN Mission in Western Sahara, and the UN Advance Mission in Cambodia....[24]

Also included in the request was initial funding for the UN Observer Mission in El Salvador, the UN Transition Authority in Cambodia, and the UN Protection force in Yugoslavia. For FY 1991, the Bush Administration asked for $350 million to meet new and anticipated peacekeeping requirements. These data certainly do not describe a nation trying to evade its UN obligations.

On the other hand, the United States would like to keep UN peacekeeping costs down because

> ... we do not view peacekeeping as the saviour of lost causes.... If new peacekeeping missions must be created, they must have as clearly defined a mandate as possible.

> ... we must make it clear to all parties that U.N. peacekeeping is not an end in itself; U.N. peacekeepers will not serve as the perpetual guarantors of an armed truce.[25]

Could he have been referring to the situation in which the Canadians find themselves in Cyprus?

More often than not, it has been Congress, not the Executive, that has expressed misgivings about the cost of UN peacekeeping operations. Historically, Congress has responded favourably to the establishment of UN peacekeeping operations but has not hesitated, in situations where it was concerned or had reservations about American participation, to use its funding powers to affect the level of participation. This has been especially evident in recent years, when budget constraints combined with policy concerns prompted Congress to reduce or impose conditions on the release of funds for UN peacekeeping. For example, the Senate Appropriations Committee recommended a reduction in US support for UNIFIL because the Committee considered it merely "a symbolic force."[26] It was not an idle recommendation. Congress supported the Committee to the effect that, as of December 31, 1989, the United States was $111,892,823 in arrears in the UNIFIL account. In the cases of UNAVEM and UNTAG, where Congress had some reservations, it required the President to certify that certain requirements had been met before American obligations to these two operations were completely paid.[27] Congress was not being obstructionist. It told the Executive that as a co-equal branch of government, it had a constitutional obligation to assert its will whenever matters of national interest were affected.

Congress has also had to face the undaunting challenge of financing the expanding number of UN peacekeeping operations. The fact is that, since 1988, more UN peacekeeping operations have been undertaken than in the previous 43 years of the UN's history. Moreover, despite the fact that the

United States has the world's largest economy, sentiment on the Capitol Hill seems to support John Bolton's assertion that "... for the United States to continue to pay 30.4 percent of the total cost of U.N. peacekeeping does seem excessive."[28] But the 30.4 percent is not the major issue. The basic question is "Where do we get the money from?" Despite Congress' image, it has tried to solve the UN funding problem creatively. For one thing, it has used "non-traditional" methods of financing, i.e. reprogramming from other parts of the international affairs budget - paying for peacekeeping by using Economic Support Funds monies allocated in past years for a specific country, but not disbursed. Another funding approach, though bitterly disputed, has been to transfer funds from the Department of Defence (DoD) to the State Department (State) for funding UN peacekeeping operations. The issue that Congress has yet to solve is whether US contributions to UN peacekeeping will be funded from the international affairs budget or from the defence function.

US Contributions to UN Peacekeeping

The United Nations has established 25 peacekeeping operations since 1948, including eight in 1991 and 1992. A review of UN peacekeeping operations and American contributions to each will reveal that the United States has hardly been disengaged from a UN activity that is currently costing $2.5 billion.

United Nations Truce Supervision Organization (UNTSO)

From an American perspective, this Middle East operation is unique in that it is rare that a UN peacekeeping operation includes US military personnel. The United States has remained supportive of UNTSO because UNTSO's corps of trained peacekeeping officers has given the UN quick start-up capabilities for establishing new missions, especially in the Middle East. In addition to providing 35 observers from 1948 to the present, the US provided aircraft free of cost to the UN from 1949 to June, 1967, and paid for maintaining the observer group by paying its regular, annual budget assessment.

First United Nations Emergency Force (UNEF I)

Secretary of State John Foster Dulles and President Dwight D. Eisenhower were receptive to a UN role for resolving the crisis caused by the British, French and Israeli invasion of Egypt in 1956 because it provided the United States with a mechanism to deal with a potentially escalating conflict involving the Soviet Union. In addition to drafting and gaining General Assembly adoption of the ceasefire resolution and making payments to the special assessment account to finance the operation, and supporting Lester B. Pearson's (Canada's Secretary of State for External Affairs) initial concept for a peacekeeping force, the United States provided a voluntary contribution of airlift services for the operation in November, 1956.

Second United Nations Emergency Force (UNEF II)

The United States supported UNEF II because the force served American interests by preventing a confrontation between the United States and the Soviet Union and because it increased stability in the Suez Canal - Sinai peninsula region. In addition to paying its special assessment for the operation, the United States (1) voluntarily provided airlift services for Irish, Finnish, Peruvian, Austrian, Indonesian and Panamanian troops in November, 1973, and (2) in October, 1978, donated $10 million in goods and services to sustain the force.

United Nations Disengagement Observation Force (UNDOF)

The creation of UNDOF was an integral part of Secretary of State Kissinger's shuttle diplomacy on the Israeli - Syrian disengagement agreement for the Golan Heights. The United States contributed to the peacekeeping effort from 1974 through the present by paying its 30.6 percent of the special assessment - $11.7 million - to the UN account financing the operation.

United Nations Interim Force in Lebanon (UNIFIL)

UNIFIL was created, in large part, in response to an American Middle East foreign policy initiative. Prime Minister Menachem Begin was due to visit Washington, D.C., in March, 1978. Finding a way for Israel to withdraw its forces from Lebanon was of paramount interest to President Carter as he worked his way closer toward the Camp David accords and the 1979 Egyptian - Israeli peace treaty. The United States, therefore, sponsored the Security Council resolution creating UNIFIL. In addition to initially supporting UNIFIL by making payments - 30.6 percent or $46.7 million annually - into the special UN account for the operation, the United States airlifted Fijian, Norwegian, Nepalese, Senegalese and Irish troops, along with Fijian equipment, to the area between March and June, 1979. However, the United States has become disenchanted with the operation to the extent that it is currently over $110 million in arrears in paying the UNIFIL special assessment.

United Nations Military Observer Group in India and Pakistan (UNMOGIP)

Through paying its regular UN budget assessment, the United States has helped to maintain the observer group. The United States has also provided an acting Chief Military Observer for the operation between July and October, 1950, and contributed aircraft for the operation between 1949 and 1954 without cost to the UN.

United Nations India-Pakistan Observation Mission (UNIPOM)

The United States supported UNIPOM because it served American interests to keep Pakistan focused on America's principal Cold War enemy - the Soviet Union. A war between India and Pakistan would have weakened the American-orchestrated encirclement of the Soviet Union. The United States supported UNIPOM materially by continuing to pay its regular budget assessment.

Mission of the Representative of the Secretary-General in the Dominican Republic (DOMREP)

The United States supported DOMREP by paying its regular UN budget assessment. Greater American involvement would not have been prudent given the wave of anti-American sentiment which swept through Latin

America during the middle 1960s, American past intervention in the Dominican Republic, and Latin American hostility toward the Monroe Doctrine.

United Nations Operation in the Congo (ONUC)

A major concern of the United States was the possible intervention of the Soviet Union in the Congo. Restoration of law and order in the Congo by an international peace force appeared preferable to using US Marines given Soviet threats to intervene in the region. When the Congo government requested US assistance, it was told that all US aid would be channelled through the UN. US policy regarding ONUC had been influenced by the election of President John F. Kennedy. A reassessment of US policy for the Congo by the new administration supported a stronger role for the UN. In addition to providing two Special Representatives to the operation, the United States airlifted food, supplies and troops from Ghana, Guinea, Morocco, Sweden and Tunisia, and sealifted troops from Malaya free of charge to the UN.

United Nations Security Force in West New Guinea (UNSF)

It was in the interest of the United States that the process of decolonization proceed as peacefully as possible. To assist the UN with the maintenance of peace and security in the territory under United Nations Temporary Executive Authority, between October 1962 and the end of April 1963, the United States contributed supporting aircraft and crews to the UN operation.

United Nations Peacekeeping Force in Cyprus (UNFICYP)

American support for a UN peacekeeping force in Cyprus came about only after President Makarios rejected an Anglo-American plan for a NATO peacekeeping force. The data seem to suggest that President Lyndon B. Johnson supported George Ball's assertion that the US did not want to get involved in Cyprus, i.e. between two NATO allies. American Cold War foreign policy required that the two NATO allies be kept at bay, and the United Nations appeared to be the mechanism by which the foreign policy objective could be achieved. In addition to providing airlift services for the operation, the United States has made some voluntary contributions to the UN peacekeeping operation.

Funding UNFICYP has been a major problem for the UN. Voluntary contributions are just not working. After over two decades of peacekeeping, a solution to the Cypriot question is no closer at hand than at the beginning of the UNFICYP. Anticipating weariness by those member states that have made voluntary contributions to pay for an endless mission, the Secretary-General suggested on October 15, 1991, that UNFICYP be funded by assessed, rather than voluntary, contributions. Despite the Security Council's unwillingness to address the proposal because "the necessary agreement did not currently exist in the Council for a decision to be adopted on a change in financing of UNFICYP," the United States indicated its willingness to engage in a thorough re-examination of the Force's finances, mandate and composition.[29]

United Nations Good Offices Mission in Afghanistan (UNGOMAP)

After paying its regular UN budget assessment out of which UNGOMAP operations were financed, the United States stood aside because American interests would not have been served. Afghanistan had become to the Soviet Union what Vietnam had been to America. With the Soviet withdrawal, a Lebanon-type situation had been left behind, and America's experience with Lebanon had been only too painful.

United Nations Iran-Iraq Military Observer Group (UNIIMOG)

Given the hatred of the United States in Iran in the aftermath of the overthrow of the Shah and the hostage crisis, prudence dictated that the United States limit its participation to the UN operation to paying its obligations to the special account financing the observer group. However, the US did supply substantial aircraft to help take the Canadian contingent to and from the theatre of operations.

United Nations Angola Verification Mission I and II (UNAVEM)

Despite the opposition of the UN General Assembly and the Security Council, the question of the withdrawal of Cuban troops from Angola was linked to the question of Namibian independence. Dr. Chester Crocker, an American envoy, led the way in trying to negotiate a set of agreements relating both to Cuban withdrawal from Angola and Namibia's independence. American policy had long sought a negotiated settlement to the Angolan civil conflict, including free and fair elections in which UNITA (National Union for Total Independence of Angola) and all other Angolan political parties were free to participate.[30] The agreement ending the conflict called for the creation of a Joint Political and Military Commission (JPMC) to implement the settlement and a Joint Verification and Military Commission (JVMC) to monitor the ceasefire. The United States, as an observer to both the JPMC and the JVMC, is supporting implementation of the agreement. But because it opposed both the Cuban-supported Luanda government and its SWAPO allies, it would have been difficult, if not impossible, for the United States to play the role of a traditional peacekeeper in this operation. The United States has not paid its full assessment to the special UN account financing the operation.

Nonetheless, the United States supported UNAVEM II - the UN peacekeeping operation mandated to oversee the Angolan peace accords. For reasons already given, the United States has prudently limited its participation in UNAVEM II to paying its special assessment of 30.4 percent - or $15 million for the initial mandate period - to the UNAVEM II fund.

United Nations Transition Assistance Group in Namibia (UNTAG)

As a member of the "Contact Group," the United States, along with Canada, France, the Federal Republic of Germany and the UK began working with South Africa, SWAPO and the "front-line states" in 1976 to implement Security Council Resolution 386 calling for free elections in Namibia supervised by the United Nations and for maintaining the territorial integrity of the country. Again, since the United States had not supported the economic boycotts that had been imposed on South Africa, America was perceived as being luke-warm in sub-Saharan Africa about Namibian independence. Hence, when the UN-brokered peacekeeping mission was worked out, there was a general consensus that the presence of Americans in UNTAG would not have served the cause of peace. Nonetheless, the United States supported UNTAG by providing airlift services and paying its assessment to the special UN account financing UNTAG.

United Nations Observer Group in Central America (ONUCA)

Except for supporting the consensus adoption of two Security Council resolutions extending ONUCA's mandate, the United States has maintained its distance from Central America, and rightly so. The outright hostility of the Reagan Administration and, to a lesser extent, of the Bush Administration to leftist activities in the region and relative acquiescence to all but the worst of rightist atrocities prejudiced American involvement in this peacekeeping operation. The United States currently has serious reservations about ONUCA. As a result, it has not paid its special assessment of $3.8 million for the operation.

United Nations Iraq-Kuwait Observation Mission (UNIKOM)

When Iraq invaded Kuwait and threatened Saudi Arabia, American interests were profoundly affected. An unchallenged Iraqi conquest of the Kuwait would have placed almost 40 percent of the world's known, recoverable oil under Iraq's control. Given the dependence of the United States on imported oil, this would have been a serious challenge to America's national security. It was only logical that the American-led coalition victory - under UN auspices - over Iraq in Desert Storm should have been followed by the creation of the United Nations Iraq-Kuwait Observation Mission (UNIKOM) to monitor the demilitarized zone between Iraq and Kuwait, and to deter Iraqi boundary violations until Iraq officially and actually accepted the Security Council resolutions on the boundary. The United States supports UNIKOM by paying its 30.6 percent of the special UN assessment for the operation - $18.5 million for the initial mandate period. On the other hand, no American interests would be served by placing Americans into the observer group given the very personal dislike that existed between Presidents George Bush and Saddam Hussein.

On a related matter, the UN effort to ensure that Iraq did not persecute its minorities - Kurds and Shiites - after the Persian Gulf War has set an important precedent for the UN, i.e. that there could be hybrid humanitarian-political intervention. The 500 security guards sent to Iraq after the war as sort of a minimal police force have the official job of seeing that the relief workers are safe. But they also act as a bridge between relief and general security. It could be argued that they foreshadowed the dispatch of troops to Somalia. But many countries, particularly those in the Third World, are appalled by the thought of yet more power being placed in the hands of the supposedly American-led Security Council under the guise of humanitarian intervention. This precedent could come back to haunt the United States if not carefully handled.

United Nations Transitional Authority in Cambodia (UNTAC)

In the aftermath of a failed war in Southeast Asia and the subsequent invasion of Cambodia by Vietnam, the United States is obviously pleased that Vietnam withdrew from Cambodia and that the United Nations was beginning to implement its most ambitious peacekeeping effort to date - the United Nations Transitional Authority in Cambodia (UNTAC).

The negotiating effort that produced the Cambodian comprehensive political settlement had been initiated by US Secretary of State James Baker III, in 1989. The agreement promoted American foreign policy goals in that it (a) may prevent the return to power of the Khmer Rouge and mitigates the resumption of genocidal violence; (2) puts into place a mechanism to verify the withdrawal of all forces; and (3) gives the people of Cambodia an opportunity for self-government through free and fair elections.[31]

In American opinion, the most critical issues confronting UNTAC are establishing a viable, nationwide UN presence, initiating priority de-mining and infrastructural improvements for timely repatriation, demobilizing as many factional forces as possible, and creating the conditions for free and fair elections. But all is not proceeding smoothly. The Khmer Rouge have resisted honouring parts of the agreement. America's UN Ambassador, Edward J. Perkins, observed that

> *... the Party of Democratic Kampuchea must permit UNTAC ... access to areas under its control and, thus, enable the United Nations to carry out immediately civil, military, electoral, and human rights responsibilities entrusted to it.... The United States believes the UNTAC plan is the best way to secure for the Cambodian people the peace they deserve.*[32]

There is little question about American support for UNTAC. Of the $801.8 million UNTAC budget, the United States has already paid its full assessment of $244.9 million.

United Nations Protection Force for Yugoslavia (UNPROFOR)

Likewise, the tragedy of Yugoslavia has brought forth a UN response in the United Nations Protection Force for Yugoslavia (UNPROFOR). As originally conceived, the UN projected an armed force of around 14,000 at a cost of $640 million in the first year. But almost immediately, some Security Council members began expressing concerns about the high costs. The assessments were eventually scaled back to $250.5 million with the US being assessed $76.4 million. Given the rapidly changing situation in the former Yugoslavia, including President Clinton's UN-approved decision to parachute supplies to beleaguered civilians in eastern Bosnia, it remains to be seen just how much UNPROFOR and its ancillary operations will ultimately cost the United States. There is little doubt that the United States was and is committed to working out a peaceful solution to the region's problems by supporting the Vance-Owen mediation efforts.

The Bosnian crisis, much like the Somalian, may be the harbinger of a new type of UN peacekeeping. Certainly, UNPROFOR has been anything but a "conventional" peacekeeping operation. For its part, the United States only reluctantly agreed that "U.N. peacekeeping in Yugoslavia as envisaged in the Vance plan can make a critical contribution to the European Community (EC) - CSCE (Conference on Security and Cooperation in Europe) - mandated efforts to promote a political settlement to the tragic Yugoslav conflict."[33]

Perceiving that the Vance plan alone would not resolve the Balkan crisis, the United States supported the Statement of Principles adopted at the 1992

London Conference, i.e. (1) all states and parties concerned were expected to comply in full with all UN Security Council Resolutions on the crisis and to do their utmost to secure their implementation; and (2) all parties were obliged to cooperate wholeheartedly in the international monitoring, peacekeeping, and arms control operations in the territory of the former Yugoslavia. Acting Secretary of State Lawrence Eagleburger remarked

> *We believe the process we've created - co-chaired by the UN and EC ... will provide the forum to bring the parties together to help define the current conflict; end the bloodshed; and, ultimately, to craft a negotiated settlement .... we have agreement to expand and strengthen UNPROFOR ... in support of humanitarian operations in Bosnia.*[34]

However, as it became apparent that the fighting in Bosnia was not abating, domestic pressures began to build on the Bush Administration to do more. Acting Secretary Eagleburger, however, cautioned, "I ... worry about ... the degree to which the United States involves itself militarily in a process for which there is no clear purpose and no clear end."[35]

Since the Serbs and their allies in the Balkans were making a mockery of UNPROFOR's humanitarian aid mission, and because the United States did not want to enter into another Vietnam-type conflict alone, the United States supported the December 17, 1992, NATO agreement to support the UN if it voted to enforce its ban on Serbian flights over Bosnia. It was not that NATO was not already involved. It had been helping to enforce UN embargoes in the Adriatic. What was new was that,

> *For the first time in its history, the Alliance is taking part in UN peacekeeping and sanctions enforcement operations.... UNPROFOR ... is using elements from the Alliance's NORTHAG (Northern Army Group, Central Europe) command for its operational headquarters. NATO ... AWACS ... are monitoring daily the UN-mandated no-fly zone over Bosnia-Hercegovina.*[36]

Introducing NATO to UN peacekeeping was a victory for American foreign policy, for the United States has consistently supported the augmentation of

UN peacekeeping operations with regional security organizations such as NATO.

Despite the steps taken by NATO, the EC, the UN and the Western European Union (WEU), the crisis in Bosnia continues. The bottom line, well-read by the Serbs, was that the Bush Administration and its European allies had little stomach for military action to stop the killing in Bosnia. In all likelihood, the Clinton Administration will not pursue a more aggressive policy for the region. Secretary of State Warren Christopher has already announced that the President had decided that the United States would actively engage in the Vance-Owen negotiations, campaign rhetoric notwithstanding. Moreover, Senator Richard G. Lugar said that American troops would go to Bosnia under UN auspices only after a new peace accord had been concluded. The *New York Times* editorialized:

> *As Mr. Clinton talks in carefully hedged terms about sending American troops into Bosnia, examples ranging from the Bay of Pigs to the Beirut barracks bombing fairly shout at him to go slowly with military initiatives unless the purposes are fully understood and supported by the American people.... This is not the time to talk about putting 15,000 American servicemen and women into a cauldron of violence that our European allies have studiously refused to take on themselves.*[37]

United Nations Mission for the Referendum in Western Sahara (MINURSO)

While Americans have remained transfixed on the crises in Somalia and the former Yugoslavia, few know much about the United Nations Mission for the Referendum in Western Sahara (MINURSO). The operation was set up to conduct a referendum on whether Western Sahara should become independent or be integrated into Morocco. The United States has supported MINURSO by paying its 30.4 percent special assessment - $43.4 million for the initial mandate period and $32 million subsequently and by supporting the effort to bring peace to a region under the auspices of the UN and the Organization of African Unity (OAU). The full deployment of MINURSO personnel includes 30 American peacekeepers.

It should be noted, however, that the United States is not terribly enthusiastic about using the OAU to promote peace and stability in Africa - even though this squares with American policy. Alluding to a recent UN discussion and vote on South Africa, the US Representative noted that although the US was pleased once again to join the consensus for General Assembly resolution 46/20, it believed that an important point had been overlooked in the resolution, notably that the General Assembly had not included any "recognition of the positive changes taking place in South Africa," and that the OAU had not seized "this moment to play a positive, active role in the historic efforts being made in South Africa to eradicate apartheid and to bring into existence a democratic, nonracial government."[38] The American statement also noted that references in the resolution to acts of regional aggression and destabilization by the South African government were outdated and that, given the independence of Namibia, the peace accords in Angola, and the on-going negotiations in Mozambique, there was no reason to retain the outmoded references.

United Nations Observer Mission in El Salvador (ONUSAL)

As with ONUCA, the United States has supported the creation of the UN Observer Mission in El Salvador (ONUSAL). The mission's original mandate had been to verify compliance with the San Jose agreement on human rights. But on January 14, 1992, the mandate was expanded to include separate peacekeeping (i.e. military) and police contingents. Because of past involvement in El Salvador's civil war, American involvement in this operation has been limited to paying its 30.4 percent share - $4.2 million for the initial mandate period - of the special assessment.

United Nations Operation in Somalia (UNOSOM)

The Somalian crisis is the first peace-enforcement operation to be carried out under UN command. It was the Bush Administration that successfully pushed the UN to lend its assistance to this novel and large-scale intervention to help the starving of Somalia. American involvement began on August 13, 1992, when the President authorized the Defense Department to offer a military airlift to transport a UN guard force of 500 and its associated equipment to Somalia. Later in the month, the US began a military airlift of emergency food supplies into Somalia from Kenya. In addition, Ambassador Peter Jon de Vos was appointed US Special Envoy for Somalia to coordinate US support with other contributors. But as the situation in Somalia continued to deteriorate, the United States decided to offer troops to secure the distribution of food and aid as part of a multinational force. Finally, on December 14, 1992, President Bush announced that American troops were being sent to Somalia under Operation Restore Hope.

According to a statement before the US House Foreign Affairs Committee, Herman J. Cohen testified that President Bush and Secretary-General Boutros-Ghali reached the decision to send a large force to Somalia almost simultaneously, but independently of one another. Since the United States was clearly the only nation that could launch the sort of effort envisioned, President Bush offered to have the US lead a military coalition under UN auspices to provide humanitarian assistance for the starving Somalis.

The American effort was an obvious UN Charter Chapter VII operation - peace making. As coalition forces began securing the country, thoughts turned from peace making to peacekeeping. The transition from peace making to peacekeeping was foreseen in Security Council Resolution 794. The transfer, however, proved to be more difficult than had been anticipated. The United States wanted the UN to begin peacekeeping as soon as was practicable since it was estimated that the operation would cost $500 billion for a two month period. On the other hand, the Secretary-General insisted that before the UN would assume responsibility for the operation, the coalition forces had to disarm the warring Somalis. He argued that the UN could not hope to bring about reconciliation in Somalia as long as the Somalis retained their "technicals." The United States responded that disarming the factions was not its mandate. It was there to protect the humanitarian aid process. The dispute dissipated when the senior commander of the American-led relief operation, General Joseph P. Hoar, announced that US forces would be more aggressive in disarming Somali gunmen who refused appeals or financial incentives to give up their weapons.

A second contentious issue that appeared concerned the timetable for the replacement of the US-led coalition with UN peacekeepers. Again, the principal issue was money. The United States is paying more than 80 percent of the cost of military operations in Somalia, and America's contingent of 24,500 troops represented 65 percent of the total foreign force. When the UN peacekeepers take over, the cost of the operation will shrink to 30 percent. Obviously, the United States would like to turn the operation over to the UN as soon as possible. But the Secretary-General has resisted. He explained that more local militias needed to be disarmed, and mines and ammunition had to be cleared away in order to create a secure environment for relief work. Until this was done, lightly armed peacekeepers would be severely handicapped in carrying our their mission. Arguably, the UN's reticence to assume control of the Somalian operation is part of a broader problem - in Cambodia, UN officials have let themselves be pushed around by both the Khmer Rouge and the Phnom Penh government; in Bosnia, UN peacekeepers let Serb gunmen shove them aside and kill a Bosnian Deputy Prime Minister; and in Angola, a UN-sponsored election has broken down into renewed civil war.

Despite some nervous moments, an agreed upon timetable was negotiated. The United States agreed not to pull out as originally threatened - at the end of January, 1993. Secretary-General Boutros-Ghali devised a plan to replace the coalition forces with a multinational force of 15,000 to 20,000 soldiers, including 3,000 to 5,000 Americans possessing logistics, communications and intelligence expertise, under the command of a Turkish general. The selection of a Turkish commander allowed Washington to rationalize its decision that it was putting American troops under a Foreign Commander by pointing out that, after all, he was a NATO officer.

UNOSOM (UN Operation in Somalia) will mark the first time that a UN-led force has intervened in a country without a specific request by a host country. An unnamed UN official said, "Certainly, this force will have more authority within this mandate, as it moves closer in the direction of an enforcement operation than the U.N. has been involved before.... This operation is precedent setting because Somalia was deemed by the Security Council as a state without a government."[39] The United States, however, does not share the official's conclusion. Ambassador Edward Perkins told the Security Council that

> *By acting in response to the tragic events in Somalia, the international community is ... taking an important step in*

*developing a strategy for dealing with the potential disorder
and conflicts of the post-Cold War world. This step must entail
unprecedented levels of cooperation amongst the international community in response to urgent humanitarian needs and
to peacekeeping, utilizing our respective military forces to do
so. Cooperation will have to occur on a case-by-case basis,
given the complexity of the post Cold War order.* [40]

The United States Measures the Success of UN Peacekeeping Operations

Like any large contributor, the United States would like to know that its in-
vestments are paying off. In her Report for Congress, Marjorie A. Brown did
an analysis of selected UN peacekeeping operations that may shed light on
how the United States evaluates the effectiveness of the operations and on
future American contributions to the peacekeeping fund(s).

Ms Brown identified three methods for measuring such success for Congress: (1) determining whether the mandate of the operation, as defined by
the Security Council, was fulfilled; (2) determining whether the operation led
to a resolution of the underlying disputes generating the conflict; and (3)
determining whether the presence of the operation contributed to the maintenance of international peace and security by reducing or eliminating conflict in the area of operation. [41] The following mandates were evaluated:

A. Peace Observation - UNTSO

B. Internal Security - ONUC, UNFICYP

C. Disarmament - ONUC, UNFICYP

D. Interposition Between Opposing Groups or Forces - UNFICYP,
    UNEF I, UNEF II

E. Buffer Zone Force - UNEF II, UNDOF

F. Border Patrol - UNEF I, UNEF II, UNDOF

Which operations were successful? [42] Using the first method for measuring success - fulfilment of the mandate - five operations might be viewed as

successful. UNEF I, ONUC, and UNEF II met their mandates and ceased to exist. UNFICYP and UNDOF arguably are continuing to fulfil their mandates. UNTSO can also be considered to be a success despite the fact that its mandate is always changing. On the other hand, UNIFIL is a failure because it has not fulfilled its mandate - even though its presence has provided some measure of security and humanitarian aid to the region.

Using the second method - the extent to which the operation contributed to the final resolution of the dispute causing the conflict - only ONUC and UNEF II can be considered successes.

The third method for measuring success - the extent to which the operation contributed to the maintenance of peace and security, or reduced or eliminated the cause(s) of the conflict - is the one preferred by the United States. In each of seven cases, the creation of a UN peacekeeping operation served US interests in promoting greater stability in a region. UNTSO seems to be helping to preserve an uneasy peace in the Middle East. UNEF II and UNDOF were necessary for the implementation of ceasefires and agreements negotiated by the United States. In this context, even UNIFIL can be considered a success. UNEF I, ONUC and UNFICYP were preferable alternatives to the possible use of American military forces in areas of major concern to America. As is apparent from this selected review of UN peacekeeping operations, it was of value to the United States to support these operations because American interests were advanced, i.e. the peacekeeping operations prevented regional conflicts from expanding and directly threatening US interests.

Obviously, American policy toward peacekeeping has changed as the demand for these UN services has increased. Acknowledging the fact that the United States did not have the wherewithal to be the world's policeman, the Bush Administration issued a statement in 1991 declaring that:

> The U.S. government welcomes the increasingly important role played by U.N. peacekeeping operations in diffusing regional conflicts.... The proliferation of these operations ... requires them to be carefully structured to complete their mission as efficiently and economically as possible.... The Administration is committed to full-funding of existing U.N.

peacekeeping operations, and payment over the next four years of all outstanding U.S. arrearages.[43]

The United States will "pay up" despite a change of administration, for presidential candidate Bill Clinton declared during his successful run for the presidency that the United States should "pay up and pay up now" the $410 million that it owed in unpaid dues and peacekeeping costs.

There are signs on the horizon, however, that suggest that the United Nations may be running out of the string of peacekeeping successes that it has enjoyed. As is well known, Secretary-General Boutros-Ghali and his aides are currently struggling to prevent the collapse of several current peacekeeping operations. In Angola, for example, the Security Council must decide whether to abandon the country or withdraw the peacekeeping force deployed since June, 1991. UN peacekeeping efforts are also beginning to falter in El Salvador, Somalia and Cambodia. The major reason for this, according to the Secretary-General, is that the United Nations was dealing with non-governmental or irregular groups whose leaders were often unable or unwilling to enforce the peace arrangements they signed, e.g. the Khmer Rouge. Likewise, UN missions are becoming increasingly complex and intrusive. For example, when the UN is drawn into internal disputes in countries like Bosnia and Somalia, the distinction begins to blur between traditional peacekeeping, which casts the United Nations in a neutral role between the belligerents, and outright military action to enforce peace, which requires the United Nations to take sides.

Improving UN Peacekeeping: An American View

A recent US General Accounting Office (GAO) report entitled "United Nations: U.S. Participation in Peacekeeping Operations," published in September, 1992, made some interesting observations and corresponding recommendations to improve UN peacekeeping.[44] What follows is a summary of that report.

The GAO's objectives in the report were (1) to determine the process of establishing, financing and implementing UN peacekeeping operations; (2) to assess the effectiveness of the State Department's oversight of US interests in these operations; and (3) to determine the role played by the Defense Department in supporting UN peacekeeping operations.

1. Regarding the implementation and financing of peacekeeping operations, the GAO concluded that the UN General Assembly peacekeeping budget oversight process needed to be strengthened. The GAO learned from members of the General Assembly's Advisory Committee on Administrative and Budgetary Questions that insufficient time and resources were being devoted to reviewing peacekeeping budgets. It also learned that member countries were not provided access to the results of UN internal audits of peacekeeping operations. The GAO suggested that special UN assessments used to finance most peacekeeping operations may need to be looked at because changes in the relative economic status of countries since 1973 raise questions as to whether the special scale of assessments based on the "capacity to pay" continues to represent an equitable basis for distributing peacekeeping costs.

2. The GAO recommended that the Secretary of State instruct the US Representative to the UN to seek other members support for (1) examining the adequacy of the process and resources used by the General Assembly committees in reviewing peacekeeping costs; (2) requiring the Secretary-General periodically to report to member countries on the status of principal internal audit findings and recommendations regarding peacekeeping operations; and (3) re-examining the basis for, and the equity of, the special UN assessment scale for peacekeeping operations.

3. The GAO recommended that the Secretary of Defense (1) account for and report DoD peacekeeping assistance to ensure that the United States received recognition for its peacekeeping contributions, including personnel costs, per diem allowances, transportation, and other related costs; (2) update policies and procedures for providing DoD logistics support to UN peacekeeping forces and ensure that (a) reimbursable costs were properly billed and controlled; and (b) the required financial activity reports were prepared and distributed; and (3) recommended that the Secretaries of State and Defense resolve

peacekeeping reimbursement issues so that the United States could respond more quickly to UN airlift requests.

Replying to the GAO, the State Department agreed with the findings and recommendations. But DoD had some reservations: (1) It replied that its participation in field-level monitoring may be appropriate when DoD personnel or resources were involved in a peacekeeping mission. The GAO agreed with its reservation. (2) Although the GAO criticized DoD for not being able to provide complete cost data on its participation in UN peacekeeping operations, DoD explained that it had not lacked this capacity. It stated that until recently, it had not been called upon to report such costs; but it would begin doing so on a monthly basis. (3) Although agreeing with the GAO that its policies and procedures for providing logistics support to UN peacekeeping missions needed to be updated, it pointed out that many of its current procedures were still valid. (4) Regarding per diem allowances, DoD pointed out that it had corrected the procedure which had allowed overpayment of per diem for US military personnel serving in UN peacekeeping operations before the GAO brought this to its attention. (5) DoD acknowledged that the peacekeeping reimbursement issue with the State Department was a serious problem that would be resolved.

The GAO analysis of the American role in implementing and financing UN peacekeeping operations included some stinging criticism of wasteful and inefficient UN budgetary procedures, including those of the Advisory Committee. The American representative on the Committee told the GAO that while the Advisory Committee had dedicated over three months in 1991 to reviewing the UN regular budget, it had spent only three days reviewing the 1992 peacekeeping budget, even though the total peacekeeping budget was larger than the regular budget. Moreover, the GAO concluded that the UN's internal review process did not adequately examine the methodology used in preparing budgets or the assumptions underlying the projected costs. Regarding UN audit reports, GAO data suggested that the UN Audit Division was located at too low a level within the UN and was not sufficiently staffed to ensure adequate audit coverage of peacekeeping operations. On the other hand, the GAO applauded some efforts taken by the UN to improve peacekeeping. For example, it observed that the State Department was supporting some of the General Assembly Special Committee on Peacekeeping Operations initiatives, including the establishment of a registry of nations capable of providing troops, material and technical resources for a peacekeeping mission, and was willing, in principle, to provide a range of military assets as part of its assistance if the Committee so recommended.

Wanting to find out for itself just how well the State Department was managing American interests in UN peacekeeping operations, the GAO made some field visits to the Middle East and Central America. In the Middle East, it learned that some peacekeeping experts believed that UNTSO duplicated the Multinational Force and Observers (MFO) in the Sinai. Confronting UNTSO with these allegations, UNTSO officials explained to the GAO that even though it did not have a formal peacekeeping role in the region, it provided a UN presence there. Paying a visit to UNDOF, the GAO learned that at least one command official was questioning UNTSO's observer role in the Golan Heights. When apprised of its findings, the UN Secretariat informed the GAO that efforts were underway to reduce the operating costs of both UNTSO and UNDOF. The GAO study was having an effect.

The GAO also looked into status of forces agreements during its field visits. Before deploying a peacekeeping operation, the UN generally negotiates status of forces agreements with host countries that provide for, among other things, the contributions of office space and living quarters at no charge to the UN. But the field visits revealed that the UN had not negotiated such agreements for UNDOF, UNTSO, or UNIKOM. Furthermore, even if status of forces agreements were signed, the GAO learned that they were not always honoured by the host countries. UN officials complained to the GAO that the UN was required to pay rent for a Central American peacekeeping mission headquarters despite the host country's agreement to provide the facilities free of charge. A UN Chief Administrative Officer told the GAO that the UN was paying VAT (value-added tax) on goods imported into a Middle East country even though the 1946 Convention on Privileges and Immunities of the United Nations provides an exemption from such taxes.

One of the costliest parts of a peacekeeping operation is related to providing support services. There are three basic ways for the UN to provide them: (1) to maintain in-house support capabilities; (2) to ask member states to provide these services on a voluntary or reimbursable basis; and (3) to contract for them. Given the current demand for UN peacekeepers, the first option is inordinately expensive. This is not to say that the UN should not maintain its current supply depots. Any significant expansion would be very costly and probably beyond the capability of the cash-starved organization. Option two has merit but it, too, must be used with discretion. At a recent meeting with Colonel Douglas Fraser, who serves at the Canadian Mission to the UN, he explained to me that the costs of moving a Canadian brigade to a peacekeeping site is usually more expensive if the brigade is moved by Canadian transport services than if moved using estimates provided by the UN. That leaves Option three. According to the GAO, contracting for support services may be more effective than maintaining an in-house capability. It learned that through competitive bidding and increased use of local subcontractors, the MFO reduced the cost of support services in 1985 by more than $9,000,000, or 42 percent. But because circumstances differ from mission to mission, individual cost analyses would be required to determine the relative cost-effectiveness of contracting out versus performing support services in-house.

There is one uniquely and exclusively American problem related to UN peacekeeping. Historically, DoD provided airlift services to the UN without charge. The cost were absorbed by the Air Force Military Airlift Command Industrial Fund. This voluntary contribution arrangement was discontinued in 1989 when the State Department asked that the UN credit its peacekeeping assessment for the value of DoD airlift services provided to UNIIMOG. The UN credited approximately $7,000,000 against the US assessment for the mission, but the State Department did not reimburse DoD. Undoubtedly, the UN credits against US peacekeeping assessments effectively represented an unauthorized transfer of funds from DoD to the State Department. The State Department defended its actions by arguing that it did not have sufficient appropriated funds to pay for all peacekeeping operations. DoD was not impressed. This inter-departmental problem has become public knowledge, much to the embarrassment of the United States.

In early 1992, the UN requested US assistance for the military airlift of equipment to Cambodia on or about February 15, 1992. DoD requested that State Department approval for the airlift be processed under a UN Letter of Assistance whereby the UN would directly reimburse DoD for the approximately $350,000 involved. The State Department agreed to approve the airlift request, but only if DoD agreed to State's request to waive UN reimbursement as permitted by the UN Participation Act so that the State Department would request that the UN credit the value of this support against the US peacekeeping assessment. While the question was being referred to the Secretary of State, the State Department was advising the UN that its airlift request could not be accommodated in the time frame requested. Subsequently, the UN arranged alternative transportation for the shipment.

The GAO's investigations have shown that there is much that can be done to drive down the costs of UN peacekeeping in order to make it more efficient. But even more could be done. One can legitimately ask if too much reliance has been placed on peacekeeping as a tool for conflict resolution. Likewise, if a registry of contributors is compiled, should countries be asked to designate specific units that could be made available to the UN on relatively short notice? Perhaps communications between the UN and potential troop contributors should be increased, particularly with those without peacekeeping experience, to explain the requirements and duties of peacekeeping forces. And why not encourage member states to institute national training for peacekeeping forces? Moreover, could not a model status of forces agreement between the UN and host countries be drafted to ease the initial deployment of peacekeeping forces? Is there a way to increase the use of civilian support staff in peacekeeping operations? These are only some of the additional issues that could be investigated to make peacekeeping less costly and more efficient.

Conclusion

US President George Bush observed that

> Never before in its four decades have the UN's Blue Helmets and Blue Berets been so engaged in the noble work of peacekeeping, even to the extent of building the foundation for free elections. Never before has the United Nations been so ready and so compelled to step up the task of peace making, both to resolve hot wars and to conduct that forward-looking mission known as preventive diplomacy..... We look to the Secretary-General to present to this Council his recommendations to ensure effective and efficient peacekeeping,

peace making, and preventive diplomacy. We look forward to exploring these ideas together.[45]

The 1991 National Security Strategy Report acknowledged that the United States will provide enhanced support for a revitalized UN to help keep the peace, improve the human condition, and ameliorate human suffering.[46]

Unfortunately, the post-Cold War period is not ushering in the millennium. On the contrary, the world appears to be awash in ethnic and religious wars. The new US administration has already learned that it cannot ignore the world. The basic question facing Mr. Clinton's foreign policy advisors in light of these conflicts is how the United States decides what and where its interests lie. At his confirmation hearings, Secretary of State designate Warren Christopher may have given some hint of an answer. He called for "preventive diplomacy" to keep conflicts from spreading. He endorsed new dispute resolution techniques, including some form of international arbitration and the increased use of UN forces to monitor and enforce agreements.

The new idea, "preventive diplomacy," being discussed by UN diplomats seems to suggest that the international community might have a right to intervene in the affairs of a country simply because that country is mistreating minority groups or for any other number of reasons. Ambassador Madeleine Albright, the U.S. Permanent Representative to the UN, suggested that "The international system is at a crossroads on the concept of what is a nation state.... We need to make sure that when a country declares independence, individual as well as minority rights are guaranteed before granting recognition."[47] Is the nation-state passe? Will or should the UN evolve into a world government? Currently, it is an inter-governmental organization. These are provocative questions. But to return to the question of this paper. Will peacekeeping remain under the Blue Flag or will it become an instrument of US foreign policy? It will remain under the Blue Flag for several reasons.

1. The Cold War is over. The need for the United States to maintain its vast military assets has diminished. As a result, American bases both at home and abroad are being closed in record numbers. If President Clinton's defence reduction plan reaches fruition, the American military will be left with the capability of fighting one and one-half Iraq-type wars simultaneously - a far cry from the one major war and two regional war capability that it possessed as late as 1990. As a result,

if several American interests throughout the world are threatened simultaneously, the United States would have little option but to use the United Nations and its peacekeeping services to protect those interests while it struggled with relevant policy questions.

2.   The United States will continue to support UN peacekeeping, but not on the basis of Secretary-General Boutros-Ghali's *Agenda for Peace.* The United States supports UN peacekeeping, in part, because it is cost effective and involves burden-sharing - both very important consideration to the United States today. The Persian Gulf War vividly illustrated this. In the area of economic assistance, 26 countries contributed $16 billion in 1990 and 1991 to the "front line" states whose cooperation was critical if the sanctions against Iraq were to be effective. In military responsibility sharing, the coalition partners committed $54.6 billion to the United States to help pay for the war. The $70 billion bill would have wreaked havoc with the American economy numerous ways if the United States had decided to go it alone.

3.   The United States will work assiduously to keep peacekeeping operations efficient and effective. However, peacekeeping operations such as UNFICYP suggest that peacekeeping may not be the only or even the principal solution to many international problems. Even though the United States considers UNFICYP a success, Canadians might think otherwise. After decades of peacekeeping in Cyprus, how much closer have the issues been brought to resolution and at what cost? Perhaps peacekeeping should be supplemented with trusteeship for places such as Cyprus, Somalia, Bosnia and the Kurile Islands. How many believe that if UNFICYP was dismantled ethnic warfare would not resume? What will it take and how long will it take to build the institutions that will enable the people of Somalia to govern themselves peacefully? If 50,000 UN peacekeepers are dispatched to Bosnia to maintain peace among the ten enclaves, how long will it take to build the political, social and economic institutions necessary to bring peace, stability and security to the nation, and what will be the human and material cost to the UN? And would not trusteeship be an excellent place "to park" problems like the Kurile Islands?

Peace making and peacekeeping are things that the United Nations does relatively well. But embarking upon something as nebulous as "preventive diplomacy" is fraught with dangers. In a move to give the United Nations a stronger role in solving disputes before they develop into armed conflicts, Secretary-General Boutros-Ghali re-assigned Under Secretary-General Marrack Goulding from his post as the top official overseeing peacekeeping missions to a post in charge of peace mediation. This decision was been interpreted as a reflection of the Secretary-General's desire to see the UN play a more active role in "preventive diplomacy." The stationing of UN peacekeepers along the Macedonian border to prevent the widening of the Balkan war also suggests "preventive diplomacy." But what if the war spills over into Macedonia? Prudence would dictate taking a long, hard look at "preventive diplomacy."

4. Chapter Eight of the UN Charter stipulates that regional organizations should make every effort to settle local disputes before referring them to the Security Council. Likewise, it directs the Security Council to encourage the use of regional arrangements to resolve local disputes. The United States has used and cooperated with a variety of such organizations for peacemaking, peacekeeping, and conflict resolution purposes. For example, even though the Conference on Cooperation and Security in Europe (CSCE) does not currently have either the mandate or the capacity to undertake peacekeeping operations, the State Department believes that the CSCE can play a role in addressing the future security concerns of a regional nature either in peace making or a policy coordination role. Likewise, the United States has supported the efforts of the Economic Community of West African Unity to bring peace to war-torn Liberia. Most recently, it has thrown its support behind the proposal to use NATO assets in a peacekeeping role in Bosnia. This US trend to use and support regional organizations will probably continue because it tends to maximize American influence.

Notes

1. Craig R. Whitney, "More Than Ever, U.N. Policing Is an American Show," The New York Times, January 17, 1993, p. E3.

2. President George Bush, excerpts from the President's address to West Point Cadets, West Point, New York, The New York Times, January 6, 1993, p. A6.

3. Loc. cit.

4. Loc. cit.

5. President George Bush, "The United Nations in a New Era," Address to the UN General Assembly, New York, New York, September 23, 1991, in the US Department of State Dispatch, Vol. 2, No. 39, September 30, 1991, pp. 720-721.

6. Leslie H. Gelb, "Shaping Change," The New York Times, January 21, 1993, p. A25.

7. Loc. cit.

8. Marjorie Ann Brown, "United Nations Peacekeeping: Historical Overview and Current Issues," Report for Congress, Washington, D.C., Congressional Research Service, pp. 4-5.

9. Ibid., p. 5.

10. Loc. cit.

11. The United Nations, The Blue Helmets, The United Nations, 1990, p. 4.

12. Brown, op. cit., p. i.

13. "The United Nations, " The Economist, December 26, 1992-January 28, 1993, p. 57.

14. Brown, op. cit., p. i.

15. Loc. cit.

16. Ibid., p. 1.

17. Ibid., p. 8.

18. Loc. cit.

19. Ibid., p. 12.

20. Ibid., p. 13.

21. Loc. cit.

22. Loc. cit.

23. US Department of State, Bureau of International Organization Affairs, United States Participation in the United Nations, Washington, D.C., August, 1992, p. 190.

24. John R. Bolton, "UN Peacekeeping Efforts to Promote Security and Stability," US Department of State Dispatch, Vol. 3, No. 13, p. 245.

25. Ibid., p. 246.

26. Brown, op. cit., p. 16.

27. Loc. cit.

28. Bolton, op. cit., p. 246.

29. United States Participation in the United Nations, op. cit., p. 33.

30. "Fact Sheet: Angolan President Visits Washington, D.C.," US Department of State Dispatch, Vol 2, No. 38, September 23, 1991, p. 702.

31. Ibid., pp. 244-245.

32. Edward J. Perkins, Statement to the UN Security Council, US Department of State Dispatch, Vol. 3, No. 32, August 10, 1992, p. 619.

33. Richard Boucher, "Yugoslavia: UN Peace Efforts," US Department of State Dispatch, Vol 3. No. 1, January 6, 1992, p. 3.

34. US Department of State Dispatch, "Materials Relating to the London Conference (August 26-27, 1992) and the Crisis in the Former Yugoslavia," Vol. 3, Supplement #7, September 1992, p. 7.

35. Ibid., p. 13.

36. North Atlantic Council Communique, NATO Headquarters, Brussels, Belgium, December 17, 1992, US Department of State Dispatch, "North Atlantic Council Ministerial (NAC)", Vol. 3, No. 52, December 28, 1992, p. 27.

37. Editorial, The New York Times, February 11, 1993, p. A30.

38. United States Participation in the United Nations, op. cit., p. 29.

39. Eric Schmitt, "Most U.S. Troops Will Leave Somalia by April in U.N. Plan," The New York Times, February 13, 1993, p. 4.

40. Ambassador Edward J. Perkins, US Ambassador to the UN, statement before the UN Security Council, December 3, 1992, US Department of State Dispatch, "Humanitarian Crisis in Somalia," Vol. 3, No. 5, December 14, 1992, pp. 877-878.

41. Brown, op. cit., p. 20.

42. Ibid., pp. 20-29.

43. "Fact Sheet: U.N. Peacekeeping Operations," US Department of State Dispatch, Vol. 2, No. 39, September 30, 1991, p. 722.

44. US General Accounting Office, "United Nations: U.S. Participation in Peacekeeping Operations," Report to the Chairman, Committee on Foreign Affairs, House of Representatives, GAO/NSIAD-92-247, September, 1992, passim.

45. President George Bush, excerpt from address before the UN Security Council, January 31, 1992, US Department of State Dispatch, "The United Nations: Power to Act for Peace and Freedom," Vol. 3, No. 5, February 3, 1992, pp. 76.

46. Fact Sheet released with President George Bush's statement, "1991 National Security Strategy Report," US Department of State Dispatch, Vol. 2, No. 33, August 19, 1991, p. 618.

47. David Binder and Barbara Crossette, "As Ethnic wars Multiply, U.S. Strives for a Policy," The New York Times, February 7, 1993, p. 14.

Main Contributors to the UN Regular Budget
(Listed by Size of Contribution)

Member State	Regular Budget Assessment* (%)	Peacekeeping Assessment (%)
United States	25.00	30.38
Japan	12.45	12.45
Russian Federation	9.41	11.44
Germany	8.93	8.93
France	6.00	7.29
United Kingdom & Ireland	5.02	6.10
Italy	4.29	4.29
Canada	3.11	3.11
Spain	1.98	1.98
Brazil	1.59	0.32
Australia	1.51	1.51
Netherlands	1.50	1.50
Ukraine	1.18	1.18
Sweden	1.11	1.11
Belgium	1.06	1.06
Saudi Arabia	0.96	0.19
Mexico	0.88	0.18
China	0.77	0.94
Iran	0.77	0.15
Austria	0.75	0.75
Republic of Korea	0.69	0.14
Denmark	0.65	0.65
Argentina	0.57	0.11
Finland	0.57	0.57
Czechoslovakia	0.55	0.55
Norway	0.55	0.55
Venezuela	0.49	0.10
Poland	0.47	0.09
Yugoslavia	0.42	0.08
South Africa	0.41	0.41
Sub-Total	93.64	98.11
Other	6.38	1.89
Total	100.02	100.00

Scale of Assessment for 1992-1994

Brigadier-General Clay Beattie, CISS Member

Dr. Eyre, I would like to see your process taken one step further. If there is any reason why people have been missing the message from these peacekeeping operations it is because there is no centre of excellence which gathers information and experience and then analyzes it. In the same way as we run war games, I think we could run peacekeeping games, and we could get a whole lot more out of the UN experience than we have in the past. It has to be institutionalized and there must be a centre of excellence established. Also, I think we should help other countries train their people for peacekeeping operations. That would help take the strain off of us in providing troops to go abroad in these situations. Second, Professor Mikulaninec, when you talk about whether the US is going to support peacekeeping or not, it was my perception that 'new world order' meant that we had come to the end of world disorder. It does not seem to be turning out that way. If the US is not going to support peacekeeping, what are they going to do, support war? These turmoils are going to continue, and no matter what you call it, it still has to be dealt with. Chapters Six and Seven of the UN Charter lay out the parameters for dealing with the maintenance of peace and security, and I would appreciate your comment on that.

Dr. Eyre

I could easily support the creation of a centre of excellence. Even if, according to my thesis, we do not know why we think that we are the best, I would think that Canada would be a perfectly appropriate country to form a centre of excellence and invite those nations that have participated historically to contribute to the process, in addition to those that are interested in doing it. I think that it is going to happen sooner than later, and if it does not happen in Canada it will happen somewhere else. There have been initiatives already. I think the time is right. As Colonel Bremner said this morning, peacekeeping is a growth industry. A centre of excellence makes eminently good sense to me.

Professor Mikulaninec

The United States has neither the wherewithal nor the inclination to be the world's policeman. I think we will be very selective in where we move in peacekeeping. I think, however, that we will have to await President Clinton's definition - or redefinition - of what American national interests are. Once redefined - and I think they will be - then I think you will see that we will move in certain directions and stay out of other areas of concern to the world community.

Mr. Peter Haydon, CISS Senior Research Fellow

I think the concept of trusteeship is fascinating, but it is obviously laden with political pitfalls. Would either of you care to comment?

Professor Mikulaninec

On the idea of trusteeship, I like what Alex Morrison said when he introduced this conference. He said that the UN is beginning to work the way it was envisioned to back in 1945, and I agree. It is only beginning to work the way it was envisioned; it is not working the way it was envisioned. It has taken 40 years to get to a beginning, and I think that it will take another 50 years to rethink trusteeship - it will not go fast.

Dr. George Bell, Chairman, CISS Board of Directors

Professor Mikulaninec, when you mentioned the potential limitations of US interest in terms of being the global policeman, you also indicated the interest of the US in supporting international operations. It seems to me that when we have examined this in this conference, that in terms of major operations it is impossible for the US not to be involved. If you discuss in Brussels with NATO officials the capacities of NATO that apply to peacekeeping, they immediately go back to communications and intelligence, transportation and logistics. I found your talk interesting, but I wondered if that self-limitation process is really possible in the role that the UN has and that the US has, in terms of supporting not only the UN but supporting NATO and other alliances.

Professor Mikulaninec

I think that we have to limit ourselves. Our budget tells us that for one thing. Second, by the election of a new president, we are going to change our priorities - and already have somewhat - from the international to the domestic. I think what President Clinton is trying to do now is to buy time. I agree that we have always been limited. We have always involved ourselves in NATO, the CSCE and through other regional organizations, but we could not grab the limelight for ourselves. The Cold War was on. I think that we are going to rethink, if only for budgetary concerns.

Lieutenant-Colonel Molife, Embassy of Botswana, Washington

I have listened to the deliberations over the last two days, and I am inclined to make a few remarks. I think that the efforts of this seminar will be futile if we do not look at the problems that necessitate peacekeeping, and I think that we all agree that Africa is dominated by a lot of conflicts. It is not that we in Africa like wars. We do not like violence - we do not want to see wars. I believe that the UN has to devise some means of stopping the flow of weapons to dictatorships in all of those countries that oppress people, otherwise the whole effort will be hopeless. We all agree that peacekeeping takes money, and this money could be employed in some meaningful form to developing countries. I sincerely believe that the developed countries can do a lot more to stop the flow of weapons to dictatorships in these lesser developed countries. The developing countries are mainly consumers, and I think the UN would be doing a lot if it could stop the flow of weapons to these areas. Angola is a typical case - war is raging on, and UN efforts to monitor the elections are being obstructed. There are a lot of countries that I can speak of. It is a concern of Africa and everyone throughout the world that something must be done to stop the flow of weapons.

Professor Mikulaninec

I agree with you. I thought it was unconscionable after the Gulf War that we sold billions of dollars of aircraft and materiel to Middle Eastern countries.

Mr. Jonathan Perkins, Carleton University

My questions are to Dr. Mikulaninec and to Dr. Eyre. We have had several command and control issues, especially in the United Nations, in the context of their relation to the United States. In the peacekeeping operations that the United States has traditionally been involved in on a large scale, they have very much played the lead role. They have organized and coordinated the forces and exercised the predominant command and control opportunities. If the United States is going to become more involved in peacekeeping, more involved in the United Nations context, do you see an opportunity or a method whereby United States forces can be integrated into a non-US commanded structure? Or do you think that is the predominant requisite for US involvement in the future? My question to Dr. Eyre is one of how the Canadian techniques of training could be diffused to other nations, whether these forms of training that we are talking about are really compatible with the training system of the allies that we would be involved with in peacekeeping operations that do not have training systems based upon our models.

Professor Mikulaninec

First, the President of the United States is the Commander-in-Chief of the American Armed Forces - that is in the Constitution. Second, with regard to putting our troops under foreign control, we have rationalized that by putting our troops under the control of a Turkish NATO general in the operation in Somalia. Third, we are presently at loggerheads with France over who might command the Bosnian operation. My crystal ball is cloudy on that last issue.

Dr. Eyre

There is always room for scenario-specific peacekeeping education and training and for instruction in general principles, practices and modalities. My solution to the education and training challenge would be to establish a central institution, perhaps with branches in a number of countries, which would pass on the Canadian philosophy, experience and expertise to others.

George Bell
Chairman, CISS Board of Directors

Concluding Remarks

Ladies and gentlemen, we have had a very full two days of wide-ranging discussion on a whole comprehensive set of activities under the broad rubric of peacekeeping. When Alex Morrison set the scene for us yesterday morning, he directed our thoughts to the dynamic change that has occurred in recent years - a period in which the UN has moved from being reactive to becoming much more of a proactive international body with the objective of maintaining peace, security and stability in this rapidly changing international environment. As a result, we have seen the expansion of the roles beyond those we had known as peace observation missions, truce supervisory operations and peacekeeping operations in the classic sense. Now we have developed an interventionist mode and expanded the scope of "peace operations" to include peace enforcement and peace restoration, humanitarian aid, and the rebuilding of government structures of societies which have broken down.

At this time, we are now looking back and saying "Oh yes, that is what the originators of the UN Charter in 1945 intended in Chapters Six, Seven and Eight." We also recognize that many activities are now involving governmental and non-governmental agencies, as well as armed forces, but that in most cases it now requires the presence and effective application of international military force in order to create the environment for these civil agencies to work. Hence, a considerable amount of our focus in this seminar has been on the role of military forces, but many of our speakers have in fact taken into consideration these other areas. Indeed, our keynote speaker Alex Mor-

rison pointed out to us that we not only had the RCMP involved in police forces, but Elections Canada helping to develop governmental election processes in newly independent countries.

Colonel Gedge's presentation, which focused significantly on the inade-
quacies of the UN headquarters structure and particularly on the supply and
logistics fields, was most important to our deliberations and should not be
forgotten. The clear facts are that we are dealing with a UN headquarters
structure and a UN Field Service structure that has not yet gone through the
reforms necessary for the efficient and effective conduct of the kinds, volume
and scope of international operations that we are experiencing today.
Canadians were proposing such changes to these structures almost thirty
years ago but UN interest has gone up and down cyclically as peacekeeping and peace operations have become of periodic concern in New York.
Since last August, Canada has aided in the building of an operations staff for
the Secretary-General, which is now growing in capacity. We are fully committed to achieving the ability to mount operations quickly. The initiatives we
have taken over the years, in terms of trying to establish a relationship between the Secretary-General's office and the Security Council - particularly
the Military Staff Committee - have been aimed at giving the organization a
contingency planning capability, a plans and operations capability and
proper logistics planning in order that international forces can be mounted.
These have been frustrated many times in the past, partly as the result of the
Cold War in the early 1970s. But present conditions dictate that we should
put considerable activity into supporting improvements in international infrastructure and the way in which the UN headquarters functions.

Ernie Regehr brought us another point of view. He focused not only on
the need to deal with peace enforcement and peace restoration, but also on
the aspect of peace building. He pointed out the difficulties within our own
national structure of dealing with the question of both international aid and
the support of our defence forces. Essentially, these international operations
are not merely a single-nation activity. The conditions which would allow the
more idealistic point of view of peace building to take place often have to be
created in the absence of stability in the areas in which we are asked to
engage. Therefore, I do not have any argument with the idealism of his approach, but I do think that in terms of the question of the re-ordering of
priorities in the current period and for the foreseeable future, we shall have

to recognize that the spectrum of conflict that confronts us now is not benign. It comprises a whole series of situations that can lead to being involved in what effectively are intensive military operations. Therefore, we have to be sure that the forces which we deploy to these operations are not only well-supported, but are well-equipped and well-trained and capable of creating the conditions for peace building to take place and for the non-governmental organizations to work with security. As we have seen both in Central America and in Somalia, these organizations, while doing good work, cannot work in a hostile situation.

David Cooper, from NATO headquarters, talked to us about the things which NATO could do for international peacekeeping operations. He explained the broad capabilities which exist within the NATO structure. When I was at NATO headquarters last May, I spent considerable hours discussing the interrelationships of these agencies and the importance of having the capabilities of the United States to transport European military forces in order that they be able to participate in major peacekeeping operations. The NATO International Staff recognized this fact of life. While it recognized that NATO has a pool of resources for command, control, intelligence, communications and political direction, one of the things that David Cooper did not speak about was the fact that NATO itself has some limitations. These limitations were highlighted later in Ambassador Peel's presentation, where he spoke about the current inability of Chancellor Kohl to change the German Constitution in order for the German armed forces to participate in peacekeeping operations. He also did not speak to us about the limitations that exist within NATO's own boundaries, nor whether some NATO countries would agree to use their forces in Europe outside their own boundaries. This is another major area for consideration.

Such considerations about the NATO countries add emphasis and importance to the broader discussion of European security which Ambassador David Peel brought to us in his review of the capabilities that are developing around the Council for Security and Cooperation in Europe (CSCE) and its role in developing an overarching area of interest in peacekeeping operations, which can embrace all the countries of NATO's North Atlantic Cooperation Committee (NACC). This CSCE function would involve NATO members and the former Warsaw Pact nations and would also provide a vehicle for interaction with those traditional European peacekeeping countries that have been neutral - such as Austria, Finland and Sweden. Quite clearly, we are talking not only about peacekeeping being a growth industry, but indeed, about the institutional mechanisms which, while imperfect, are in fact helping to deal with the various political dimensions of the problems that still exist. Some of these are a result of the post-Second World War settlements with Germany and Japan. As our Japanese colleagues pointed out, these account for the long time that it has taken for them to be able to move from these post-Second World War arrangements with the west to the point where they can now participate in international peacekeeping.

In respect of the foregoing, I was particularly pleased with the contribution of our Japanese colleagues, Mr. Hagi and Professor Takai, who were very clear and precise about the capabilities of Japan, the limitations of its International Peace Co-operation Law, and the process of learning what they were going through in terms of how to participate now and how to move forward to broader involvement. I am hopeful that their experience will be as it was for Austria. When Austria, a neutral country, first participated in Cyprus, it contributed civil police forces. Later on an infantry battalion group was sent, and later on still Austrian generals were commanding brigade group-sized forces in the Golan Heights and also in Cyprus. There is obviously a need for an evolution for a neutral country, or one that has been restricted by its constitutional process, when moving into this type of international activity. I think we should be careful to understand the developments that are taking place in Japan and look forward to the 1995 discussions to bring about broader participation.

Our colleague Peter Haydon gave us a very articulate presentation on the role and possibilities for maritime and air forces in peacekeeping operations. We have to recognize that peacekeeping operations, by character, depend upon individual and particular situations. But there is a clear role for all three forces, and there is a need for us to be looking seriously at the capacities for joint planning to ensure that, as we plan for operations, the interests of all parties are taken into consideration, and that the capabilities that we are developing are such that multi-force capability can be achieved. There are precedents for looking at the maritime and air sides. If we refer to Ken Eyre's presentation, he reminded us that we must have an institutional memory and that we must learn from our doctrines and our experiences. Peacekeeping is not a role exclusive to the army, but it is one in which it has had a predominant part, and a major role in which it continues to have to provide, by far, the greatest amount of the manpower for most operations.

Col. Bremner gave us a very good presentation on the current guidelines and preparation and planning for our Canadian Forces. It would have been useful to also have heard about the restrictions that are placed on us by the UN. Part of our experience has been that in some of the operations in which we have participated, we have been limited by the UN as to what equipment we can take into the operational area. To the UN, some equipment either appears to be too aggressive, or is the type of surveillance equipment that could cause the parties to the conflict to say that one or the other is receiving intelligence from the peacekeeping force as a result of observing them with surveillance systems. Despite this, there is a need to be sure that we provide our forces with the highest level of capability to be able to meet all potential situations which they might have to confront. For example, we are dealing right now in the former Yugoslavia with a situation where the competing forces have equipment which is far more lethal and far more effective than the equipment that our own forces possess.

This brings me to focus on the remarks of our guest speaker at lunch on the first day of the seminar. When Major-General MacKenzie was pointing out the need to look seriously at the equipment that we have, he emphasized the need to see that we are properly equipping our armed forces. He also suggested that we look at whether the organizational programmes - in terms of training time and space to develop capabilities are indeed right, and that in doing so we must ensure that Canada has the operational capabilities to deal with the high end of the spectrum of peace enforcement and peace restoration operations as well as for low and mid-intensity situations.

Jeffrey Tracey's presentation on the topic of remote sensing and the use of surveillance systems in peacekeeping demonstrated that these are very strong potential tools for peacekeeping operations or any kind of international military operations. The questions, as he pointed out, are clearly timeliness, the resolution that you can get from the images, and, of course, the acceptability of this process to the parties in conflict. Most people know that some countries have objected to images of their national areas being given to other countries. This sensitivity must be taken into account and dealt with in a sensible way. There is also the question of how one deals with providing the resources for the continuous processing of these capabilities over time, because it will build up to be a major task. Consequently, affordability is a major concern. This means that the international organization or a country that had such capabilities should be persuaded to develop a structure to supply these kinds of services to the UN because they are not low in cost and most states cannot afford them.

Ken Eyre brought something of importance to mind in his presentation on training - what in his view is a lack of institutional memory and analyses of lessons learned from peacekeeping operations. He asserted that our involvement in a large number of operations at the same time has often been used as a justification for only devoting a limited amount of time to such evaluation analyses. I would suggest that this problem may have been over-dramatized, because considerable work has been done in this respect. Many of the doctrines that are in place in the United Nations now in terms of their guidelines for peacekeeping were in fact contributed to by Canadians. Many of the documents were originally written by Canadians, and many items are on the curriculum of our staff colleges and the staff colleges of NATO members because of the diverse nature of the countries participating in the operations. If you look at the doctrines of the UNEF I or UNEF II, any staff officer coming from a Commonwealth country or indeed NATO could function within them. Others coming from the Warsaw Pact had difficulty and it was necessary to provide training for them. Those coming from the Organization of American States countries probably had worked with similar processes. Despite these efforts, however, there continues to be a need for development of doctrine, procedures and training programs. There is a need for much more distillation and dissemination among UN members. There is a need to look at new techniques that are required, particularly when we are talking about training in negotiation and critical roles that individual observers and low level commanders now have to play in some of these operations.

The question of command and control of international forces came up in Dr. Mikulaninec's presentation in a number of ways, and I would just like to remind you that the question of mounting headquarters for international forces is something that has been dealt with by the UN over time, and the United States has not been backward in looking at that problem. I remember that about 20 years ago, when the Americans were looking for a solution in the

Middle East, they were looking at developing a force structure which would include US military troops and a range of forces from other countries, including the Soviet Union, under a non-American or non-Russian international commander, backed by a capable multinational staff to conduct such operations. So they are not blind to the nature of the problem and they do know that there are operations in which having a multinational command would be absolutely essential. This has been looked at a number of times and in a number of ways.

Dr. Mikulaninec presented us with a very interesting set of problems. He pointed out something that is real in the United States, something to which we have to pay attention. I think that it is quite clear that while the UN cannot count on the US being its total bankroller, or that the US will freely take on the role of world policeman, I think that the United States will continue to realize that it is the one member state with the capacity needed to make major operations work. NATO is quite clear that US participation is essential in air transportation, communications and intelligence and airborne warning systems. There are all sorts of things which only a major power like the United States can provide, particularly the capabilities of a deep sea navy with aircraft carrier capabilities. I think that his talk was interesting because it also focused us on the need to look at a number of these issues, not only "Who is paying the bills?" or "Who will participate, but how do we provide the support for other smaller forces that will participate?" Who will provide the logistics support to them? Many of you may not remember, but when UNEF I was formed it had a Brazilian battalion. That battalion would not have been in Egypt had it not been for the capacity of the US not only to equip it, but to transport it from the Latin American area. It is of interest to note that, when the US looked at the question of peacekeeping in Vietnam in the early 1970s, the Rand Corporation found that there were only seven out of 51 countries studied that, despite the size of their armed forces, had the capacities for supporting a battalion group offshore. Therefore, for some time, you will have to look at the northern group of nations in terms of NATO and the North American nations as being the prime suppliers of the major capabilities to deployed forces of other nations. Even countries like India, as big as the Indian Forces are, do not have the real capacity to maintain forces offshore. Their forces in the Sinai and other areas were partly supported by Canadians and others. We need to look at the question of what things the US can do, what things other NATO countries can perform, and what things other major countries of the world can support. This may again be an avenue for Japan to find other ways of participating in the operations.

We have come away from these two days with a new list of ways of talking about the subject of peacekeeping. We are now talking about preventive diplomacy, preventive deployment, peacemaking, peacekeeping, peace restoration, peace enforcement and peace building. All of these are important, and we need to look at not only the military side of peacekeeping, but at the comprehensive set of responsibilities between governments and non-governmental agencies needed to make it all work.

I am impressed by the exhibits which the industry people have put up in the Centre, and the direction they have taken in terms of peace operations. I am also quite conscious of the fact that outside is a whole group of protesting people who hold different views. It is evident, therefore, that we still have the major task of creating with them and with the rest of the Canadian public a broader understanding of what maintaining international security and stability, in relation to our own national interests, is all about. I do not think that we Canadians are doing as good a job of educating our own population about these processes as we should be doing. We should be much more proactive.

I want to thank you all for being here, and for making the seminar an active forum. I would like to thank our speakers for their key talks. I would like to thank our moderators for controlling the discussion and debate. I would like to thank Baxter Publishing and the Canadian Institute of Strategic Studies for sponsoring this activity, pointing out the work of Al Geddry, Alex Morrison and his staff, our President Don Macnamara and the exhibitors and their representatives who helped to make the whole event possible.

GLOSSARY

ALO	Air Liaison Officer
ASW	Anti-Submarine Warfare
CIDA	Canadian International Development Agency
CAO	Chief Administrative Officer
CAPS	Conventional Armaments Planning System
CCD	Charged-Coupled Device
CDS	Chief of the Defence Staff
CLO	Chief Logistics Officer
CPC	Conflict Prevention Centre
CPO	Conflict Procurement Officer
CO	Commanding Officer
CSBM	Confidence and Security Building Measure
CSCE	Conference on Security and Co-operation in Europe
C^{3}I	Command, Control, Communications and Intelligence
DoD	Department of Defense (US)
DND	Department of National Defence

FLIR	Forward-Looking Infrared
FOV	Field of View
GAO	General Accounting Office (US)
IAEA	International Atomic Energy Agency
IEPG	Independent European Programme Group
LDC	Lesser-Developed Country
LOROP	Long-Range Optical Photography
MFO	Multinational Force and Observers
MINURSO	United Nations Mission for the Referendum in Western Sahara
MTI	Moving Target Indicator
NACC	North Atlantic Co-operation Council
NGO	Non-Governmental Organization
NTM	National Technical Means
ONUC	United Nations Operation in the Congo
ONUCA	United Nations Observer Group in Central America
ONUSAL	United Nations Observer Mission in El Salvador
PKF	Peacekeeping Force
PKO	Peacekeeping Operation
PSS	Performance Support System
RAR	Real Aperture Radar
RCR	Royal Canadian Regiment
RPV	Remotely Piloted Vehicle
SAR	Synthetic Aperture Radar

SASS	Small Aerostatic Surveillance System
SLAR	Side Looking Radar System
SOP	Standard Operating Procedure
SOR	Statement of Requirement
SPOT	Systeme Pour l'Observation de la Terre
STOL	Short Take-Off and Landing
UNAVEM	United Nations Angola Verification Mission
UNDOF	United Nations Disengagement Observation Force
UNEF	United Nations Emergency Force
UNFICYP	United Nations Peacekeeping Force in Cyprus
UNGOMAP	United Nations Good Offices Mission in Afghanistan
UNHQ	United Nations Headquarters
UNIFIL	United Nations Interim Force in Lebanon
UNIIMOG	United Nations Iran-Iraq Military Observation Group
UNIKOM	United Nations Iraq-Kuwait Observation Mission
UNIPOM	United Nations India-Pakistan Observation Mission
UNMOGIP	United Nations Military Observer Group in India and Pakistan
UNOGIL	United Nations Observation Group in Lebanon
UNOSOM	United Nations Operation in Somalia
UNPROFOR	United Nations Protection Force for Yugoslavia
UNSCOM	United Nations Special Commission
UNSF	United Nations Security Force
UNTAC	United Nations Transition Authority in Cambodia

UNTAG	United Nations Transition Assistance Group in Namibia
UNTSO	United Nations Truce Supervision Organization
VAT	Value-Added Tax
VFR	Visual Flight Rule
WEU	Western European Union

Peacekeeping '93: The Exhibition

*Note: The information contained in this section has been adapted from the
official programme of Peacekeeping '93: Exhibition and Seminar, published
by Baxter Publications.*

**Active Gear Co. of Canada Limited, 201 Shidercroft Road, Concord ON,
L4K 2J9. Tel: (416) 669-2292, Fax: (416) 660-1927, Mr. Howard Malach,
Exhibit Coordinator.**

Active Gear Co. of Canada Limited has provided products and services to
support the requirements of the Canadian Defence Department and that of
original-equipment manufacturers for over 30 years. They have extensive experience in the following systems: drive train, fuel, filtration, exhaust, electrical and special emphasis on cold weather operations. They have a systems
approach to technical, operational and logistical requirements.

**Adga Systems International Ltd., 116 Albert St., Ste. 601, Ottawa ON,
K1P 5G3. Tel: (613) 237-3022, Fax: (613) 237-3024, Ms Kim Koebel, Corporate Mgt and Mktg.**

The Adga Group is a leading source of Canadian systems-engineering expertise. The pace of technological change over the last decade has been
breathtaking and it will continue as new and emerging technologies become
dominant forces in our society. The selection, implementation and use of
these technologies often presents significant challenges to users. ADGA's
mission is to enable its clients to exploit these new technologies fully by
providing innovative solutions.

AirSep Corporation, 290 Creekside Drive, Buffalo NY 14228-2070. Tel: (716) 691-0202, Fax: (716) 691-0707, Mr. Frederick Morgan, Dir. of Mktg.

AirSep Corporation is a leading manufacturer of medical and industrial oxygen-generating systems. Their products, commonly referred to as oxygen concentrators in medical markets, and oxygen generators in industrial markets, utilize a unique pressure swing adsorption (PSA) air separation process to produce up to 95 per cent pure oxygen. AirSep now sells or distributes to more than 55 countries.

Allen Testproducts, 405 Britannia Road E., Ste. 100, Mississauga ON, L4Z 3E6. Tel: (416) 890-8047, Fax: (416) 890-3094, Mr. Bill Stafford, V.P.

A division of the Allen Group Canada Ltd., the Allen Testproducts Division started in 1921 with the original "Growler," and has been the leader in diagnostic technology since then. Today's engine/systems analyzer is designed to collate all functions of all under-hood systems together in order to enhance diagnostic accuracy with the ability to produce over 18,000 diagnostic results. The Allen Smart Engine Analyzer can check the engine functions, sensor response, wiring integrity and the on-board computer reaction to the sensor "automatically."

Allied Signal Aerospatiale Canada Inc., 200 Laurentien Blvd., Montreal PQ H4M 2L5. Tel: (514) 744-2811, Fax: (514) 748-4419, Mr. Timothy Heaney, Mktg. Mgr.

Allied Signal Aerospatiale Canada Inc. has established an international reputation for its expertise in the design, development, manufacture and support of electro-optical systems. The thermal-imaging products utilize infrared technology to detect and classify heat emissions, working in the far infrared spectrum (8-12 microns). These devices are ideally suited for day or night surveillance, search and rescue, peacekeeping, drug interdiction and numerous defence applications, such as weapon sights and targeting systems.

Ancom Electromagnetique Ltee., 9665 Cote de Liesse, Dorval PQ H9P 1A3. Tel: (514) 633-9679, Fax: (514) 633-9681, Mr. Christian Dube, Pres.

Sectors of specialization: electromagnetic compatibility consulting and testing. Ancom provides expert consulting and testing services in the areas of electromagnetic technologies, interference control (EMI), TEMPEST, radiation hazards and antenna performance. Services are offered to system integrators and equipment manufacturers requiring expert assistance in the control of electromagnetic interference.

Associated Marine Equipment Ltd., 11 Thornhill Drive, Dartmouth NS B3B 1R9. Tel: (902) 468-6001, Fax: (902) 468-3163, Mr. Darren Trites, Sales and Svc. Mgr.

Recognized as a leading manufacturer of military marine and commercial pyrotechnics, Pains-Wessex has the experience of over 100 years in the industry. Company records show that its first patent for a naval distress flare was granted in 1873. Since 1840 the company has developed many specialist pyrotechnic devices and continues to manufacture a wide range of equipment for armed forces and supplies the British Ministry of Defence and many governments worldwide.

ATS Aerospace Inc., 1250 Marie-Victorin, St. Bruno PQ J3V 6B8. Tel: (514) 441-9000, Fax: (514) 441-6789, Ms. Johanne Choquet, Marketing.

ATS Aerospace Inc. is a high-tech engineering company focusing on aerospace and defence technology. ATS has two divisions: the aerospace division specializes in the development and production of fully integrated air traffic control (ATC) instructional systems; Ballistech Systems (BSI) specializes in defence-related testing and trials services, and research and development of aerial targets and aeronautics.

Aviation & Aerospace, 310 Dupont St., Toronto ON M5R 1V9. Tel: (416) 968-7252, Fax: (416) 968-2377, Mr. Garth Wallace, Editor.

Aviation & Aerospace is a bi-monthly journal covering all aspects of the aviation and aerospace industry. Feature articles cover aircraft manufacturing, including transport airplanes, light aircraft and helicopters, avionics, airlines, corporate aviation, military aviation, blue-collar aviation, aviation training, airports, airshows, space, and all the industry suppliers, supporters and maintainers that contribute to making this an important and vibrant sector of Canadian business.

Avl List Gmbh, Klesstrasse 48, Graz AUSTRIA A-8020. Tel: 0316-987, Fax: 011316-987-700, Mr. Gert Wresnig, Engineer.

(No text provided)

Belcan Tech Inc., 316 Knowlton St., Knowlton PQ J0E 1V0. Tel: (514) 243-6144, Fax: (514) 243-0572, Mr. John Aiken, Exhibit Coordinator.

Belcan Technologies is a Canadian company providing engineering, research and development and test and evaluation services as they relate to ordnance products. The company is staffed with highly skilled engineers and technicians with particular expertise in long-range artillery weapons and ammunition. It has extensive in-house analytical capabilities in all areas of ordnance engineering and analysis.

Bell Helicopter Textron, 12,800 Rue de l'Avenir, St. Janvier PQ J0N 1L0. Tel: (514) 437-2729, Fax: (514) 437-6888, Mrs. Vicki Stuart, Mktg. Coordinator.

A division of Textron Canada Ltd., Bell Helicopter Textron currently produces commercial light helicopters for delivery worldwide. The company designs and produces helicopters at its Mirabel, Quebec, facility. It also maintains a distribution centre in Calgary and a sales office in Ottawa. Bell manufactures about half the components that go into its aircraft. In addition to the design, machining and production facilities at Mirabel, the company also has a ground and flight-testing centre there along with a pilot training facility.

Biocarb Technologies, 14163 - E, Route 117, St. Janvier, Mirabel PQ J7L 1M3,.Tel: (514) 979-3300, Fax: (514) 979-3366, Mr. Robert Perry, Account Executive.

BIOCARB is Canada's leading manufacturer of the TRIOSYN family of iodinated biocidal resins for purification of potable water and waste-water treatment. The company offers state-of-the-art, medical-class laboratories; advanced R&D facilities; and expert engineering and product-design assistance to Original Equipment Manufacturers (OEM) for filtration/purification systems.

BR Communications, 222 Caspian Drive, Sunnyvale CA 94089. Tel: (408) 734-1600, Fax: (408) 734-1671, Mr. Foster Paulis, Show Coordinator.

BR Communications designs, develops and manufactures high-frequency equipment that helps communicators achieve and maintain superior HF communications. The product line includes a series of proven Chirpsounder equipment including the AN/TRQ-42 (successor to the AN/TRQ-35), AN/URQ-39, XCS-6 Chirpsounder transceiver and the 4280 Tactical

Chirpcomm Transceiver. The 4280 brings to the field the proven power of Chirpcomm for unprecedented HF message reliability.

Bytown Marine Limited, P.O. Box 11397, Station H, Ottawa ON K2H 7V1. Tel: (613) 820-6910, Fax: (613) 726-0266, Mr. T.J. Mason, Mktg. Mgr.

Bytown Marine Limited (BML) is an Ottawa-based company and the Canadian representative for several leading manufacturers of marine electronics and communications equipment. The products sold by the company include INMARSAT Satellite Communications Terminals, GPS Receivers, HF Surveillance Receivers, Tactical Antennas, Satellite Weather Imaging Systems, Laser Distance Measuring Instruments, Militarized Compasses/Heading Sensors and Solar Energy Systems.

CAE Electronics, 8585 Cote de Liesse, Saint-Laurent PQ H4T 1G6. Tel: (514) 341-6780, Fax: (514) 341-7699, Mr. Robert Hodge, Mgr - Sales Support.

CAE produces flight, tactics and mission simulators for fixed-wing and rotary aircraft for today's most advanced fighters, helicopters, heavy transport and patrol aircraft. CAE has supplied Canada's armed forces with simulators for the CF-100, CP-107 Argus, CP 140 Aurora, CT-114 Tudor, C-130 Hercules and CF-18 Hornet. CAE also provides software engineering support for the CF-18.

Canadian Air Cushion Vehicles Ltd., P.O. Box 1390, Shediac NB E0A 3G0. Tel: (506) 532-3986, Mr. Ray Stevens, President & GM.

A new company registered in New Brunswick, CACV Ltd.'s line includes craft made by NEPTUN of Moscow. These vessels have proven themselves in several years of service in Russia and other countries, and will be fitted with engines compatible with customers' requirements and the latest in instrumentation and electronics. Special equipment can be installed for customer-specified requirements at time of order. A series of variations to meet specialized military and civil uses have been designed, as well as enlargements of the basic range and a 10-ton cargo carrier.

Canadian Defence Quarterly, 310 Dupont S., Toronto ON M5R 1V9. Tel: (416) 968-7252, Fax: (416) 968-2377, Mr. Cliff Caunter, Dir. of Mktg.

Now in its 22nd year of publication, Canadian Defence Quarterly is recognized as the premier independent military journal in Canada, providing information, informed comment and opinion from highly qualified writers on

Canadian defence policy, strategic issues, tactics, arms control, peacekeeping, military organization, armaments, equipment and technology, military history and other defence-related issues. More than 85 per cent of Canadian Defence Quarterly's circulation is distributed by the Department of National Defence to senior officers of the Canadian Forces in Canada and abroad.

Canadian Institute Of Strategic Studies, 76 St. Clair Ave. W., Ste. 502, Toronto ON M4V 1N2. Tel: (416)964-6632, Fax: (416) 964-5833, Mr. Alex Morrison, Executive Director.

The Canadian Institute of Strategic Studies is a non-profit voluntary organization which enjoys wide recognition throughout Canada and abroad as the nation's foremost source of independent information and research on a broad range of security issues. Through its programmes in public education, student activities, publications and media relations the Institute enhances the basis for informed choice by citizens and governments.

CPAD Holdings, 11 Tristan Court, Unit D, Nepean ON K2V 8B9. Tel: (613) 224-9939, Fax: (613) 224-2418, Mr. Ron McAdam, Business Development.

CPAD Holdings Ltd. is a Canadian centre of excellence in the field of trace compound detection, including instruments to detect concealed bombs. The Explosives Detection Security System (EDSS), invented by CPAD, is a world leader. It detects a full range of explosives, including plastics such as Sentex. EDSS is fast and accurate, taking less than ten seconds to complete an analysis. Its sensitivity is comparable to detecting one drop of water in a million barrels of oil.

Dalimar Instruments, 89 Don Quichotte, #12, Isle Perrot PQ J7V 6X2. Tel: (514) 453-0033, Fax: (514) 453-0554, Mr. Daniel LaRose, Technical Sales Rep.

Represented in Canada by Dalimar Instruments Inc., AVL provides innovative solutions to complex and unique problems at the forefront of knowledge and technology. The business-segment high-pressure instrumentation covers a wide spectrum of sensors, systems for data acquisition and evaluation, static and dynamic calibration systems, equipment for small-, medium- and large-calibre testing in interior, exterior and terminal ballistics and application software.

Dew Engineering & Development Limited, 3429 Hawthorne Road, Ottawa ON K1G 4G2. Tel: (613) 736-5100, Fax: (613) 736-1348, Mr. Frank Robillard, Vice-President.

DEW Engineering and Development Limited is a Canadian company incorporated in 1978 to provide a vehicle systems engineering capability to the federal government. The company has prospered over the years and now operates out of its own 11-acre industrial site with a fully equipped 60,000-square-foot manufacturing facility in Ottawa, a few miles from Parliament Hill.

Diemaco (1984) Inc., 1036 Wilson Ave., Kitchener ON N2C 1J3. Tel: (519) 893-6840, Fax: (519) 893-3144, Mr. Maurice Clermont, Mktg. Dir.

A 100 percent Canadian company, Diemaco is a wholly owned subsidiary of Devtek Corporation of Markham, Ontario. Diemaco is Canada's Centre of Excellence for Small Arms and has been serving the military small-arms community since 1976. The company employs approximately 100 people at its 48,000-square-foot combined engineering office and manufacturing facility located at 1036 Wilson Ave., Kitchener, Ontario. Diemaco is most widely recognized as the producer of the C7 family of combat weapons and related training equipment.

E.T.M. Industries Inc., P.O. Box 610, 266 Hall Ave., Renfrew ON K7V 2E4. Tel: (613) 432-6136, Fax: (613) 432-9547, Mr. Bob Graham, Vice President.

Supplier of precision machined parts to Boeing, Haley Industries, Gearbox Machining. Manufacturer of sheet-metal assemblies. Capability/Products: Conventional and CNC machining; special fixture and jig building; precision honing, boring; tool making; aircraft sheet-metal subassemblies; plastic injection mold design and construction; plastic injection molding; CAD/CAM design; exclusive manufacturer of Watkin Vacuum Fingerprint Chamber for law enforcement; riot shield with video mount.

EZ4U Systems, Comp. 43, 385 Wilsey Road, Fredericton NB E3B 5N6. Tel: (506) 457-1525, Fax: (506) 458-5827, Mr. Glenn Briggs, Exhibit Mgr.

The Briggs Port-A-Fold is a multi-purpose, portable building that collapses to a 12" height for shipping and storage. The Port-A-Fold is lightweight, rigid and strong, corrosion resistant, inorganic and resists cracking. It also offers low flame spread, materials that won't bubble or wrap, cost effectiveness, durability, good import strengths, low water absorption, easy-to-clean surfaces, sanitary walls and ceilings and resistance to chemicals.

Firearms Training Systems, Inc., 110 Technology Parkway, Norcross GA 30092. Tel: (404) 448-7318, Fax: (404) 242-6962, Mr. Karmin McKay, International Sales.

In November 1992, Firearms Training Systems, Inc. (FATS) further consolidated its worldwide leadership in the design and production of small- and supporting arms simulators by winning both the British and Netherlands Ministry of Defence contracts for small-arms simulators. FATS has sold its off-the-shelf, indoor small-arms simulators to 24 countries including Canada. Judgmental training on FATS simulators is now mandatory in many police forces around the world.

Fuji Photo Film Canada Inc., 275 Britannia Road E., Mississauga ON L4Z 2E7. Tel: (416) 890-6611, Fax: (416) 890-6446, Mr. John Abbott, Mgr - Special Projects.

Since its inception, it has been the primary objective of Fuji Photo Film Co. Ltd. to develop and manufacture superior products of the highest quality. From advanced films, papers and other imaging materials, we will endeavour to maintain our leadership through research and technology. Featured in the show were Fujinon's superior line of military/marine binoculars including the Fujinon Stabiscope (Gyro Binoculars) and Starscope (Night Vision Monoculars).

General Motors Of Canada Limited Diesel Division, P.O. Box 5160, London ON N6A 4N5. Tel: (519) 452-5054, Fax: (519) 452-5688, Ms Hazell Booker, Mktg. Co-ordinator, Defence Products.

Diesel Division, General Motors of Canada Ltd., is a major designer and manufacturer of armoured vehicles for the Canadian, U.S. and Australian armed forces. The LAV is an eight-wheel-drive, amphibious vehicle, tested and driven in snow, mud, sand and extremely rocky terrain. The LAV is currently in service with the Canadian Army peacekeeping forces in Europe and Somalia, and has supported the U.S. National Guard in various counter-narcotic operations.

Hagglunds Vehicle AB, 100 Sparks St., Ste. 400, Ottawa ON K1P 5B7. Tel: (613) 237-7496, Fax: (613) 238-5519, Mr. Svante Andersson, Director-Government Relations.

Hagglunds Vehicle of Sweden is a leading supplier of military and civilian all-terrain carriers worldwide. The BV206 is the all-terrain carrier preferred by peacekeepers from many nations including the Netherlands (in Cambodia), France (in Yugoslavia), Sweden, Finland and Norway (in Macedonia and Honduras). Great Britain and Italy plan to deploy the BV206 in UN missions in Bosnia-Hercegovina and Mozambique, respectively.

Harris Corporation, 1680 University Ave., Rochester NY 14610. Tel: (716) 244-5830, Fax: (716) 325-1572, Mr. Bob Tubbs, Trade Show Mgr.

Harris RF Communications Group has been a major supplier to military, government agencies and commercial customers in more than 100 countries of the free world for more than 30 years. Harris equipment is used for critical long-haul, HF voice and data communications, high-speed data and video over HF, adaptive HF communications, strategic and high-performance computer-based command and control systems, as well as advanced VHF-FM and UHF-AM transceivers for secure communications.

Hughes Leitz Optical Technologies Ltd., 978 Merivale Road, Ottawa ON K1Z 6A4. Tel: (613) 725-1570, Fax: (613) 725-5178, Mr. David Reed, Sales Mgr, Govt Accts.

Hughes Leitz Optical Technologies Limited has a tradition of excellence spanning more than 140 years. The company has set many benchmarks in the application of precision optics in industry, medicine, photography and science research. Hughes Leitz occupies a unique position in the North American market as one of the world's leading suppliers of precision optics for both defence and civilian applications.

Hutchinson Corp., 460 Southard St., Trenton NJ 08638. Tel: (609) 394-1010, Fax: (609) 394-2031, Mr. Pascal Seradarian, Manager.

Hutchinson is a worldwide manufacturer and supplier of run-flat devices for pneumatic tires. Designed and manufactured in co-operation with vehicle builders and government engineers, Hutchinson offers a full range of run-flat devices and beadlocks, giving the maximum tire footprint in sand, mud, snow and soft-soil conditions. Hutchinson is proud to supply run-flat protection to

80 percent of the militaries of the free world, including vehicles such as the HMMWV, LAV, FMTV and PLS.

IMP Aerospace Limited, 2651 Dutch Village Road, Halifax NS B3L 4T1. Tel: (902) 873-2250, Fax: (902) 873-2249, Mr. Michael Garvey, Mktg. Mgr.

IMP Aerospace Ltd.specializes in depot-level inspection and repair of CP-140/140A Aurora and Arcturus long-range patrol aircraft and CH-124A/B Sea King Helicopters. The company has an extensive aircraft-systems-installation capability supported by an avionics repair, overhaul and spacecraft wire harness systems. The company repairs and overhauls aircraft structural components and produces aircraft and spacecraft sheet metal, composite and precision machined parts in individual or small lots or volume production.

Information Handling Services (Canada) Ltd., 1940 Oxford St. E., #7, London ON N5V 4L8. Tel: (519) 659-1400, Fax: (519) 659-1426, Ms Robyn Smith, Mktg. Administrator.

Information Handling Services Canada Limited maintains its head office in London, Ontario, with representatives across the country. A leader in technical-information services for more than 34 years, IHS provides the world's largest collection of technical documents in a number of formats. IHS provides more than information. We also train your people quickly and thoroughly right at your site and are committed to reliable service and support at no additional cost.

Ingersoll Machine & Tool Company Ltd., 347 King St. W., Ingersoll ON N2C 3K6. Tel: (519) 485-2210, Fax: (519) 485-2163, Mr. Mike Moore, Director - Sales & Mktg.

IMT's forging and machining capabilities combine to provide an efficient production facility for the manufacture of a wide range of defence-related products. Large-calibre ammunition projectiles up to 155mm, suspension components for the General Dynamics M1A1 Abrams tank, drive components for the General Motors LAV and suspension components for BMY Combat systems are just a few of the many defence-related products manufactured by IMT.

Ingersoll-Rand Canada Inc., 51 Worcester Road, Rexdale ON M9W 4K2. Tel: (416) 675-5611, Fax: (416) 675-6920, Mr. Frank Sova, Sales Mgr.

The ARO Life Support Products Division has been manufacturing, assembling, repairing, overhauling and testing life support equipment on a continuing basis since 1952. The division is a major supplier to military forces, the Department of Transport, aircraft and military vehicle manufacturers, and services commercial and business aviation industries throughout the world. The company is certified AQAP-4, Certification of Compliance, Department of Transport/FAA, Department of National Defence, US9858, and FAR Publications.

Intergraph Canada Limited, 2580 Matheson Blvd. E., Mississauga ON L4W 4J1. Tel: (416) 625-2081 Ext.277, Fax: (416) 625-6445, Ms Jill Gowland, Mktg. Events Mgr.

Intergraph is the world's largest supplier of interactive graphics systems. Intergraph Canada Ltd. is the Canadian subsidiary of Intergraph Corporation. We will provide demonstrations of Intergraph's solutions for the Architecture, Engineering and Construction disciplines as well as CAFM (Computer Aided Facilities Management). We will show how Intergraph's fully integrated CE environment facilitates the co-ordination and implementation of a variety of tasks.

Iotek Inc., 1127 Barrington St., Halifax NS B3A 3R3. Tel: (902) 420-1890, Fax: (902) 420-0674, Mr. Terry Doyle, Dir. of Business Development.

Iotek is a seven-year-old Halifax-based company that designs, manufactures and services specialized hardware and software for applications in advanced sonar and radar systems. Iotek currently manufactures the AN/UYS-501 signal processor and a high-resolution, 2048x2048 pixel-imaging display system. The company has also developed a Gallium Arsenide ASIC (Application-Specific Integrated Circuit) that acts as a serial receiver and serial-to-parallel converter.

Istec, 1810 Highway 6 North, Hamilton ON L9J 1H2. Tel: (416) 529-5132, Fax: (416) 529-5311, Mr. Michael Wlodek, Mktg. Mgr.

Istec Inc. manufactures the WESCAM stabilized airborne camera system. The Wescam is available in three different models (12D, 24D and 36D) and is used to provide imaging from applications which use broadcast (3 CCD), film (35mm), low light level (LLTV) and thermal-imaging (FLIR) cameras. All

WESCAMs are isolated from the vibration of the aircraft and gyro-stabilized from the motion of the aircraft, resulting in jitter-free images.

Ivor Macleod Training Systems, 27 A College Crescent, Barrie ON L4M 2W4. Tel: (705) 726-5091, Fax: (705) 726-5091, Mr. Ivor MacLeod, President.

Since 1984, Ivor Macleod Training Systems has provided experienced, practical instruction in all aspects of professional small-arms use to police, military and civilian armed guard agencies. The company is also dedicated to the design, development and production of innovative products such as the extremely useful, all weather, plastic shooting targets which have been supplied to the Canadian Forces, the RCMP and other police forces. Large quantities of the IMTS-designed Plastic Shot Hole Markers (produced by ETM Industries) have been supplied to DSS contracts.

Kaufman Footwear, 410 King St. W., Kitchener ON N2G 4J8. Tel: (519) 576-1500, Fax: (519) 742-0034, Mr. Bruce Holliday, Industrial Sales Mgr.

Kaufman Footwear, Canada's largest footwear manufacturer, has crafted quality products since 1907. Product lines include Sorel cold weather boots, leather and rubber work boots and industrial rainwear. As a world leader in the development of materials and designs for cold weather footwear, Kaufman was proud to have been a sponsor of the recently completed Weber-Malakhov North Pole expedition.

Leblanc & Royle Telcom Inc., 514 Chartwell Road, P.O. Box 880, Oakville ON L6J 5C5. Tel: (416) 844-1242, Fax: (416) 844-8837, Mr. Brian Gray, Account Executive.

LeBlanc & Royle Telcom Inc. specializes in the design, fabrication, furnishing, installation and maintenance of communication towers and antenna systems. Now in its third decade of business, Leblanc has supplied and installed equipment in more than 60 countries. Manufacturing facilities are found in Canada, the United States, Australia and Singapore. LeBlanc is also the Canadian distributor for Cablewave Systems (transmission line, microwave and broadcast antennas) and has the licence to manufacture Xit Rods (electronic ground rods).

Lexi-Tech Inc., 10 Dawson Ave., Moncton NB E1A 6C8. Tel: (506) 859-5200 Fax: (506) 859-5205, Mr. Ronald Fournier, President.

Lexi-Tech Inc. is the only fully integrated translation and publishing company of its kind in North America. Our full-time staff of 102 people in Moncton and Montreal offers a complete translation and publishing service from English to French and English to Spanish. Your requirements are met using state-of-the-art imaging and desktop-publishing software and equipment.

Magnavox Overseas Ltd., 1313 Production Road, Fort Wayne IN 46808. Tel: (219) 429-8268, Fax: (219) 429-7600, Mr. Arthur Dailey, Regional Mgr Int'l.

Magnavox Electronic Systems Company is a broad-based organization dedicated to the development and manufacture of electronic systems. As a major supplier to defence establishments worldwide, including the Canadian Department of National Defence as well as the U.S. DoD, the company has an established reputation for excellence in military communication, battlefield command and control, anti-submarine warfare, and electronic combat systems; ordnance electronics; display and electro-optics.

McDonnell Douglas Aerospace, Int.Mail Code 217A-400, 1510 Hughes Way, Long Beach CA 90810-1864. Tel: (310) 522-2542, Fax: (310) 522-2572, W. D. Kelly, Mgr C17 Domestic Mktg. Transport Aircraft.

McDonnell Douglas Corporation is a global aerospace company with a tradition of delivering the highest-quality aerospace products. MDC is the world's leading producer of combat aircraft, including the F-4 Phantom, F-15 Eagle, F/A-18 Hornet, AV-8B Harrier and AH-64 Apache. MDC is also a leader in missiles, including the Harpoon, Tomahawk and SLAM. MDC has played an integral part in America's space programme, including SpaceStation Freedom and the Delta rocket.

Mercedes - Benz AG, P.O. Box, Stuttgart GERMANY. Tel: 49 71 117 54940, Fax: 49 71 117 32167, Mr. Gerd Hannak, Director of Cross Country Vehicles.

Mercedes-Benz AG, a division of the Daimler-Benz group, exhibits its cross-country vehicle in the configuration employed in UN missions. Mercedes-Benz engineering, rugged construction and superior performance have convinced seven NATO countries to acquire our cross country vehicle for military and para-military uses. An additional eleven non-NATO countries, whose armed forces frequently support UN missions, also rely upon the Mercedes-Benz.

Mercedes-Benz Canada Inc., 849 Eglinton Ave. E., Toronto ON M4G 2L5. Tel: (416) 467-2285, Fax: (416) 423-5027, Mr. Alfred R. Zeeb, Procurement, Mgr. Special Projects.
(See Mercedes-Benz AG)

Michelin Tires (Canada) Ltd., 175, Bouchard Bvld., Dorval PQ H9S 5T1. Tel: (514) 633-4716, Fax: (514) 633-8415, Ms Laurette Vachon-Shaw, Communications Mgr.

The commercial division of Michelin Tires (Canada) Ltd. has a history that goes back 80 years with the establishment of the first commercial office in Canada. The manufacturing division of Michelin Tires (Canada) Ltd. began production for the North American market in 1971 when its Canadian executive offices and its first Canadian manufacturing plant opened in Granton, Nova Scotia. Based in Dorval, Quebec, Michelin manufactures and distributes quality tires for both commercial and government applications.

MIL Group, 22 George D. Davie St., Levis PQ G6V 6N7. Tel: (418) 837-5841, Fax: 1(418)833-9492, Mr. Steve Kack, Mktg. Asst.
(No text provided)

MIL Group, 1600 Carling Ave., Ste. 700, Ottawa ON K1Z 8R7. Tel: (613) 722-2247, Fax: (613) 722-3505, Ms Sharon Howard, Business Devt.

The MIL Group ranks among Canada's leading industrial manufacturers, offering services in conceptual and detailed design, engineering, manufacturing, construction, installation and quality assurance testing for a wide range of heavy-equipment and high-technology products. MIL's principal markets are in the defence, shipbuilding, industrial and offshore fabrication sectors. Products offered include military and commercial vessels on a turn-key basis, offshore structures and a wide range of other heavy equipment, as well as design and other engineering services.

Mining Resource Engineering Limited, 1555 Sydenham Road, RR #8, Kingston ON K7L 4V4. Tel: (613) 545-0466, Fax: (613) 542-8029, Mr. Bill Bauer, GM.

MREL is a 100 percent Canadian-owned small business specializing in explosives/ordnance related projects. MREL's explosives testings, warhead casting, and fuse-assembly facilities have supported a wide variety of R&D and delivery contracts for the defence and industrial communities in Canada and abroad. MREL also produces a unique patented liquid explosive foam, LEXFOAM, ideally suited for EOD, minefield clearing and special operations.

Mobile Telesystems, Inc., 300 Professional Drive, Gaithersburg MD 20879. Tel: (301) 590-8509, Fax: (301) 590-8558, Ms Rania Habbaba, Exhibit Mgr.

Mobile Telesystems Inc. is a privately held company in the United States that develops, manufactures and services a series of satellite-communication terminals operating exclusively with the INMARSAT Network. The International Maritime Satellite Organization (INMARSAT) operates a system of geostationary satellites over the Atlantic, Pacific and Indian Oceans providing complete global coverage that permits our products to be operated anywhere, anytime.

Motorola Inc. Government Electronics Group, 8201 E. McDowell Road, Scottsdale AZ 85252. Tel: (602) 441-4159, Fax: (602) 441-2806, Mr. David Evanitz, Exhibits Mgr.

Motorola Military and Aerospace Electronics Inc. will feature, among other products and systems, both SATCOM and line-of-sight radios, modular surveillance radar, ranging systems and secure telephone and fax products designed to meet the sophisticated requirements of international peacekeeping operations.

Munters Corporation Cargocaire Defense Division, 79 Monroe St., P.O. Box 640, Ames Bury MA 01913-4740. Tel: (508) 388-0600, Fax: (508) 388-3767, Mr. Hansi Kruger, Defense Division Mgr.

Desiccant Wheel (DEW) Technology, a maintenance revolution, it is a simple, portable, durable and cost-effective maintenance concept that extends system life, reduces logistic support costs and ultimately increases weapons-systems availability. This amounts to true maintenance productivity enhancement.

Mustang Industries Inc., 3810 Jacombs Road, Richmond BC V6V 1Y6. Tel: (604) 270-8631, Fax: (604) 270-0489, Mr. Michael McGraw, Co-ordinator - Defence Projects.

Mustang has more than 25 years of experience designing and manufacturing safety and survival equipment for airborne, land and marine operations.

Various forms of immersion suits, anti-exposure coveralls, aviation coveralls, inflatable life preservers, life vests and buoyant coats form the basics of Mustang's product line. With head office and main manufacturing facility in a modern 75,000-sq.-ft. factory in Richmond, B.C., Mustang employs an exceptional work force of skilled and dedicated workers.

National Standards Association, 1200 Quince Orchard Blvd., Gaithersburg MD 20878. Tel: (301) 590-2340, Fax: (301) 990-8378, Ms Meredith Hagerty, Secretary to the President.

National Standards Association exhibited PARTS-MASTER logistics support system on CD-ROM and available on line; SPECMASTER full-text Mil-Specs, Mil-Stds, industry standards and vendor (industrial) catalogs on CD-ROM. Both systems can be installed on a network. Founded in 1946, National Standards is a U.S.-owned small-business high-technology publisher.

Natural Aid Products Ltd., Bay #6, 4063 - 74 Ave. S.E., Calgary AB T2C 2H9. Tel: (403) 279-8881, Fax: (403) 279-8885, Ms Loryhl Gutman, Export Development.

When you move your people into the field, how do you deal with human waste? The waste itself is a threat to the health of your troops and local civilians, and chemicals used to treat the waste are a hazard to people and the environment. If you have the problem, we have the solution. Sept-Aid, used by the Canadian military, greatly reduces odours and speeds the natural breakdown of waste into harmless fertilizer. Sept-Aid is easy to apply, non-toxic, non-irritating and harmless to the environment.

New Brunswick, Economic Develop. & Tourism, P.O. Box 6000, 670 King St., Fredericton NB E3B 5H1. Tel: (506) 453-2875, Fax: (506) 453-7904, Mr. Steve Kelly, Project Executive.

Your inquiries are welcome for subcontracting, partnerships, industrial-benefit offset requirements, alliances, joint ventures and investment. New Brunswick industry is "Open for Business." World-class industry in New Brunswick includes shipbuilding technologies, software, computer-based training, electronics, English-language electronic translation, engineering, research and development, precision machining, as well as specialized products in the medical, food and textile industries.

Newfoundland & Lab. Gov't Dept. Of Industry, Trade & Technology, P.O. Box 8700, St. John's NF A1B 4J6. Tel: (709) 729-5594, Fax: (709) 729-5936, Mr. Phillip Smith, Sr. Promotion Officer.

The role of the Strategic Procurement Division of the Department of Industry, Trade and Development is to help the private sector expand and diversify the economy of Newfoundland and Labrador through public- and private-sector procurement.The Division identifies markets for local products and services that may be accessed through provincial procurement, federal procurement, major capital projects, and procurement.

Newtech Instruments Ltd., 63 Thorburn Road, Box 13635 Station "A", St. John's NF A1B 4G1. Tel: (709) 576-6666, Fax: (709) 576-7635, Mr. Tom Binden, Director of Market Development.

NewTech Instruments Ltd. is an electronics design and manufacturing company providing quality products and services to the marine, communications and defence industries. The company currently employs approximately 40 at its St. John's facility manufacturing a wide range of products of its own design as well as others under manufacturing contracts. These include marine safety lights, electronic rodent deterrents, cable assemblies, military vehicle components, naval ship components, electronic whale alarms and electronic crustacean devices.

Nico Pyrotechnik, Bei der Feuerwerkerei 4, P.O. Box 12 27, Trittau GERMANY 2077. Tel: 4154/805 0, Fax: 01114154/2451, Mr. Heiko Burmeister, PR Mgr.

(No text provided)

North Atlantic Treaty Organization, 1110 Brussels, BELGIUM. Tel: 32 2 728 50 46, Fax: 01132272842, Mr. A. Soares, Head - Photos & Visual Aids.

The North Atlantic Alliance plays a central role in the pursuit of stability and in efforts to maintain peace in Europe. The Alliance was founded on the basis of the 1949 Treaty of Washington, signed by ten European states and the United States and Canada. Four more European states subsequently joined the Alliance. The Treaty commits each member country to sharing the responsibilities and benefits of collective security and stipulates that no member shall enter into any other international commitment which might conflict with the Treaty.

Nova Scotia Dept. Of Industry, Trade & Tech., P.O. Box 519, 1800 Argyle St., Halifax NS. Tel: (902) 465-2877, Fax: (902) 424-5739, Mr. Peter Giffin, Trade Development Officer.

(No text provided)

Primex Defence Products Ltd., 275 Bamburgh Circle, Scarborough ON M1W 3X4. Tel: (416) 498-5963, Fax: (416) 498-0566, Mr. Tom Finan, Pres.

Primex Defence Systems Limited, an Ottawa-based company, is engaged in providing international representation services for foreign and domestic high-tech manufacturers for commercial and military product areas. Primex represented two companies at Peacekeeping '93. One was NOWAR GmbH, a German manufacturer specializing in state-of-the-art security equipment for military and police use. The second was Digital Eclipse Inc., which is a single-source advanced solution of multimedia applications and hardware.

Quimpex Ltd., 5450 St. Roch, Drummondville PQ J2B 6V4. Tel: (819) 472-3326, Fax: (819) 477-9423, Mr. Jack Jennings, VP Mktg.

Founded in 1973, Quimpex soon became a dominant force in the design and manufacture of quality rubber tracks. Faced with a rapidly expanding market, Quimpex launched a research and development programme resulting in some of the most highly creative and innovative track designs ever developed.Quimpex has made substantial contributions in revolutionizing track technology.

Racal Filter Technologies Ltd., 1175 California Ave., P.O. Box 665, Brockville ON K6V 5V8. Tel: (613) 345-0111, Fax: (613) 345-2639, Mr. Julien Kusek, Marketing.

Racal Filter Technologies Ltd., a member of the Racal Health and Safety Group, designs and manufactures industrial and military respiratory filter canisters for world markets. Located in Brockville, Ontario, the company has a flexible manufacturing facility capable of producing aluminum and plastic canisters. The company also has a substantial R&D capability for new-product design and innovation.

Rosemount Instruments Ltd., 16 Concourse Gate, Nepean ON K2E 7S8. Tel: (613) 727-5752, Fax: (613) 224-1937, Mr. Tony Bockman, Aerospace Manager.

The Rosemount Group is one of the world's largest manufacturers and marketers of high-precision measurement and analytical instrumentation, distributed-control systems and valves for the processing and aerospace industries. The Rosemount Group consists of ten operating units brought together in 1986 by its parent company, Emerson Electric Co., to provide its customers with leading-edge technology, practical and reliable products and superior service and support.

Royal Canadian Legion, 359 Kent St., Ottawa ON K2P 0R7. Tel: (613) 235-4391, Fax: (613) 563-1670, Mr. Greg Hogan, Secretary Dominion Command.

(No text provided)

S.A.B.C.A., 1470, Chaussee de Haecht 1130 Brussels BELGIUM 1130. Tel: 02 729 55 11, Fax: 01132221615, Mr. Pierre Pellegrin, Mktg. Mgr.

S.A.B.C.A., the oldest aerospace company in Belgium, is involved in optical and electronic applications. For 25 years, S.A.B.C.A. has developed Fire Control Systems for Main Battle Tanks. This fire control system was used in the Canadian Leopard 1 tanks at the beginning of their operations. S.A.B.C.A. supplies maintenance and training equipment and provides engineering, logistic and customer support.

Saco Defense Inc., 291 North St., Saco ME 04072. Tel: (207) 283-3611, Fax: (207) 283-1395, Mr. Tom McNamara, Mktg.

Saco Defense Inc. is the sole supplier of the MK19 MOD 3 40mm machine gun system, the 7.62mm M60 machine gun series and the M2HB .50 cal machine gun series to the U.S. Armed Forces. The firm also produces barrels ranging in size from 5.56mm to 40mm.

Saint John Shipbuilding Limited, 300 Union St., Saint John NB E2L 4L4. Tel: (506) 633-4444, Fax: (506) 632-5915, Mr. Ian Jones, Dir. of Mktg.

Saint John Shipbuilding Limited is Canada's largest privately owned shipbuilding facility. The facility is situated in the sheltered, ice-free harbour of the Port of Saint John. SJSL is the prime contractor for the Canadian Patrol Frigate Programme. SJSL's overall responsibility for the $6.2-billion dollar contract is to provide the Canadian government with 12 fully operational frigates.

Samsonite Canada Inc., 753 Ontario St., Stratford ON N5A 6V1. Tel: (519) 271-5040, Fax: (519) 273-4650, Ms Carol Edmunds, Mktg. Svcs. Mgr.

Samsonite's engineered products division, backed by its extensive luggage heritage, has become one of North America's leading producers of custom-moulded components and specialty cases. The company's exhibit attracted visitors with the display of a thermoplastic moulded blank artillery shell, the first to be manufactured in North America. Also displayed was the moulded transportable trunk locker, already in service with Canadian and British Armed Forces.

Scepter Manufacturing Company Limited, 170 Midwest Road, Scarborough ON M1P 3A9. Tel: (416) 751-9445, Alan R. Newman, Mgr. Defence Products.

A Canadian leader in plastics design and manufacturing, Scepter is an innovator, putting corrosion-proof, waterproof, lightweight, virtually indestructible plastics to work building the most advanced and most comprehensive family of plastic containers for military ammunition, fuels and water. Scepter has more than 20 years experience supplying NATO armed forces with approved containers.

Schiebel Elektronische, 61 Spruce St., Stittsville ON K2S 1P8. Tel: (613) 836-3548, Fax: (613) 836-7479, Mr. John Knowles, Agent.

Schiebel, an Austrian electronics company located in Vienna, has developed the highly sensitive, lightweight, AN-19/2 metal detector, primarily used for the safe location of buried anti-personnel and vehicle mines. While the AN-19/2 may be used in several metres of water, a deep-water version is now in evaluation. Major procurements of the hand-held AN-19/2 have been made by the armed forces of most NATO countries. The detector is used by UN forces in the Persian Gulf, Lebanon, Afghanistan, Cambodia, Somalia and the former Yugoslavia.

Schiebel Elektronische Geraete GmbH, Margareter strasse 112, A 1050 Vienna AUSTRIA. Tel: 43 1 546 260, Fax: 43 1 545 2339, Mr. Hans-Georg Schibel, Managing Director.

(No text provided)

SEI Industries Ltd., 7400 Wilson Ave., Delta BC V4G 1E5. Tel: (604) 946-3131, Fax: (604) 940-9566, Mr. Greg Emry, Mktg. Mgr.

Since January 1983, the company has focused its expertise on the design and manufacturing of structural-engineered fabric products and systems to the aviation and remote-site logistics-supply industries. Since 1990, SEI Industries has introduced technological advances creating opportunities in the environmental and permanent containment markets utilizing on-site fibreglass manufacturing of tanks, structures, piping and vessels.

Select Business Network, 5000 Dufferin St., Unit E. 2, Downsview ON M3H 5T5. Tel: (416) 739-0009, Fax: (416) 739-1713, Mr. Boris Velman, President.
(No text provided)

Siemens Electric Limited, 1180 Courtney Park Drive, Mississauga ON L5T 1P2. Tel: (416) 670-6358, Fax: (416) 564-5855, Ms Alice Abt, Asst. Mgr. - MC & PR.

Siemens-Albis develops and manufactures civil and military equipment together with communications, electronic and electrical systems and installations. Out of a total work force of 4,000, more than 600 are engaged in development and quality control. A rigorous quality-control department, staffed by highly qualified and dedicated personnel, assures products that meet the most stringent requirements. Along with our products and system, Siemens-Albis also manufactures equipment under licence.

Siemens-Albis AG, Freilager strasse 38, CH-8047, Zurich SWITZER-LAND. Tel: 41 1 195 3111, Fax: 41 1 495 3816, Mr. Robert Zwicky, Department Head Communications.
(No text provided)

Simunition, 366 Bruyere St., Ottawa ON K1N 5E7. Tel: (613) 789-7010, Fax: (613) 789-0227, Mr. David Luxton, Mktg Mgr.

Simunition is the recognized world leader in small-calibre training ammunition. This division of SNC Industrial Technologies has introduced a complete line that opens new horizons in training for military, para-military and police forces. Developed in co-operation with special military forces and police emergency-response teams, our product line is designed to meet today's training needs. Simunition cartridges are available in the most widely used small-arms calibres.

Skylink Aviation & Transport Services, 593 Yonge St., Ste. 234, Toronto ON M4Y 1Z4. Tel: (416) 922-2831, Fax: (416) 922-0081, Mr. Kenneth Swartz, Mktg. Communications.

Skylink provides helicopters, aircraft, aviation management and transportation services to UN missions and other non-governmental organizations. A fleet of 100 fixed-wing aircraft and helicopters from the West and the Eastern Bloc are currently working with international organizations in seven global hot spots: Angola, Cambodia, Croatia, Kuwait, Mozambique, Somalia and Western Sahara. Skylink also specializes in co-ordinating the international movement of peacekeepers and their equipment on scheduled and chartered flights.

SNC Industrial Technologies Inc., 5 Montee des Arsenaux, Le Gardeur PQ J5Z 2P4. Tel: (514) 581-3080, Fax: (514) 582-6267, Ms Lise Laberge, Marketing.

SNC Industrial Technologies has been producing high-quality ammunition and other defence products for more than a century. Today, we provide conventional and training ammunition, as well as protective equipment, to military, special forces, and police in Canada and abroad. SNC Industrial Technologies is the designated supplier to the Canadian Forces.

Steelcor Industries Inc., 1 Main St., P.O. Box 208, Buchans NF A0H 1G0. Tel: (709) 672-3351, Fax: (709) 672-3564, Mr. Sean Power, President.

Steelcor Industries Inc. is a custom manufacturer offering quality service in the sheet-metal, machining and fabricating industry. Steelcor recognizes the individual requirements of each customer and is committed to meeting those requirements through a quality assurance and quality improvement programme. Steelcor operates in several industries, including aerospace and defence.

SURNAV Corporation, 89 Auriga Drive, Nepean ON K2E 7Z2. Tel: (613) 723-1830, Fax: (613) 723-0786, Mr. Harold Tolton, V.P. Mktg.

Surnav Corporation, based in the Ottawa area, supplies technologically advanced equipment to the Canadian geomatics and navigation marketplace. Clients include the federal and provincial governments, DND, and companies involved in surveying and mapping, resource exploration, forestry, dredging, aerial applications and aircraft manufacturing. Surnav's representation includes Trimble Navigation, the leading supplier of Global

Positioning System products for commercial and military applications with more than 50,000 GPS units sold worldwide.

Thyssen Henschel Department VSO, Henschelplatz 1, D-3500 Kassel GERMANY. Tel: 0561-801-6486, Fax: 0114910561-801, Mr. Werner Hofmann, Public Relations.

Thyssen-Henschel, located in Kassel, Germany, is a division of Thyssen AG, a major German industrial and trading corporation. (Thyssen BHI is the sister Canadian subsidiary.) The company is an established designer and manufacturer of advanced technical products, including wheeled and tracked armoured vehicles. Over the years they have produced vehicles for Germany and NATO allies, and for military and security forces worldwide.

Trans-Lite Inc., 10 Battery Road, Ste. 202, St. John's NF A1A 1A4. Tel: (709) 722-3772, Fax: (709) 722-3442, Mr. Paul Edison, Mktg. Director.

Trans-Lite produces a marine safety light (Digi-lite A12M) for personal floatation devices to aid in search and rescue operations at night and in poor-visibility conditions. The Digi-lite A12M is amongst the world's smallest personal rescue lights for marine use. It activates upon contact with water and will last in excess of 12 hours. It is attached to a personal floatation device by means of a plastic tie wrap. The Digi-lite can be used as an all-round safety light and is also available in infra-red.

U.S. Foreign Commercial Service, U.S. Embassy, 100 Wellington St., Ottawa ON K1P 5T1. Tel: (613) 238-5335, Fax: (613) 233-8511, Mr. Rick Tachuk, Sr. Commercial Specialist.

The U.S. Foreign Commercial Service, American Embassy Ottawa, organized a USA SHOWCASE Catalog Exhibition featuring products and services of several dozen U.S. companies that could not exhibit on their own this year. Some of these companies are new to this market; others had products being introduced for the first time. All were reliable potential partners and suppliers to this important new sector.

W.L. Gore & Associates Inc., 297 Blue Ball Road, P.O. Box 1130, Elkton MD 21922,. Tel: (410) 392-3700, Fax: (410) 392-4452, Ms Heather McLennan, Advertising Associate.

Gore products have been tested and specified to meet the challenges faced by today's soldier. Gore's technology, coupled with state-of-the-art garment manufacturing, provides the most technologically advanced protective-clothing items available. From Arctic storms to the desert of Saudi Arabia, Gore products have proven effective. From cold-water immersion to fire fighting, to a chemical and biological environment, Gore products are engineered for survival.

Wab Purification Products, 9015 Avon Road, Unit 2001, Montreal PQ H4X 2G8. Tel: (514) 483-5386, Fax: (514) 483-6235, Mr. Nory Laderoute, President.

WAB produces purification products for the military, for consumers and for industrial/commercial markets. WAB products contain the powerful TRIOSYN iodinated biocidal demand release resin that kills water-borne viruses, bacteria, parasite and protozoa. Some products on display: Passport Water Purification Cup, Passport Water Purification Hand Pump I, Passport Water Purification Hand Pump II, Passport Water Purification Jug I, Passport Water Purification Jug II.

Weatherhaven Resources Ltd., 5700 Marine Way, Burnaby BC V5J 5C8. Tel: (604) 451-8900, Fax: (604) 451-8999, Ms Denise Fisher, Sales & Mktg. Co-ordinator.

Weatherhaven designs and manufactures rugged, versatile, portable shelter systems. Lightweight but strong, Weatherhaven insulated fabric structures are currently deployed in the world's extreme locations, some accessible only by helicopter, and at over 100 UN peacekeeping sites around the world. Turn-key services are a specialty with integration of preharnessed electrical, mechanical, furnishings, water supply and waste management.

Webasto Thermosystems (Canada) Ltd., 4450 Mainway, Burlington ON L7L 5Y5. Tel: (416) 335-4143, Fax: (416) 335-6958, Mr. Douglas Jacques, Sales Mgr.

Webasto will be showing its line of air and coolant heaters, which have been successfully tested at -40 degrees C and were selected for Canadian Forces HLVW, AVGP and BISON vehicles. Established more than 90 years ago, the company has sold over two million heaters around the world to armies and commercial organizations. Used extensively by NATO forces in Europe, Webasto heaters are reported to deliver performance and cold-start capability in both tracked and wheeled vehicles, as well as stationary diesel engines.

Western Star Trucks Inc., 2076 Enterprise Way, Kelowna BC V1Y 6H8. Tel: (604) 868-6363, Fax: (604) 860-1443, Mr. Ted Mills, Int'l Sales Mgr.

Western Star Trucks Inc. is a manufacturer of custom transport equipment. Vehicles produced range from the LSVW unit for the Canadian military through the mid-sized 4x4 Range fire-fighting vehicle, up to Heavy Duty Prime movers for tank transport use. Western Star specializes in complete packages -- fully rigged oilfield units, crane trucks, dumps etc. -- and is active throughout North America and the world, with current exports and after-sales support to over 20 countries on every continent.

Westinghouse Electronic Systems, P.O. Box 17319 MS A255, Baltimore MD. Tel: (410) 765-6465, Fax: (410) 993-7528, Mr. David Pierson.

Westinghouse Electronics Systems develops, manufactures and supports electronic systems for the U.S. government, and for commercial, civil and international customers. Product and systems focus is on advanced technology in solid-state devices, and digital systems and processors. Products featured were the AN/TPS-63 and AN/TPS-70 Tactical Air Defense Radars, TAC 90 Color Raster Display and Theatre Missile Defense Systems.

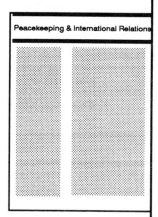

Peacekeeping: An Annotated Bibliography
by Peter Jones

This informative and educational book identifies and summarizes a wide variety of articles on international peacekeeping which have appeared in the major English language journals since the end of the Second World War. It is designed as an introductory research tool. The index has three sections: 1) National Views on Peacekeeping; 2) Histories of the Various Peacekeeping Missions; and 3) Special Topics and Concerns.

$15

BUY BOTH OF THESE BOOKS NOW
AND PAY ONLY $20
(Please use order form at the back)

Peacekeeping, Peacemaking or War: International Security Enforcement
Edited by Alex Morrison

**Proceedings of the CISS Spring Seminar
held in Toronto in May 1991**

Presentations include "Canada and International Security Enforcement"; "Latin America and Peacekeeping: Future Prospects"; "The Future of Peacekeeping: A Military View"; "The Challenges of Ethnicity and Tribalism in Muslim Countries"; "International Security and International Finance"; "The Economics of Canadian Defence"; "A Chinese View of the United Nations in International Security"; "International Security and Conflict Management"; "International Security Enforcement: Challenges and Opportunities"

$10

The
Canadian
Institute
of Strategic
Studies

L'Institut
Canadien
d'Etudes
Stratégiques

CISS Publications

The Canadian Institute of Strategic Studies (CISS) provides the forum for and is the vehicle to stimulate the research, study, analysis and discussion of the strategic implications of major national and international issues, events and trends as they affect Canada and Canadians.

For membership and seminar information contact

The Canadian Institute of Strategic Studies
76 St. Clair Avenue West, Suite 502
Toronto, Ontario M4V 1N2
Telephone (416) 964-6632
Facsimile (416) 964-5833

Executive Director
Alex Morrison, MSC, CD, MA

The CISS

The Canadian Institute of Strategic Studies is committed to the enhancement of the national security of Canada. Through a programme of seminars, publications, educational activities and media relations the CISS improves the basis for informed choice by the Canadian public and its leaders on a wide range of issues affecting national and global security.

The Institute draws members from all regions and constituencies of Canada. In common they are concerned about such vital issues as the formulation of sound foreign and defence policies, national and international economic strategies, and a range of social and environmental issues.

The CISS is a non-profit, non-partisan, voluntary organization which maintains an independent posture. It has been granted the status of a registered charity by Revenue Canada. All donations and membership fees are tax deductible.

Current Research

The CISS is currently working independently or in conjunction with related organizations in a number of fields. These include:

- **Canadian security and sovereignty;**
- **Peacekeeping in all its aspects;**
- **Canadian constitutional issues;**
- **Arms control and disarmament;**
- **Canada-US co-operation;**
- **Regional security studies;**
- **Social issues, such as the drug trade, global economic disparities, human rights;**
- **National and international environmental issues.**

Order Form

The Canadian Institute of Strategic Studies
76 St. Clair Avenue West, Suite 502
Toronto, Ontario M4V 1N2
Telephone (416) 964-6632
Facsimile (416) 964-5833

QTY/TITLE

[ ] _____ $_____

[ ] _____ $_____

[ ] _____ $_____

[ ] _____ $_____

SHIPPING (10% of order value, $3 minimum) $_____

SUBTOTAL $_____

GST (7% OF SUBTOTAL) $_____

TOTAL PAYABLE $_____

Ship To

Name _____

Address _____

_____ Postal Code _____

Telephone No. _____

Payment

* (NB: payable in US funds outside Canada)

[ ] Cheque enclosed

[ ] VISA**   [ ] Mastercard**

** $15 minimum order required

Card No _____

Expiry Date _____

Signature _____

CISS Publications

CISS Books

* The following CISS publications are provided free to members and are available for purchase by non-members:

* **The Canadian Strategic Forecast**
  Published each autumn.
  Purchase Price: (see list)

* **Spring Seminar Proceedings**
  Each year a particular issue in Canadian foreign and security policy is examined in depth.
  Purchase Price: (see list)

* **Strategic Datalinks** (occasional)
  A series of concise 2-4 page briefs providing detailed analyses of important security issues.
  Purchase Price: $1 each
  $5 for 10

* **The CISS Bulletin** (4 per year)
  The Institute's newsletter providing members with current news on CISS programmes, book reviews, articles and member news.
  Purchase Price: $5 each
  $20/year

* **Strategic Profile: Canada**
  A quick reference data card providing up-to-date information on Canada's comparative strength and strategic position in the world.
  Purchase Price: $1 each
  $5 for 10

* The following CISS publications are available by subscription:

* **The McNaughton Papers (The Canadian Journal of Strategic Studies)** (2 issues per year)
  Each issue is a collection of essays addressing a particular security theme.
  Subscription: $25/year
  $40/2 years

* **Peacekeeping and International Relations (6 issues per year)**
  This independent journal offers facts and opinions on all aspects of peacekeeping. Written by experts for peacekeeping troops, diplomats, politicians, UN officials, academics and others interested in this subject.
  Subscription: $15/year
  $10 /single issue

* **Regional Seminar Proceedings**

Current

* The Canadian Strategic Forecast 1993 - Adapting for Survival: Global Security from Sarajevo to Maastricht to Rio (1992) ($20)

* A Continuing Commitment: Canada and North Atlantic Security (Spring 1992) ($20)

* Canada, The Navy and Shipbuilding: Is There a Future? (Regional 1991) ($15)

* The Canadian Strategic Forecast 1992 - Divided We Fall: The National Security Implications of Canadian Constitutional Issues (1991) ($10)

* Peacekeeping, Peacemaking or War: International Security Enforcement (Spring 1991)(Photocopy format only) ($10)

Back List   ($3 each)

* The Canadian Strategic Forecast 1991 (1991)
* Canadian, American and Mexican Free Trade: Issues and Implications of Trilateralism (1991)
* International Security in a Changing Global Order (1990)
* Partners in Defence: US-Canadian Cooperation in Meeting Security Challenges of the 1990s (1990)
* The Canadian Strategic Forecast 1989 (1989)
* A Grand Strategy for the United States? (1987)
* High Tech and the High Seas (1985)
* Nuclear Strategy and the Superpowers (1984)
* The Grand Strategy of the Soviet Union (1984)
* The Canadian Strategic Review 1983 (1984)
* War in the Eighties: Men Against High Tech (1983)
* Canada's Strategies for Space: A Paradox of Opportunity (1983)
* Arms Limitation and the United Nations (1982)
* Superpower Intervention in the Persian Gulf (1982)

Strategic Datalinks

* Change, Challenge & Commitment -- 1989: A Strategic Review (January 1990)

* Security in a Complex World: Iraqi Invasion Demonstrates Need to Renovate Military (November 1990)

* Deployment of Troops to Gulf Raises Many Strategic Questions (December 1990)

* Crisis in the Baltic States (January 1991)

* Overview of the Gulf Crisis: A Perspective from India (January 1991)

* The United Nations and the Persian Gulf Crisis (January 1991)

* India in Dire Straits: Prognosis and Perspective (May 1991)

* The Crisis in Yugoslavia (August 1991)

* At Last - A Stable Defence Policy for Canada? (September 1991)

* Gunfire in the Balkans, Ricochets in Lahr: Why We Still Need Canadian Troops in Europe (November 1991)

* Canada's New Frigates: Have We Missed Something? (November 1991)

* An Analysis of the New Military Strategy of USA President Bush: Perspectives of a Chinese Scholar (February 1992)

* The Government Policy Process and the Military: Pressures and Priorities in Democratic Societies (March 1992)

* Thinking About the Unthinkable: Strategic Studies (April 1992)

* The Franco-German Corps: The Seeds of a European Army are Sown (July 1992)

* The Strategic Legacy of St. Pierre-Miquelon and the Atlantic Fishery Dispute (September 1992)

* Naval Peacekeeping? (December 1992)

Also Available

The Quebec Plot, Leo Heaps ($6)

Memories of the Forgotten War: The World War I Diary of Pte. V.E. Goodwin
David Pierce Beatty ($15)

The Vimy Pilgramage July 1936
David Pierce Beatty ($8)

My Mom the Sailor
Norra Taylor, (Illustr. Calvin Laur) ($16)

ORDER FORM

Publications may be ordered from
The Canadian Institute of Strategic Studies, 76 St. Clair Avenue West, Suite 502
Toronto, Ontario M4V 1N2, Tel: (416) 964-6632 Fax: (416) 964-5833

Books

[ ] Peacekeeping: An Annotated Bibliography   *@$15 $_____

[ ] Peacekeeping, Peacemaking or War...   *@$10 $_____
    *Special offer: both books for combined price of $20 $_____

[ ] The 1962 Cuban Missile Crisis: **@$20 $_____
    Canadian Involvement Reconsidered
         (**@$15 if ordered before 15 September 1993)

Shipping	*(10% of order value, $3 minimum)*	$_____
	Subtotal	$_____
GST (Cdn residents only)	*(7% of Subtotal)*	$_____
Book order total		**$_____**

Subscriptions (Shipping/GST incl in prices)

[ ] The McNaughton Papers (2 issues/year)   (1 year)$15 $_____

[ ] Peacekeeping & International Relations $_____
          One year $25 (CISS members pay $20)
          Two years $40 (CISS members pay $30)

                              *TOTAL ENCLOSED*** $_____

SHIP TO:

Name   _____

Address _____

_____Postal Code _____

PAYMENT

(**NB: payable in US funds outside Canada**)

[ ] Cheque enclosed   [ ] Visa*   [ ] Mastercard*
Card No. _____ Expiry Date_____/_____
Signature* _____

The Canadian Institute of Strategic Studies

76 St. Clair Ave. W., Ste. 502, Toronto, Ontario M4V 1N2

Membership Application

Categories	Annual dues	Entrance Fee
Regular - Canadian citizen	$ 60	$ 10
Associate - citizens of other countries	$ 60	$ 10
Student - full-time students	$ 30	$ 5
Corporate A*	$550	$ 50
Corporate B*	$225	$ 25

* Corporate A members may designate up to five individuals to exercise membership. Corporate B members may designate up to two persons.

Members receive a copy of each of the Canadian Strategic Forecast, the Proceedings of the Spring Seminar, the Institute's newsletter, Strategic Datalinks, occasional publications and the annual report, as well as discounts on seminar fees and other CISS publications.

Annual membership spans the calendar year.

The CISS is a registered charitable organization and all membership fees and other donations qualify as an income tax deduction.

I/We apply for membership in the Canadian Institute of Strategic Studies:

Name: _____

Address: _____

Telephone:(Residence) _____ (Business) _____

Citizenship:_____

Firm and Position: _____

I/We enclose an entrance fee of $_____

An annual membership fee of $_____

Total membership fee $_____

Donation

I believe that the Institute makes a vital contribution to the understanding of Canadian national security needs. I would like to help with an income tax deductible contribution of:

$_____

Total $_____

Enclosed is my cheque for $_____

Charge to Visa #_____ Expiry Date _____

Charge to Mastercard #_____ Expiry Date _____

Signature _____

[ ] Please send me a CISS Publication Catalogue